DATE DUE

~~NO 1 '01~~			
~~JE 10 '02~~			

DEMCO 38-296

Reclaiming Myths
of Power

Reclaiming Myths of Power

Women Writers and the Victorian Spiritual Crisis

Ruth Y. Jenkins

Lewisburg
Bucknell University Press
London and Toronto: Associated University Presses

n to photocopy items for internal or personal
se of specific clients, is granted by the copyright
f $10.00, plus eight cents per page, per copy is
earance Center, 222 Rosewood Drive, Danvers,
[0-8387-5278-0/95 $10.00 + 8¢ pp, pc.]

ed University Presses
440 Forsgate Drive
Cranbury, NJ 08512

Associated University Presses
25 Sicilian Avenue
London WC1A 2QH, England

Associated University Presses
P.O. Box 338, Port Credit
Mississauga, Ontario
Canada L5G 4L8

The paper used in this publication meets the requirements
of the American National Standard for Permanence of Paper
for Printed Library Materials Z39.48-1984.

Library of Congress Cataloging-in-Publication Data

Jenkins, Ruth Y., 1959–
    Reclaiming myths of power : women writers and the Victorian
spiritual crisis / Ruth Y. Jenkins.
        p. cm.
    Includes bibliographical references and index.
    ISBN 0-8387-5278-0 (alk. paper)
    1. English fiction—Women authors—History and criticism.
    2. Literature and society—Great Britain—History—19th century.
    3. Women and literature—Great Britain—History—19th century.
    4. English fiction—19th century—History and criticism.
    5. Fiction—Religious aspects—Christianity. 6. Power (Social
sciences) in literature. 7. Nightingale, Florence, 1820–1910.
    8. Spiritual life in literature. 9. Christianity and literature.
    I. Title.
    PR878.W6J46 1995
    823'.8099287—dc20
                                                    94-20113
                                                    CIP

PRINTED IN THE UNITED STATES OF AMERICA

for my parents

Contents

Abbreviations

<dl>

B   *The Brontës: Their Lives, Friendships and Correspondence.* The Shakespeare Head Brontë, ed. Thomas James Wise and John Alexander Symington, 4 vols. (1933; reprint, Oxford: Basil Blackwell, 1980).

D   Sarah Stickney Ellis, *The Daughters of England: Their Position in Society, Characters, and Responsibilities* (New York: D. Appleton, 1842).

DD   George Eliot, *Daniel Deronda* (Harmondsworth: Penguin, 1982).

E   Sarah Stickney Ellis, *Education of the Heart: Woman's Best Work* (London: Hodder & Stoughton, 1869).

FH   George Eliot, *Felix Holt* (Harmondsworth: Penguin, 1982).

GEE   George Eliot, *Essays*, ed. Thomas Pinney (New York: Columbia University Press, 1963).

GEL   George Eliot, *The George Eliot Letters*, ed. Gordon S. Haight, 9 vols. (New Haven: Yale University Press, 1954–78).

LG   Elizabeth Gaskell, *The Letters of Mrs. Gaskell*, ed. J. A. V. Chapple and Arthur Pollard (Cambridge: Harvard University Press, 1967).

M   George Eliot, *Middlemarch* (Harmondsworth: Penguin, 1979).

MB   Elizabeth Gaskell, *Mary Barton* (London: Penguin, 1985).

MF   George Eliot, *The Mill on the Floss* (New York: New American Library, 1965).

NS   Elizabeth Gaskell, *North and South* (Oxford: Oxford University Press, 1982).

R   Elizabeth Gaskell, *Ruth* (Oxford: Oxford University Press, 1985).

</dl>

RE   Mrs. Humphry Ward, *Robert Elsmere* (Oxford: Oxford University Press, 1987).

S   Charlotte Brontë, *Shirley* (Oxford: Oxford University Press, 1986).

ST   Florence Nightingale, *Suggestions for Thought to Searchers After Religious Truth*, 3 vols. (London: Eyre & Spottiswoode, 1860).

Acknowledgments

No piece of writing is solitary in its birth, and this book is no exception. The ideas were conceived years ago and nurtured by various communities. I am indebted to Susan Squier, Helen Cooper, and Adrienne Munich for introducing me to feminist theory and most significantly welcoming me into that community. Their careful readings of and challenging questions about the earlier versions of this book enabled the ideas to grow and find voice. Virginia Sickbert and Elizabeth Fay contributed discerning responses, opportunities for dialogue, and sustained encouragement. Important revisions would not have been possible without time provided by a generous research award from California State University, Fresno.

I would also like to thank Bucknell University Press, especially James Heath for the care with which he shepherded my manuscript and Karen Chase for her insightful suggestions.

I am grateful for permission to reprint material essential to this study: to the trustees of the Henry Bonham-Carter Will Trust for permission to quote from Florence Nightingale's *Suggestions for Thought to Searchers After Religious Truth*; to Basil Blackwell Publishers for permission to quote from *The Brontës: Their Lives, Friendships, and Correspondence*, edited by Thomas James Wise and John Alexander Symington; and to Yale University Press for permission to quote from the *George Eliot Letters*, edited by Gordon S. Haight, copyright 1955. An earlier version of a portion of the Nightingale chapter appeared in *Weber Studies* as "Rewriting Female Subjection: Florence Nightingale's Revisionist Myth of 'Cassandra.'"

Special thanks to John Moses for his invaluable help in preparing the manuscript and for consistently offering honest and perceptive readings of the book at every stage of the process. This book would not have been possible without the unwavering support of my family during my own crises of faith. And finally, I must thank Kathryn Jenkins-Moses for providing me with a context that grounds my understanding of female spirituality.

11

Reclaiming Myths
of Power

1

Introduction: Reclaiming the Word

It *is* unnatural, and the most selfish of all ties *if* the tie is to be, as Milton has put it, "He, thy God, thou mine."
— Florence Nightingale, *Suggestions for Thought*

Go not to Milton, or the Fathers, but to the Word of God.
— Sarah Josepha Hale, *Woman's Record*

The late eighteenth and early nineteenth century in Britain witnessed a widespread religious revival of Low Church Evangelicalism, which preached unmediated access to God.[1] Concurrent with this resurgence of reformation Christianity, however, were scientific advances and capitalistic expansion: the first, shaking the foundations of doctrinal infallibility; the second, redefining middle-class power and position. The complexities of this combined sacred empowerment and secular realignment produced an unprecedented opportunity for individuals to challenge dominant ideologies.

For one of the first times in Protestant England, organized religions allocated women a vocational place in the Church; even the Anglican church initiated a deaconess movement. (The advent of this enterprise, however, must be kept in context: while it did sanction a hierarchical place for women within the Church, this campaign also helped to absorb "redundant" women, which the 1851 census identified.)[2] The newly established ecclesiastical status that resulted, however, was short-lived, as conservative forces rallied to limit women's active role within the Church's hierarchy.[3] Even in some of the Evangelical sects, which initially allowed female preachers, women were soon returned to their secondary positions.[4] In short, the "unnatural" ties that Florence Nightingale identifies in Milton's hierarchy—"He, thy God, thou mine"—were soon reestablished.

Although women's expanded clerical role was temporary, men,

in contrast, found their spiritual privileges fortified by the Evangelical movement. The "right of private judgment," which Charlotte Brontë's character Caroline Helstone identifies in *Shirley*, remained the central tenet of England's state religion—a prerogative reserved for men. For women, husbands and fathers continued to be the exclusive interpreters of both the natural and supernatural worlds. In fact, woman's "natural" place (that which was believed to be divinely assigned) became the focus of much of Victorian England's conservative energy. In this context, institutionalized religion endorsed a pre-Reformation relationship between women and God, telling them that, like their Catholic forefathers, God's word could not be understood without a mediator—in this case, a man. Organized religion, then, especially the Church of England, reinforced dominant patriarchal values; rather than reenfranchise those that the world had marginalized, the established church actively abetted a patriarchal appropriation of sacred myth. So, even if any individual woman could enjoy a private and/or mystical spirituality independent of clerical edicts or closed hierarchies, institutionalized religions severely restricted, even denied, her a voice in the dialogues that shaped theological doctrines and informed secular mores.

Just as the Church marginalized women from spiritual power, conservative lay forces limited the opportunities for women, especially from the middle and upper classes, to pursue their culture's secular salvation—work. Carlyle transformed the question voiced by Bunyan's Christian—what is my place in this world—into a cultural call to preserve social and economic hierarchies, and as the prophet of this conservative ethic, he espoused the need to embrace (and be content with) one's established position and the work apportioned to it. In concert with Carlyle's rendering of social and spiritual duty, Sarah Ellis articulates its application to women:

> Whether you are rich, or poor, an orphan or a child of watchful parents—one of a numerous family, or comparatively alone—filling an exalted or an humble position—of highly gifted mind, or otherwise—all these points must be clearly ascertained before you can properly understand the kind of duty required of you.[5]

She continues, joining this class-defined basis for determining one's duty to gender: "As Christian women. . . . the first thing of importance is to be content to be inferior to men" (*D*, 8). Consequently, women's "Christian" duty meant accepting first one's so-

cial position and then the superiority of similarly stationed men.[6]
Carlyle and Ellis's directives meant, in other words, for the working classes, often difficult labor; for women, domesticated duties.
In this way, accepting one's place—whether laborer or female—
became as much a spiritual duty as a social one. The symbiotic
relationship between the tenets of Protestantism and capitalism
cannot be ignored, therefore, especially in the light of their complicitous reinforcement of women's subjection:

> the ethical components of Protestantism . . . and the Calvinist doc-
> trine of the Elect . . . proved particularly congenial to the spirit of
> capitalism.[7]

> Puritanism and capitalism are closely connected. . . . Puritanism laid
> great stress both on hard work and on moral discipline.[8]

In the abstract these twin qualities endorsed by both Puritanism
and capitalism—"hard work" and "moral discipline"—could be
applied to women and their work within the domestic sphere; in
reality, however, they faced *different* standards for their salvation:
as Ellis conveys in her guides for women, gender, not talent,
served as primary arbitrator in interpreting the appropriate arena
for an individual's divinely appointed duties—public or private.
For women, these gender-distinct spheres were translated into a
complicated pattern of behavior; women lived in a culture that
revered an active life of good works and industry, but defined
and evaluated the female by a passive model. While women, as
Sarah Ellis would instruct, should never be "trusting to the day
to provide its own occupations" (D, 29), they should also never
focus their attention toward themselves or their own desires; instead, women's all should be "to enliven and interest others" (D,
29). Consequently the means by which and the scope in which
women demonstrated their "moral discipline" and "hard work"
were gender bound.

Thus, many women found themselves in a community that
spiritually circumscribed their salvation by patriarchal mediators
and socially restricted their opportunities to answer Carlyle's cry
to work in the ways open to their male contemporaries. And, as
the Victorian public arena became more and more the arena of
mammon, competition, and profit, the differences between public
and domestic spheres, intensified in this way, exaggerated
women's secular disempowerment as the private domain became
gradually divested of an equal social power and prerogative. As

a consequence of this physical distinction, the home evolved into a recognized symbol of purity, thus fixing the character of women and the domestic sphere as separate and undefiled by the world.[9] Yet, ironically, while wives and daughters were not to enter the workplace as participants, their assets often became the means to the husbands' capitalistic venture: the dowries of future wives, significantly, served as a means for investment.[10] So, paradoxically, while a woman should remain unadulterated by the public workplace, her money could escape the same restrictions, fueling the very activity deemed improper for her—just as a woman should actively pursue *selfless* deeds, thus maintaining her passivity.[11] The interconnected nature of these secular and spiritual ideologies—both exploiting women—limited women's access to power and, subsequently, the requisite authority necessary to evoke substantive change.

As a result, when faced with such restrictive models of behavior, many women experienced spiritual crises: how could they enact what they believed to be God's plan for them when it conflicted directly with clerical and social edicts for female behavior? When He charged them with a vocation that defied these cultural demarcations? This study analyzes the conflict between four Victorian women and their culture, their ethical beliefs, and the limited opportunities to enact their faith; specifically, this project examines the manifestation of this conflict in the lives and writings of Florence Nightingale, Charlotte Brontë, Elizabeth Gaskell, and George Eliot.[12] In a culture that endorsed a passive social model for women, these women found themselves with talents and abilities, which were traditionally validated only in men, but no sanctioned place to develop and pursue them satisfactorily.

Heretofore the spiritual conflicts that these women writers experienced have not been considered, even though the Victorian spiritual crisis has been the subject of extensive analysis. While I would not wish to oversimplify or essentialize the complexities of the spiritual crises experienced by Victorian men, scholars have identified two predominant patterns—either a condition of skepticism (of "Believing where we cannot prove") or one of despair from perceiving nature's indifference to humanity.[13] To illustrate this sociohistorical phenomenon, critics point to the world Arnold represents in "Dover Beach" with "neither joy, nor love, nor light, / nor certitude"; to Tennyson's description in *In Memoriam* of nature as "red in tooth and claw" and "careless of the single life"; to Carlyle's image in *Sartor Resartus* of a purposeless universe as "one huge, dead, immeasurable Steam-engine, rolling on, in its dead indifference, to grind [one] limb from limb"; and to the despair that Mill records in his *Autobiography* as he contemplated life with "nothing left to live for."[14] Reading these male writers and analyzing their crises remain central to understanding the complexity of Victorian religious and ethical attitudes, but by omitting women writers (and consequently female experience) from this inquiry, and thereby assuming a singular perspective, scholars have misconstrued the full scope of Victorian spirituality. This omission can be demonstrated in the two central scholarly works on this phenomenon. John Holloway in *The Victorian Sage* (1953) and George P. Landow in *Elegant Jeremiahs* (1986) provide important analyses of the prophetic nature of many Victorian texts. Whereas Landow expands and clarifies distinctions between fiction and nonfiction that Holloway does not, neither of these scholars identifies what I see as significant differences produced by the Victorian writer's gender. Neither Holloway nor Landow recognizes that many women's spiritual crises and their related writings attribute humanity's apparent falling away from God to a patriarchal appropriation of the sacred, forcing women to become Christian martyrs under androcentric hegemony.

Regardless of the possible causes that have contributed to the absence of female experience in analyses of the Victorian spiritual crisis, any consideration of the relationship between gender and such crises has been missing. Although feminist literary and religious scholars have recreated a matrilinear heritage by disinterring lost voices and reexamining traditional standards to include female experience, the major project of analyzing Victorian women writers' reclamation of patriarchally appropriated religions has barely begun.[15] This study, by analyzing the paradigm that I have identified, reexamines the Victorian spiritual crisis from the perspective of these women. Doing so, I extend the parameters of Victorian scholarship by revealing a more complex, multivoiced dialogue concerning the relationship of God or ethical beliefs to various individuals than has previously been argued.

A closer analysis of the gender-based spiritual patterns of behavior that informed Victorian culture is necessary to understand fully the basis for these writers' conflicts. Theological scholarship during the Victorian period advanced toward a more liberal interpretation of Christianity, transforming biblical exegetics from a typological to a historical project; this evolution of perspective revealed the human subjectivity that affected biblical hermeneutics.[16] Although intellectual theology may have recognized the historically determined components of biblical truths, practical,

organized religion and its institutions often reflected the imperialism of Victoria's reign: the majority of society remained under
the psychological burden of Puritanism.[17] Just as industrialization
reinforced gender distinctions among the middle class by remov-
ing the economic workplace from the home, so, too, much of the
period's manifestations of Christianity reinforced gender-distinct
characteristics. Citing Charles Kingsley as a prime example,
Houghton writes that much of Victorian England believed in what
Kingsley named "a healthful and manly Christianity, one which
does not exalt the feminine virtues to the exclusion of the masculine"; this brand of Christianity, subsequently, demanded its
prophets ready for the "good fight."[18]

In contrast to this militant version of spirituality, the Victorian
home represented a hallowed place of worship with women functioning as passive symbols of purity. "The Victorian home,"
Houghton writes, "was not only a peaceful, it was a sacred, place.
When the Christian tradition . . . was losing its hold on contemporary society, and the influence of the pastorate was declining,
the living church more and more became the 'temple of the
hearth.'"[19] Even Kingsley, who exhorted middle-class women to
be "manly" Christians by going out and inspiring the lower
classes to piety and the clean life, would assert that when it came
to female suffrage women would gain more by "patience" and
"private influence" than by the kind of militant activities he ordained for spiritual enfranchisement.[20] The conservatism inherent in his vision is also revealed by his belief that woman's mission
was fulfilled through marriage, even to the extent that he favored
the married St. Elizabeth to the unmarried Teresa, a preference
that strengthened any enshinement of the home.[21] However,
whatever the factors that contributed to the developing worship
of the home—whether sacred or secular—the result proved fertile
ground for reinforcing both women's powerlessness and capitalistic enterprise:

> Having confined all those virtues inappropriate within the stock mar-
> ket or the boardroom to the hearts of their women folk, middle-class
> men were then left free to indulge in all these unfortunate vices neces-
> sary for successful bourgeois enterprise. The fate of women and
> Christian selflessness having been thus bound together, the depend-
> ency and social powerlessness of the first become a virtual guarantee
> of the social irrelevance of the second: once God had settled into the
> parlour, Mammon had free range in public life—and the exclusion of
> women from virtually all arenas of public existence guaranteed that
> this tidy division was maintained. An ideal of femininity which com-

bined holy love with social subordination not only served to suppress women, it also tamed and contained the anticapitalistic implications of Christian love itself. Domesticated Christianity, like domesticated womanhood, was the most comfortable kind for a bourgeois man to live with.[22]

This spatial division of behavior—aggressive competitiveness in the workplace, gentle beneficence in the home—evoked attention both from those with conservative and radical perspectives. Sarah Ellis, for example, believed that the way to ensure cultural morality was by "maintaining a strict separation of the domestic and social spheres, arguing that women develop their moral superiority only by their exclusion from the marketplace," that "men and women have separate places in creation."[23] Elizabeth Gaskell, in contrast, wanted to eliminate moral distinctions between the two spheres of activity, arguing for a less competitive social dynamic. But where Sarah Ellis would point to women's cloistered lives as the foundation of their allegedly higher morals to argue for maintained ghettoization, Gaskell preferred instead to extend "domesticated" values into the public sphere, regardless of gender; in contrast to people like Kingsley, who worried about the "effeminacy" of the middle class and the need of women to be freed from "sentiment," Gaskell envisioned a community liberated from gender-based distinctions that, if anything, privileged traditional female characteristics and values for all of its members.[24]

The secular and sacred division by gender—spatially and behaviorally—contributed further to the objectification of women as angels or emblems of purity themselves, filling, as Houghton names it, a "vacuum" of worship.[25] This reorientation of worship from the supernatural to the natural in turn established the role of the angel-of-the-house or the virginal vessel as the models for female behavior. Kristeva's description of motherhood—an "impossible elsewhere, a sacred beyond"—illustrates the complicated and debilitating relationship between women, reproduction, and Christianity that also informed the Victorian perspective.[26] Unable to achieve this impossible, sacred quality, women found themselves "essentially identified with Eve," humanly unable to emulate the virgin birth. This bifurcation, Daly writes, "has served to separate the 'feminine' ideal of good from the active role attributed to Jesus," leaving women disassociated from the divine.[27] By defining women's salvation through this negative condition, the Church and her clerics secure their own power because

"Woman, while the passive object of His redeeming work, can never actively represent Him as mediator of God's word and deed."[28] If, in institutionalized religion, women can never act as spiritual mediators, they can never possess sacred authority, and consequently can never effectively challenge patriarchal constraints implemented in the name of God.

Yet ironically, especially in the role of mothers, women became the cultural mediators for men's salvation. Voices like Ruskin's would perpetuate this phenomenon by charging women with the responsibility of manipulating moral behavior, even while he warns against women engaging in theology.[29] So, although women were judged unable to participate in a true reformation Christianity—men must interpret the word, must mediate their salvation—women functioned as channels and conduits for the men's salvation; both symbolically and physically, then, women functioned as cultural filters. By teaching their children the symbolic codes that in fact disempower and devalue themselves, women complicitiously perpetuate patriarchal standards. In this capacity, however, women, while instructing their own exploitation, gain a distorted power in their relationship to the dominant ideology; although enshrined and worshipped, women cannot tap this position for their own empowerment.[30] In other words, women, who serve as socializing agents, cannot use their "social" position to empower themselves because, by definition, that act would be antisocial. Just as the bifurcated models of female behavior render women powerless, so, too, the patriarchally informed role of motherhood, with its appropriated, sacred association, invests women with a meaningless power.

The work of twentieth-century feminist theologians show this pattern to be one that runs through the history of western religion: patriarchal cultures eliminate women's active and authoritative place within sacred myth and the resulting institutions.[31] "The more Christianity became a genuine part of the patriarchal Jewish or Greco-Roman society and culture, the more it had to relegate women's leadership to fringe groups or to limit women's functions."[32] This diminishment of the female in religious narratives occurred in a variety of ways, most commonly through the transfiguration of the images associated with female deities into the new patriarchal religion as symbols of evil—such as the serpent figure or the apple from the tree of knowledge, both associated in the Judeo-Christian tradition with sin.[33]

These transformations and devaluations of the female deities also parallel the suppression of the nonpatriarchal Gnostic gospels. Both point to political motivations behind the presumption of neutrality and divine inspiration in the Judeo-Christian tradition. Exposing the patriarchal ideology that informs the standardized narratives of this religion identifies the human agenda that produces "sacred" doctrines; otherwise, a patriarchal community—sacred and secular—can monopolize sacred language, the power associated with it, and the authoritative use of both. Stone's analysis of ancient religions has important consequences for the entire history of religion:

> Judging from the production of religious mythology of the royal scribes and priests found in the archives of palaces of the Indo-European-ruled nations of the historic periods, often in the languge of the conquered populations, we may surmise that political aims, rather than religious fervor, may well have been the motivation. The prevalence of myths that explain the creation of the universe by the male deity and the institution of kingship, when none had existed previously, strongly hints at the possibility that many of these myths were written by priests of the invading tribes to justify the supremacy of the new male deities and to justify installation of a king as the result of the relationship of that king to the male deity.[34]

Similarly the result of suppressing the Gnostic gospels strengthened Christianity's hierarchical economy of authority by eliminating any competing sacred power. Denounced as heresy by orthodox Christians in the second century, buried, and not disintered until 1945, some fifty-two manuscripts identified as the Gnostic gospels delineate a competing vision of Christianity. In *The Gnostic Gospels* Elaine Pagels considers the political suppression of these texts that threatened a patriarchally informed theology by identifying female as well as male aspects of the deity and the trinity as Father-Mother-Son.[35] Gnosticism, which stresses the process of knowing over the attainment of a body of knowledge, stands in sharp contrast to the concept of a fixed doctrine based on *the* word, which determines values and standards.[36] Embracing a multiple perspective, these egalitarian gospels invested women with the same spiritual authority as men.

> The virtue of gnosticism is that it retained the early Christian sense of a redemption set over against oppressive hierarchies. It cultivated a spiritual egalitarianism among the redeemed. This meant that it took seriously the belief that redemption in Christ made women and men equal. Women had the same spiritual authority as men and could share the same ministries for most gnostic groups.[37]

The crucifixion and resurrection, the central tenets of Christianity, can be interpreted from a radically different and nonhierarchical perspective than that producing the canonized version: the Gnostic gospel of *Truth* "sees the crucificixion as the occasion for discovering the divine self within, and the gospel of *Mary* asserts that Mary Magdalene was the first to see the risen Christ."[38] The patriarchal rendering of the resurrection in contrast "serves an essential *political* function: it legitimizes the authority of certain men who claim to exercise exclusive leadership over the churches as the successors of the apostle Peter"; as such, the patriarchally inscribed gospels limit the number of believers who hold an incontestable position of authority.[39] This creation of a hierarchical structure, based on one God with access to Him invested in an elite few, replicates the sociological patterns attributed to the shift from polytheism to monotheism and the subsequent "changing attitudes toward female sexuality."[40] In contrast, the Gnostic gospels would prove subversive to any patriarchal hierarchy; by offering each believer direct access to God, an elite band of priests or scribes becomes unnecessary.[41] The Gnostic gospels not only empower every individual believer but also identify Mary Magdalene as one of the chosen successors, thus giving women a central position in mediating and interpreting God's word. As such, the revolutionary potential of such a gospel represented so great a threat to the patriarchal economy—particularly by sanctioning women as mediators of God's word—that the Gnostic gospels had to be divested of sacred authority.

Building on Pagels's ground-breaking scholarship, Christine Froula delineates fundamental differences in male and female images of authority. She asserts that before the patriarchally inscribed literary canon can be reinscribed as historically and culturally determined works, not sacred texts, these differences must be acknowledged and elucidated. The differences she identifies produce striking parallels to the differences between the canonized scriptures and the Gnostic gospels: male respect and female questioning of a mystified authority; patriarchal mystification of history, which invests spiritual authority in an elite few; the image of a male creator, which subordinates the visible to the invisible, experience to mediated knowledge, and silence to the word. With male authority the cornerstone of the sacred and secular worlds, marginalized individuals can never gain the requisite power to challenge the status quo and render changes; with this self-protecting factor, patriarchal edicts, whether sacred or secular, appear not only to be of divine design but also irrevocable.

This patriarchal appropriation of sacred imagery and the power associated with it devalues, transfigures, and even eliminates female imagery and experience from the central and defining myths of the culture; as the clerics translate religious narrative into written texts, biblical and secular, the patriarchal production becomes *the* version—its narrative, *the* word. This appropriated myth nonetheless becomes the standard against which identity and value are measured. The cultural reinforcement of this patriarchal agenda reaffirms the biblical texts; this in turn perpetuates the scriptural canon, which compounds the belief in the divine authorship of these sacred texts.[42] As such, the sacred canon establishes an exclusionary model of text standard and selection.

As the Judeo-Christian myth is transubstantiated into a culture's ethical standard through the written word, the actual ideology that tailored the myth for a patriarchal agenda is renamed divine through the fabricated "intrinsic" authority that sacred language and rhetoric produce. This "divine" authority extends not just to the secularized texts and language but to the antecedents as well. If in the Christian myth the Word is God, then texts that claim divine authority possess an unapproachable and unchallengable value system and structure. The political and clerical complicity in the monopolization of language and its function to define and manufacture "reality" enables these patriarchal institutions to claim a sacred, even though androcentric, place in language's role to represent cultural value. The Western literary canon, an extension and secularization of sacred literature, replicates and perpetuates this illusion of intrinsic authority and superiority; as such the Judeo-Christian narrative, serving as an ur-text, produces a patriarchal image of authority that claims divine authority to exclude and devalue authentic female experience.[43]

Without realizing that they were restoring the earlier suppressed, female-inclusive aspects of the Judeo-Christian tradition, Victorian women reclaimed the power associated with this religious narrative. Prohibited from authoritative positions and relegated into the margins both through access to language and language itself, women recognized that they would need just such an authority to sanction their critique and revision of the formidable superstructures of Church and state. Nightingale, Brontë, Gaskell, and even the unbeliever Evans—as well as many of their female contemporaries—reappropriated the substance and the language of the Judeo-Christian narratives to authorize their subversion of patriarchal institutions.[44]

At the same time that these women reappropriated sacred imagery, the nineteenth century witnessed another, yet compatible, movement that attempted to resurrect the female aspects of God, even to the extent of prophesizing a female messiah, tapping the historic privilege Christianity had given the oppressed to challenge the world.[45] This privilege provided women a vehicle through which to challenge male hegemony by reclaiming Christianity—naming the patriarchal appropriation of sacred narrative heretical and themselves the "handmaidens of the Lord," both appellations subverting institutionalized religion.[46] In this way, they aligned themselves with and consciously participated in an extant tradition of Christian prophets, who voiced truths whether or not they were listened to or believed. As a rhetorical strategy, reclaiming this myth enabled women to depatriarchalize the language justifying their marginalization and to reinscribe that language and the companion narratives with female experience. Invested with this reappropriated authority, the act of writing often served women as either a vehicle for their own empowerment, as for Nightingale, whose revisionist theology justified her rejection of cultural roles, or empowerment itself, as for Brontë, whose belief that her ability to write was a God-given talent demanding attention.

By reclaiming the Judeo-Christian myth, then, women writers authorized their participation in literary production and the subsequent cultural dialogues even if their culture denied them the opportunity.[47] If a matrilinear literary heritage was absent, an extant prophetical one existed. Associating themselves with this heritage, women could subvert one basis for their subjection— the allegedly divine design. This enabling heritage allowed these women to circumvent the anxiety of authorship, which Gilbert and Gubar identify as the debilitating fear that the act of writing will destroy them because no recognizable female literary tradition exists.[48] But, to understand fully the subversion of patriarchal authority that Nightingale, Brontë, Gaskell, and Evans engage in through their use of the Judeo-Christian myth, it is crucial to distinguish their reclaimed and reinscribed myth from the patriarchally appropriated one: by using sacred allusion, these women are not necessarily subscribing to the androcentric construction; instead, they allude to a non-patriarchal imaging of Christianity.

This use of sacred allusion by Nightingale, Brontë, Gaskell, and Evans in their writing also needs to be differentiated from another larger Victorian phenomenon. At the same time that religious discourse became infused with dissent and doubt, secular literature became saturated with biblical allusions to such an extent that "the use of literary and biblical allusion should be recognized as an important convention in Victorian fiction."[49] This grafting of sacred to secular reflects the simple fact that, even if the certainty of traditional theological beliefs was being questioned, the Bible remained the only common book between writer and reader, the one book that the writers could assume their increasingly divergent audience would know. Barry Qualls contends that the Victorian novel became, like earlier religious literature, a medium through which to school humanity in finding a remnant of the godlike in the physical world—a natural supernaturalism. But unlike earlier religious literature, the Victorian novel superimposed these sacred values onto the secular genre.[50] Because of this, Victorian writers created fictional pilgrims who no longer had the luxury of finding their purpose in life through religious allegory; instead these Victorian pilgrims needed to progress through the sordid realities of a secular fiction.

During this period, in fact, the religious novel became a respectable and popular genre.[51] Qualls explains this proliferation of religious rhetoric and suggests that "Lacking Bunyan's assurance, readers and writers held all the more tenaciously to his language."[52]

> Of the roughly 45,000 books published in England between 1816 and 1851, well over 10,000 were religious works far out-distancing the next largest category—history and geography—with 4,900, and fiction with 3,500. There was also an immense circulation of religious periodicals and tracts. A good many middle-class readers would read nothing but devotional works; many more were deeply concerned to get religious material into the hands of the lower classes—hence the ingenious efforts at distributing tracts, from single copies tucked into baskets by benevolent ladies to distributions of over 40,000 tracts among crowds gathered at public executions.[53]

In short, fiction became the vehicle through which to disseminate and reinforce moral and ethical standards. Yet while Qualls's study helps to explain the predominance of biblical allusions in Victorian literature, it fails to identify or explain this complementary feminist appropriation of sacred allusion.

Although Nightingale, Brontë, Gaskell, and Evans claimed a greater authority and an extant tradition in which to write, these women nevertheless had to negotiate the canonized patterns of myth, narrative, and social behavior. Gilbert and Gubar emphasize the extent to which these patriarchal literary constructs pervaded women writers' lives: "the question of Milton's misogyny was not in any sense an academic one. On the contrary . . . it was only through patriarchal poetry that they learned 'their origin and their history'—learned, that is, to define themselves as misogynistic theology defined them."[54] This symbiosis between fictional plots and social scripts, between canonized texts and cultural standards, suppresses genuine female experience. If women authors were to write authentically about their experience, then the narrative itself, as Rachel Blau duPlessis has argued, had to be changed.[55] Circumscribed by patriarchal constructs—whether narrative plots or the abstracted symbolization of the word—women writers, writing from their own experience, would transform canonical patterns—even by simply reproducing them as women.

In recent scholarship, feminist theorists have begun to analyze such narrative strategies used by women to translate canonical plots into ones that reflect female experience. Lucy Irigaray identifies the mimicked or exaggerated narrative patterns that result when women reproduce male plots, theorizing that when women reproduce the standard plots, the plots will inevitably be transformed. Analyzing modern female authors who write beyond the traditional ending of the romance plot, duPlessis asserts that these women consequently produce alternative scripts that better account for female experience. Nancy K. Miller has studied the substitution and "plausibility" of such alternative plots in relation to standardized narrative scripts. And, identifying what she names "mother / daughter" language, Margaret Homans reveals female language patterns in texts by women. This project of "breaking the sequence," as Virginia Woolf called women's narratives, evokes comparative and consequently devalued receptions. When considered against other canonized texts, which are named intrinsically superior because of their claimed dissemination from the Word, women's narratives are often dismissed as flawed and consequently denied a central place in the canon, replicating on the secular level the fate of the Gnostic gospels. Even though the "constructs behind literary plots are male, not universal," as Miller writes, those constructs assume intrinsic value.[56] Even when women's narrative patterns predate their male contemporaries—Dorothy Richardson's experimental stream of consciousness, for example—the male writers' works become canonized as they ultimately produce fiction more compatible to the extant canon. Consequently, when women's texts diverge from the canonized pattern—whether by endorsing domesticated values, as Jane Tompkins has shown, or by producing alternative plots, as Miller and duPlessis contend—women's writing is viewed substandard because the patriarchal patterns have become synonymous with the Word, synonymous with literature.[57]

Reclaiming the Word (and the rhetorical power that resides in sacred language) both in the spiritual and secular spheres, Nightingale, Brontë, Gaskell, and Evans attempt to reconstruct narrative patterns and the (replicating) social models from the beginning, from the ur-text. If language is used to represent reality, then the ascribed authority of sacred language enables women to reclaim the power of myth for their own empowerment; language, consequently, is revealed as subjective with no intrinsic antecedent. Instead of *the* Word and *the* plot, these writers produce alternative words, patterns, and scripts. With sacred myth the moralizing force of a culture, reappropriating this language could affect not just the symptomatic results of a patriarchal ideology, but could also reconstruct the primary text used for women's subjection. Writing with "literary" conventions but out of a foregrounded theological tradition as well, these writers revise not just the literary canon but also its theological foundation.

2

Florence Nightingale's Revisionist Theology: "That Woman Will Be the Saviour of Her Race"

[Florence Nightingale] seems as completely led by God as Joan of Arc. . . . it makes one feel the livingness of God more than ever to think how straight He is sending his spirit down into her, as into the prophets & saints of old.

—Elizabeth Gaskell

In 1852 Florence Nightingale wrote that "Women [have] passion, intellect, moral activity . . . and a place in society where no one of the three can be exercised," that the "unity between the woman as inwardly developed and outwardly manifested" no longer exists.[1] Locating the cause for this discrepancy—between women's talents and social opportunities to articulate that talent—Nightingale identifies culture, not nature, as the oppressive force. That is, if, as she believed, God had endowed women with natural capacities that cannot be tapped or acknowledged in her patriarchal community due to gender-distinct roles, Nightingale concludes that it is man who prevents their development; in short, society interferes with divine design rather than enhances it. Thus, with this premise of cultural limitations, Nightingale deduces a conflict not only between women and their society, but also between that patriarchal society and God.

Although she perceives a spiritual conflict between her community and her God, and, consequently, experiences one herself, Nightingale does not participate in the spiritual *disillusionment* that has been traditionally ascribed to the Victorian period. In fact, while many of her contemporaries struggled with religious doubt, Florence Nightingale never questioned God's presence; her spiritual crisis did not involve the loss of faith at all. Instead, she structured her life around trying to work actively in His service, and it is the conflict already identified between Nightingale's desires and the limited opportunities to fulfill them that produced the crisis she experienced. Her spiritually driven life, however, must be clarified, and the competing forces of her faith and her community's institutionalized religion, which had to be reconciled before she could enact her beliefs, must be considered. Although Nightingale embraced her God, she rejected her culture's organized religion, differentiating between their missions and their directives. Functioning as an established institution, the Church, she believed, no longer attempted to advance God's word; instead, the Church reinforced doctrine and advanced dictates that sustained itself, rejecting and excommunicating voices that would challenge its dogma.

Believing in God but disbelieving in organized religion's efficacy or accuracy in interpreting His word, Nightingale found her spirituality at the heart of her conflict with her culture when she attempted to enact her faith. Because she was female, her nation's Church offered Nightingale no sanctioned vocation other than serving God by serving family, father, or husband.[2] To work for God *through* someone else, however, did not fulfill her spiritual needs; she felt compelled to serve God directly. Just as the Reformation had rejected mediators between God and man, Nightingale rejected mediators between God and woman—no longer should women's access to God be circumscribed by their husbands. That is, Nightingale rejected the popular Victorian borrowing of Milton's phrase "He for God only, she for God in him" to determine women's lives. But before she could serve God directly, Nightingale had to gain opportunity and authority to challenge the complicitous forces of her Church and state.

She obtained neither easily because of her social position and religious upbringing; consequently, a consideration of Nightingale's family history and its impact on her can provide context for both her frustrations and actions. As upper middle class and Anglican, Nightingale may have lived within authoritative communities, but because of her gender, she remained powerless. Born into a wealthy family, Nightingale experienced the fruits of privilege, but female, she could never wield its power or shape its course. Raised in the Church of England, Nightingale witnessed its sanctioned doctrines, but female, she could never participate as more than an observer. Her religious heritage further exaggerated this twin marginality, the dynamics of which instigated the split she would define as that between her God and her culture. Unitarian by descent, Fanny Smith Nightingale raised her daughters in the Church of England. Even though Florence's maternal grandfather was influential in the repeal of the Corporation and Test Acts, giving Unitarians religious freedom for the first time in English history, her mother accepted the dominant religious viewpoint of her day, conforming to the Church of England. In contrast, Florence's father, William Nightingale, retained his dissenting beliefs and attempted to educate his daughters from that liberal perspective.[3]

This schism between Established Church and Unitarianism, really between mother (and mother-church) and father (and Spiritual Father), reveals competing influences in Nightingale's life. She saw her mother as oppressive, too much concerned with society's opinions and too little concerned with her daughter's desires. While Fanny Nightingale relentlessly endeavored to train her daughter properly in the functions and obligations associated with their position, Nightingale resisted these gender-distinct duties. Consequently, she and her mother could never agree on the proper sphere for female, specifically Nightingale's, activity; in concert with her culture's patriarchal values, her mother continually attempted to socialize her into those same values.[4]

Just as Nightingale saw her mother as an agent of patriarchal values, she saw her also as representative of another, just as oppressive, social force—the Established Church. In this way, Nightingale's mother represented the two cultural forces which restricted and imprisoned her—patriarchy and institutionalized religion, both repressing, rather than reinforcing, what she believed to be her God-given talents. Because of this, Nightingale stood in contention with not just her mother (as complicitous with patriarchy) but also the culture and church she represented.

In contrast to the oppressive force that Nightingale attributed to her mother, she saw a degree of liberatory potential in her father. From a very early age, she aligned herself with him, rejecting the role of petite angel-in-the-house that her sister embraced. Instead of accepting her culture's prescriptions for women, she preferred to study Greek and Latin under her father's tutelage. And it was he who eventually enabled Nightingale's independence, bestowing upon her an annual maintenance of fifty pounds, even though his wife protested.[5] Throughout Nightingale's life, her father remained an important confidant as she agonized over her ethical beliefs and inability to enact them: there exists extensive correspondence between them about her religious ideas in which she would use him for a sounding board; in turn, he responded with long, thoughtful letters.[6]

Significantly, this childhood preference for father over mother—for intellectual enterprise and action over selfless private servitude, for opposition to the Established Church over complicity in its androcentric agenda—continued throughout Nightingale's life. This history of their relationship suggests that in her father, as in God-the-Father, Nightingale found what her culture denied her. In him, with his rejection of the Established Church as well as its conservative social vision, Nightingale recognized a possible model for confronting the forces, including her mother and the mother-church, that restricted her. As a daughter of her class, however, even with her father's model, she had only a limited number of preordained alternatives for her life, and those she found stifling.

These family dynamics frustrated Nightingale, precipitating intense suffering for her. Until she liberated herself from the need to answer cultural expectations, a freedom from even tacit approval, she could only fantasize about God's plan for her. Sir Edward Cook writes in his biography of Nightingale that "The constant burden of her self-examination . . . was that she was forever 'dreaming' and never 'doing.'"[7] Lytton Strachey, reflecting on her rejection of a marriage proposal, writes that "She would think of nothing but how to satisfy that singular craving of hers to be *doing* something."[8] For nearly sixteen years, until she was thirty-three, Nightingale had to repress her dreams and silently plan and consider her future.[9]

Her passion to do this became an obsession; she could no longer be content simply to reject her culture's sanctioned roles for women. More than resist her "heretical" world, a resistance of somewhat mute articulation since it could be interpreted as displaying the passive behavior culturally sanctioned for women, Nightingale wanted, needed, to enact her faith. She felt compelled to work actively and directly for God in part because she believed that He had spoken to her at four different times during her life.[10] The first of these divine revelations occurred just before Nightingale's seventeenth birthday, marking what she would call "the dawn of her true life."[11] Recording this event in her journal, Nightingale wrote: "On February 7, 1837, God spoke to me and called me to His service."[12] Some eight years later, in an attempt to follow His call, Nightingale envisioned a religious community in which nurses would be trained; but, when she asked her parents to allow her to study nursing for three months at Salisbury

Infirmary only a few miles away, Nightingale's mother and sister were shocked and appalled, accusing her of having an affair with some "low vulgar surgeon."[13] Nightingale details both this rejection of her plan by her mother and the subsequent despair she experienced in a letter to her cousin Hilary Bonham Carter, which explains the intended project and includes one of the many allusions that parallels her life to Christ's:

> I thought something like a Protestant Sisterhood, without vows, for women of educated feeling, might be established. I wonder if our saviour were to walk the earth again, and I were to go to Him and ask, whether He would send me back to live this life again, which crushes me into vanity and deceit. Oh for some strong thing to sweep this loathsome life into the past.[14]

The six years following Nightingale's first call from God fed and starved her dreams. God's initial call inchoate to her, Nightingale suffered under self-imposed patience until she would interpret her call as the reform of nursing. While traveling abroad, she visited a hospital run by a Protestant religious order in Kaiserswerth, Germany, which confirmed Nightingale's belief that nursing could be a moral, even religious profession. But however enticed by what she saw in Germany, Nightingale still could not act upon her vision if she wanted support and approval from her family; quite simply, they forbade it. Rather than encourage or even allow her to study nursing upon returning to England, Nightingale's mother insisted that she embrace the very role of dedicated daughter and devoted sister that she sought to escape. This continued resistance to her desires became harder for Nightingale to bear—precisely because she not only now knew what her spiritual vocation was to be but had seen the possibility in the Kaiserswerth order.

During this period of deep despair and near suicidal depression, Nightingale wrote her three-volume *Suggestions for Thought to Searchers After Religious Truth*, which contains embedded within it "Cassandra."[15] Here, Nightingale details her rejection of organized religion, identifying its failings and appropriations, the resulting harm to the individual believer who wants to seek actively after a better relationship with God (especially if that individual is a woman in Victorian society), and an alternative vision of women's relationship to the divine. Writing this theological discourse proved to be a crucial step in gaining her independence—both in earthly and spiritual terms. *Suggestions* became not only a working out of her personal beliefs but also the authority to act on those same ideas.

The theological struggle and liberating effect contained in *Suggestions* (both marked by rich autobiographical allusions) underscore Nightingale's complex and difficult life, illuminating her own struggle for religious and social independence. Analyzed in conjunction with this text, Nightingale's own life reads as a narrative—the story of one Victorian woman struggling to escape from her culture's oppression. Reclaiming God from a patriarchal appropriation, Nightingale uses Him to empower her desires and fantasies, to authorize her rejection of cultural values, and to revitalize His place in her world.

A closer analysis of *Suggestions* will clarify both how the document functioned to enable Nightingale and how she perceived her relationship to God as well as her culture. Here, she exposes what she believes to be at the heart of this conflict: although claiming divine design, patriarchal culture enlists the family and organized religion to serve as its agents for its agenda. In contrast to these conventional forces, Nightingale delineates what she believes to be the appropriate role of the individual in relationship to the divine—a personal, almost mystical relationship with God, which taps the talents He has given. In this way, *Suggestions* not only describes the conflicting forces the individual must face but also envisions her subsequent rejection of patriarchy's appropriation of God.

Suggestions reveals these tensions—between the individual believer and her culture—both in its style and content. Although the work can be roughly summarized by volume (volumes 1 and 3 explain and define her more abstract beliefs as they relate to the working class and natural laws, and volume 2 applies these theories specifically to daughters in Victorian culture), Nightingale's manner of developing these ideas defies a traditional, linear argument. Acknowledging her work's layered and circumlocutious rhetoric, Nightingale begins the second volume with the following note to her readers:

> In the hope of reaching different minds, the same subjects have been differently (and not always consecutively) dealt with in the several portions of this book. A feeling of their extreme importance has dictated, and it is hoped will excuse, this course, which has rendered repetition, even to the frequent use of the same phraseology, unavoidable. (*ST*, 2)

Fulfilling this promise, Nightingale reiterates her observations about women in her Victorian culture in the semi-autobio-graphical "Cassandra" at the end of volume 2. Identifying herself as "poor Cassandra" in a letter to her cousin, Nightingale reveals the personal history which saturates this angry and frustrated narrative.[16] Just past the midpoint of the work, this focused energy completes the inward movement of perspective—from society, to families, to daughters, to one daughter in particular, before shifting the focus back to more generalized abstractions of her culture. With the narrowed focus of "Cassandra" comes a powerful refinement of the ideas Nightingale has considered elsewhere in *Suggestions*. Here she fuses the frustration of a specific daughter to the frustration of any individual trying to answer God's call, exposing with her greatest passion the appropriation of women's talents by patriarchy, significantly, within a sacred context.

The style in which Nightingale presents her ideas—nonlinear, recapitulative, and fragmented—evidences another aspect of *Suggestions'* subversive impact. Julia Kristeva's semiotic approach to language provides a useful theoretical method from which to analyze the revolutionary potential present in the articulation of Nightingale's ideas. Building upon Lacan's division of language into the symbolic (that which operates within the conventions of grammar and syntax, which he labels the Name-of-the-Father) and the imaginary (that which operates outside these rules), Kristeva redefines Lacan's "imaginary" as "semiotic," emphasizing its tie to the presymbolic language of the preoedipal period. Because of established conventions for communication, after the speaker enters into symbolic discourse, she must repress the semiotic or else risk psychotic behavior; the suppression of this earlier language produces a split between psychological processes and social constraints.[17] Since the semiotic must be suppressed to realize symbolic conventions, it becomes, by definition, marginal to the dominant language system, just as female is marginal to male in patriarchal culture.[18] Any discourse which allows the semiotic to erupt, then, becomes revolutionary in that it defies the conventional rules which should suppress it. In this way the revolutionary writer, while operating within the symbolic, transforms that "symbolic order of orthodox society from the inside."[19]

For Nightingale, engaging in the traditionally male domain of theological speculation—the symbolic rendering of the primary symbol—represents both an attempt to participate in that exclusionary vocation as well as to revise it.[20] This is especially evident in her desire and efforts to publish *Suggestions*, which would transform her ideas from a personal exploration of faith into a public articulation of her word, her gospel; that is, publication becomes prophecy, investing those ideas with a spiritual authority and making her efforts analogous to Christ's. After many years, her manuscripts for this work had been read by only a few friends; it was not until 1858 and 1859 that she returned to the manuscripts. Cook writes that Arthur Hugh Clough (who was a cousin by marriage) encouraged the resumption of Nightingale's religious speculations.[21] She sent manuscripts of *Suggestions* to both John Stuart Mill and Benjamin Jowett for their opinions. Mill loved the book and urged publication, but Jowett argued against publication and for "moderation, conciliation, and suavity."[22] Although Nightingale never revised the manuscripts after they were privately printed, Cook notes that in her testamentary instructions (made in early 1862) she asked that this work be revised according to Jowett's and Mill's suggestions, but because Clough was then dead, she did not know who would be able to do it. In April of 1865 she asked Jowett to edit *Suggestions* for her, but he still insisted that it was "rather the preparation or materials of a book than a book itself."[23]

Nightingale's style in *Suggestions*, which Jowett interpreted as unpolished, reveals her double motive of participation in and revision of theological doctrine. Such conflicting energies mark her discourse with expressions of a kind of semiotic articulation interwoven in the symbolic representation of her beliefs and experiences. While Nightingale's discourse never breaks down to a pure semiotic level, by which I mean a nearly incommunicable degree of nonconventional syntactic or grammatical aberrations, it can reveal her marginal position to the conventions of theology; instead, the eruption of the nonlinear, fragmented "Cassandra" in the treatise's center, framed on either side by more traditional discourse, indicates the tensions inherent in her enterprise.[24] In Nightingale's discourse the semiotic impulse takes the form of a shift in genre, rhetoric, and coherence, each of which underscores the revolutionary perspective voiced most sharply in "Cassandra." And, while much of the whole of *Suggestions* contrasts in its presentation to the rigorous, logical rhythm of most theological enterprises because of its circumlocution and digressions, "Cassandra" provides the most striking example of a cacophonous counterbeat. Here in this shift from abstract to concrete in the history of Cassandra, the discourse proceeds with marked breaches of continuity; nearly impressionistic in its presentation of scenes or moments that are left to the reader to deduce not only their controlling idea but also their connection to juxtaposed sections, the narrative of "Cassandra" seems nearly devoid of transitions, developed not by causal or traditionally logical relationships, but by the association of accumulated fragments. Although the parabolic style has a rich history of association with Christian teaching, Nightingale is not just interpreting canonical stories, she is writing one: Nightingale's voice echoes earlier, sacred ones by articulating this new parable of women in patriarchal culture. In this way, Nightingale conflates the position of concrete and abstract: at the core of her treatise reverberates the impulses of the oppressed woman in patriarchy, not the symbolic delineation of God's word; she provides experiential illustration, not protracted, logical reasoning. In short, Nightingale not only interprets the world around her but also produces new parables to be interpreted. Thus with the act of writing and the manner in which she does write *Suggestions*, Nightingale challenges her culture at its most phallocentric: she challenges the Law-of-the-Father as her culture constructs it by representing the relationship between the believer and her God not just as that of the Word in need of interpretation but also as that of experience and feeling. (This revolutionary aspect present in *Suggestions* is clarified by a closer analysis of "Cassandra," which I turn to later.) In creating an alternative text to reveal the position of believers in her world, Nightingale elaborates her criticism of orthodox beliefs by revising its doctrines to account for women's experiences; radically subverting traditional maxims, she rewrites, in "Cassandra," the incarnation myth to envision a female Christ. With this provocative revision, Nightingale challenges patriarchy's exclusive position in sacred myth and subsequently its appropriation of Judeo-Christian religion. Thus, she revises, rather than completely rejects, the orthodox religious myth, both explaining women's powerlessness and identifying ways to regain greater power.

Before Nightingale rewrites the incarnation myth, however, she establishes the necessity for her revisionist theology: she exposes the complicity of organized religion and the state in suppressing God's gifts—both in workers and women—and details the prevailing sexual double-standard, regardless of class. By clarifying her culture's androcentric agenda, she gains some degree of authority to challenge that ideology, for she disagrees not with God but a heretical community, and, consequently, her challenge of patriarchal edicts is transformed from a personal to a spiritual dimension.

Nightingale reached these conclusions when, finding the Church of England inadequate for her needs, she undertook an analysis of Western religions in search of one that would empower her. For some time, Nightingale even flirted with Catholicism because she perceived in that faith two virtues absent in Protestantism—first, the continued recognition of a sacred vocation for women and, second, the continuing belief in a mystical relationship with God.[25] What she discovered, however, by this analysis was the overall inefficacy of organized religion, beginning with its inability to accurately represent the divine. "The perfect God," she writes, "is so unlike that of the Protestants and Roman Catholics" (ST, 2:40), who, she believed, distort His true character. In contrast to the institutionalized anthropomorphization, Nightingale envisions that:

> He is such an entirely different being, that we too may almost feel as if we were doing Him good service when we laugh at "their gods." At all events, there is such an absolute separation between them, such an opposition of natures, that we are no more laughing at Him,—Him the infinite wisdom, the perfect love, than when we speak of Jupiter and Juno, or of Egyptian cats. (ST, 2:40)

By categorizing modern Christianity with so-called pagan religions, Nightingale demystifies the power of sacred institutions and introduces both historical context and a sense of Christian duty to reject their precepts: the established churches of her day are no closer to the Truth than if they still worshipped Jupiter, Juno, or cats. Nightingale uses this technique of juxtaposing "Christian" beliefs with "pagan" ones to reinforce what she saw as the antiquated status of organized religion and the necessity of a Christianity that evolves as its believers progress, remaining true to God, but reflecting the impact of growth and time. Later in *Suggestions*, Nightingale would return to this technique when she evokes Greek myth. Titling her narrative "Cassandra," she underscores the image of that ancient, prophetic woman. The story of Cassandra becomes a powerful symbol for women, whose silenced voices could also hold truths. Like the mythical Cassandra, who is punished with the gift of unbelieved prophecy for rejecting Apollo, women whose words may be ignored still serve their cause—and God's—as prophets of the Truth. Strikingly, Nightingale reclaims one aspect of these "defunct" beliefs— Cassandra as prophet—to inform and clarify her revisionist Christianity. Through this allusion to Greek myth, like the earlier allusions to Juno and Jupiter, Nightingale inverts the traditional view of religious progress by paralleling the contemporary

Church's devaluation of women with now defunct beliefs. In other words, the Truth has evolved beyond what the Church preaches, and, subsequently, true believers should challenge these edicts.

In effect, Nightingale points to what she believes to be the stagnation of organized religion: the Church, self-assured that it holds the Truth in its laws, no longer seeks a higher truth; satisfied with the security of an institutionalized position, it no longer seeks confrontation with worldy values. Nightingale boldly asserts that "The Church of England is no training-ground for a discoverer of religious truth" (*ST*, 2:83). Rather, the Church restricts those who question its customs and provides no educational mechanism for a serious pursuit of the interpretation of God's word; instead, the Church retains that privilege for its select few. With a metaphor of Church as mother, Nightingale explains the impetus of this shortcoming by suggesting that it is a reaction against the "over-busy mother" of the Catholic church; that, in contrast, "the Church of England is expected to be an over-idle mother, who lets her children entirely alone" (*ST*, 2:96–97). This provocative analogy reveals a great deal about Nightingale's perception of the forces that limit her desires, basic tensions that would operate through much of her life, and ironic, paradoxical inversions that complicate any analysis of her life and faith. Not only does this analogy imply greater spiritual opportunity for the member of the Catholic church precisely because of its "interference" in the believer's life, challenging the ideal of the Protestant Reformation, but it exposes the significant presence of the mother in her life.

Nightingale perceived the Church as resting on its ordained laurels rather than revitalizing humanity's spirituality. In this way, then, Victorian religion, Nightingale believed, had become the perfect mouthpiece for a conservative and patriarchal ideology. As a voice for her androcentric culture, the doctrine espoused by institutionalized Christianity not only endorsed but also encouraged the marginalization of women and, even more significantly, that of God. Simply put, the adherence to radical Christian ethics—those that embraced individual needs and desires and those that Nightingale sought—would stifle the industrial energy and the competitive spirit upon which an increasingly market-driven economy would depend. As Barbara Taylor explains, the nineteenth century "domesticated Christianity," freeing man and mammon to rule the workplace.[26] Still, even if in this domestication the traditional patriarchal ideals dismissed Christian values of compassion and community and relegated them to the private (now predominantly female) sphere, religious power remained with men: the authoritative, rule-giving Church hierarchy never included women, and only in the earliest days of the Evangelical movement did women preach.[27] The Church, then, no longer serving God, not even really including women, appropriated His word but nonetheless claimed the history of divine authority for a patriarchal agenda.

As a result, Nightingale believes that nothing resembles the true essence of Christ—regardless of the number of relics or chapels—because humanity has long since given up searching after His truths. Unlike the sciences, which continually seek to advance more factual data from that held by previous generations, religion, she asserts, has stagnated with half-truths and outdated dogma. Troubled by this absence of any real spiritual inquiry, Nightingale would return to this in "A Sub-Note of Interrogation: What Will Be Our Religion in 1999?" where she considers the state of religion in future generations. Framing her inquiry by the solar eclipse of 1873, she wonders what the state of religion will be for the next total eclipse, in 1999:

> Will religion consist then, as now, not in whether a man is "just, true, and merciful"; whether the man seeks to know God, and what He is, and what He wishes us to do; whether the man seeks to be a fellow-worker with God, and for this purpose to find out God's plans; but whether the man "had believed what he was told to believe?" had gone to church "for what he called prayers," and "had duly paid the fees to the temple?"[28]

Victorian religion, then, it seems to her, depends not on scholars dedicating their lives to advancing theological truths but on docile believers obeying the status quo. Although her culture possesses the potential to better ascertain God's laws than any previous generation, theological scholarship has become retarded, even rigid, petrifying and enshrining now outdated and primitive values. She asks:

> What is morality to be referred to? Is it not to our sense of right? But we have referred it to a book, which book makes many contradictory assertions. Discoveries are being made every day in physical science; but in the most important science of all no discoveries are made or can be made. Why? because [the Bible] is final. Supposing Moses had written a book about mechanics, and this book was regarded as the ultimatum, we should have made no progress in mechanics. Aristotle was supposed to have written such a book, and for 1,800 years people

disbelieved their own actual experience before their eyes, because they could quote chapter and verse of Aristotle to a contrary effect. Yes, with the sound of two weights falling simultaneously in their ears, they maintained that the weight which was ten times heavier than the other fell in one-tenth of the time of the other, because *Aristotle had said-so.* Is not this an exactly parallel case? (*ST*, 2:24)

Using Aristotle as the source to which early scientists clung unquestioningly, Nightingale evokes an interesting analogy—especially given her non-Aristotelian development and presentation of spiritual beliefs—to suggest the foolishness of organized religion holding fast to an equally outdated dogma. Christian rules may indeed be inscribed in stone, but, she argues, humanity's understanding of them is far from sufficient or complete: the longer organized religion clings to these primitive values, the more difficult it becomes to supplant those outdated beliefs with more accurate ones, with beliefs closer to the Truth. Established as *the* Truth and implicitly sanctioned by heaven, these archaic values, which Nightingale ascribes to the Church, continue to shape organized religion and dictate people's lives. With the absence of a living ethic, present-day believers can only passively act on their faith; instead of developing an individual understanding and relationship with God, these followers become circumscribed by ancient interpretations. Too often used as a pacifier of the oppressed, religion has ignored issues of poverty, imperialism, education, and legal reforms (*ST*, 2:29). No longer a medium through which to achieve a more compassionate world, organized religion becomes both a tool for the powerful to justify their desires and to exclude individualistic participation in shaping its creed. And while Nightingale was not naive enough to believe that atrocities had not occurred before in the name of God, she would not condone complacency in those shortcomings; failing to advance, Victorian religion not only vindicated systemic problems but also perpetuated them.

This travesty of religion becomes mirrored, she believes, in the dynamics of the Victorian family. Early in *Suggestions*, Nightingale establishes this connection, writing that "The two questions concerning the relation [of the individual] to God and the relation to the parent are one. You cannot separate the inquiry about religion and about the family" (*ST*, 2:245). Just as her culture replicates Western religion's hierarchical structure, the family recreates the same, with father as lord (or, in Nightingale's case, with her mother representing patriarchy, as I have already argued). The power of God becomes implicitly transferred to the domestic ruler, and, because of this, the family, Nightingale insists, is the Protestant form of idolatry (*ST*, 2:179): children and wives serve the father, nearly worship the sons. She develops this analogy between the family and the church by pointing to their shared desire for uniformity among its members. Just as the Church rejects dissenting and nonconforming members, so does the family. In contrast, Nightingale suggests that rather than be threatened by challenging voices, the Church and the family should grow strong by the diversity of these members: "The parent, like the Church," she asserts, "must allow for varieties of character, *whilst* he retains his absolute authority"; otherwise, the parent "will turn out John Wesley," or a Florence Nightingale, "instead of being strengthened by his earnestness and zeal" (*ST*, 2:239–40). Regardless, then, of the child's dreams or even of God's plans, the family appropriates its members' talents for self-serving goals (*ST*, 2:198): "The family uses people, *not* for what they are, not for what they are intended to be, but for what it wants them for— its own uses. It thinks of them not as what God has made them, but as something which *it* arranged that they shall be" (*ST*, 2:389).

The family, Nightingale believes, has "Too narrow a field for the development of an immortal spirit, be that spirit male or female. The chances are a thousand to one that, in the small sphere, the task for which that immortal spirit is destined by the qualities and the gifts which its Creator has placed within it, will not be found" (*ST*, 2:388–89). Declaring that the family limits both male and female individualization, Nightingale extends the criticism of her culture beyond just the oppression of women's gifts to the oppression of God's gifts. She asks, "What is [the family's usurpation of the individual] but throwing the gifts of God aside as worthless and substituting for them those of the world?" (*ST*, 2:389).

With organized religion exposed as flawed and the family indicted through parallel failings, Nightingale considers the place of women and especially daughters, in both. In the family:

> It is vaguely taken for granted by women that it is to be their first object to please and obey their parents till they are married. But the times are totally changed since those patriarchal days. Man (and woman too) has a soul to unfold, a part to play in God's great world. (*ST*, 2:219)

Like outdated religions, this antiquated pattern must be changed;

but, just as theology, in her opinion, failed to evolve with humanity, the position allowed women in patriarchal society has shown little progression. "Jesus Christ," she insists, "raised women above the condition of mere slaves, mere ministers of God. He gave them moral activity" (ST, 2:404). Really asking what women have done that society should make them slaves, Nightingale inverts the issue, querying "What has 'society' done for us?" (ST, 2:209).[29] "What has mankind done for us?" she continues, this time providing an answer: "It has created wants which not only it does not afford us the opportunity of satisfying, but which it compels us to disguise and deny" (ST, 2:210–11). Rather than encourage women to develop their capacities, her culture, Nightingale contends, has instead offered them the role of slave, or, at best, that of prisoner. "The prison which is called a family, will its rules ever be relaxed, its doors ever be opened? What is it, especially to the woman? The man may escape, and does" (ST, 2:198). In contrast, the woman's sentence, she believes, is stricter, her pardon more circumscript:

> Daughters are now their mothers' slaves . . . they are considered their parents' property; they are to have no other pursuit, nor power, nor independent life, unless they marry; they are to be entirely dependent upon their parents—white slaves in the family, from which marriage alone can emancipate them. (ST, 2:224)

"There is no tyranny," she concludes, "like that of the family, for it extends over the thoughts" (ST, 2:200).[30]

And, because her class and culture sanction no profession for women, only one option for escaping familial domination exists—marriage—and, echoing her earlier complaints, Nightingale sees in her state religion no viable alternative. "To the woman," she writes, "Protestantism offers nothing but marriage; she may leave home to marry, but for nothing else. . . . To justify herself she must take a husband" (ST, 2:180). So according to Nightingale's observation, daughters have but two options: to be married or to be forever a daughter (ST, 2:229). Neither, for Nightingale, offers anything appealing: "It is the hardest slavery, either to take the chance of a man whom she knows *so little*, or to vegetate at home, her life consumed by *ennui* as by a cancer" (ST, 2:59). Yet, she wonders, is marriage—especially as her culture defined it—really what God would intend for His daughters? God instituted marriage as a choice, Nightingale believes, not a mandate, for Jesus never married (ST, 2:284). And it would be unnatural to serve one man when one could serve humanity through God's works: "it is unnatural, and the most selfish of all ties *if* the tie is to be, as Milton has put it, 'He, thy God, thou mine,' if they are to serve and divinify one another" (*ST*, 2:44).

Nightingale acknowledges, however, that many women do choose marriage over remaining in their fathers' homes. She reflects upon their motivation: "three things on which marriage is generally founded,—a good opinion of a person, a desire to love and be loved, and a wish to escape dissatisfaction at home" (*ST*, 2:230). And regardless which of the three foundations a marriage is based on, the woman receives little more freedom as wife than what she had as daughter. "A woman doesn't really gain independence with marriage; she only becomes 'property' of her husband, who gets all her wealth" (*ST*, 2:278). For the man, who becomes the secular lord, the family life revolves around him and his activities. He acts; he controls; he masters. In contrast, a wife from Nightingale's social station produces nothing except perhaps children—and even they will be raised by their nanny, taught by their governess. Nightingale concludes that "A married woman's life consists in superintending what she does not know how to do": she orders dinner, rather than prepares it; she inspects the larder and store room, rather than supplies it; she visits the poor rather than acts to alleviate poverty (*ST*, 2:291). And all the while the daughter suffers, parents "hope that if [daughters] don't marry, they will at least be quiet" (*ST*, 2:59–60). Again assigning the suffering of Victorian daughters' sacred status, Nightingale hypothesizes whether "Christ, if He had been a woman might have been nothing but a great complainer" (*ST*, 2:408); and, doing so, she points to the fact that in her culture gender, not action, determines rights. As a man, Christ could detach himself from his earthly family's demands and follow his God-given mission; a woman, Nightingale believes, who would follow hers is accused of "destroying the family tie" and "obligation of home duties" (*ST*, 2:409). Implicit in this desire by parents for acquiescence is the view of daughters as worthless in themselves—the daughter is seen as a burden because parents refuse to (or cannot) see their daughters as productive members of the family or society. The work they do perform is undervalued, the work they might do lost. This point of difference between daughters and sons signals to her not only the incongruity between God's will and man's interpretation of it but also the subsequent impossibility for women to develop their talents in a patriarchal society.

In contrast to this exploitation, Nightingale presents an alternative for women. "Unmarried women," she claims, "should have every facility given them by parents to spend their time and faculties upon any exercise of their nature for which it has an attraction, which can be pursued in harmony with God, which can answer, in short, any good purpose" (*ST*, 2:256). The reality of women's lives, however, is that their "life is spent in pastime, men's in business. Women's business is supposed to be to find something to 'pass' the 'time'" (*ST*, 2:213). Nightingale elaborates:

> The maxim of doing things at "odd moments" is a most dangerous one. Would not the painter spoil his picture by working at it "at odd moments?" If it be a picture worth painting at all, and if he be a man of genius, he must have the whole of his picture in his head everytime he touches it, and this requires great concentration, and this concentration cannot be obtained at "odd moments." (*ST*, 2:65–66)

This, she adds, is as ridiculous as telling people not to take regular meals, but to eat at odd times (*ST*, 2:66). Given only "odd moments" to develop their talents, women's abilities will never be realized, and the woman, when finally free to pursue her own desires, "will be too wasted to employ herself" (*ST*, 2:69).

Nightingale's own life illustrates the degree to which she did not want to work at odd moments or expend her primary energy tending to others' needs. Rather than become complicit in what she perceived as a cultural devaluation of God's plan for her, Nightingale rejected the acceptable patterns of behavior for a woman of her position. She refused what would have been considered a suitable marriage proposal from Richard Monckton Milnes, explaining:

> I have an intellectual nature which requires satisfaction, and that would find it in him. I have a passionate nature which requires satisfaction, and that would find it in him. I have a moral, an active nature which requires satisfaction, and that would not find it in his life. Sometimes I think I will satisfy my passional nature at all events, because that will at least secure me from the evil of dreaming. But would it? I could be satisfied to spend a life with him in combining our different powers in some great object. I could not satisfy this nature by spending a life with him making society and arranging domestic things.[31]

This reasoned rejection to Milnes's marriage proposal, which privileges her "active nature" even above passion or familial escape, is echoed by many passages in her journals concerning women and marriage. At the end of one of these entries, she pledges to make a better life for women.[32] This "better life" meant the opportunity for women to determine for themselves the course of their own life, to find avenues to satisfy their active natures and their untapped talents—independent of marriage. So when faced with what appeared to her to be the choice to either defy her God or her family, Nightingale boldly defied the latter by refusing to marry. This meant, however, that she would need to identify and pursue another channel for fulfilling her vision of God's plan.

Nightingale bolsters her argument by suggesting patriarchal edicts oppress not only women but also men who feel called in nontraditional ways, thus preventing the appearance of a purely personal agenda. She establishes this by analyzing the extent to which her culture suppresses the individual's God-given talents among the working class; in fact, she even dedicates the first volume of her *Suggestions for Thought* to "The Artisans of England." Their needs unmet or unaccounted for by a religion complicit in the capitalistic doctrines of industrialization, many working class men and women rejected orthodox beliefs and, in doing so, proved threatening to their economic superiors, who would have benefited from a meek acceptance by the workers of hard conditions softened by capitalistic interpretations of the doctrine of work.[33] This lack of "faith" appeared to the upper classes to be a complete abandonment of morality and God—and not incidentally a recognition of their place. Nightingale, herself dissatisfied by her place both in culture and in traditional religion, attempted to clarify this apparent atheism in a way that suggests a projection of her own beliefs onto these workers: "What the most conscientious among our working men seem to be doing now, is renouncing religious error, not announcing religious truth; they seem not to be seeking after light, but giving up darkness" (*ST*, 2:39). The working class, Nightingale believed, was not rejecting God, but rejecting the dark state of religion, just as she was. Explaining the workers' apparent atheism in this way, Nightingale contextualizes her criticism of her culture's treatment of women.

Middle-class daughters and workers, she would contend, held positions analogous to each other in society. Just as capitalism and industry demanded obedience and uniformity, so, too, the family expected loyalty and devotion. While daughters like Nightingale did not face the real threats of poverty or the physical exploitation that the workers did, they still suffered from their culture's self-serving agenda, which had appropriated religious doctrine for authority. Just as many workers had turned away from organized religion—not because they were atheists but because they recognized the Church's failings—so, too, must daughters like Nightingale, who found neither comfort nor support in its oppressive preachments. Equating women's suppressed talents (and workers' exploited ones) with God's, Nightingale not only builds her case by revealing the widespread exploitation of believers but also by citing divine authority for their emancipation. Criticizing patriarchy in this way, she undercuts any easy authority from secular to sacred parallels; while patriarchal hierarchy may appear to replicate the paradigm of the traditional Judeo-Christian myth with God as father, it merely replicates the pattern, not the divine intent or sacred mission; consequently, she diagnoses female subjection, not as woman's proper role, but the result of a clerical misreading of God and a cultural appropriation of the associated power. Elevating her suffering as a daughter of patriarchy to sacred dimensions, Nightingale acquires not only the power to challenge that subjection but also the authority to voice alternative social and spiritual dynamics.

After exposing and detailing this cultural, as opposed to divine, subjection of women, Nightingale produces an alternative doctrine: she creates a revisionist incarnation story that accounts for women's pain and struggle, and she calls for female prophets to dedicate their lives to advancing this vision. Nightingale begins "Cassandra":

> One often comes to be thus wandering alone in the bitterness of life without. It might be that such an one might be tempted to seek an escape in hope of a more congenial sphere. Yet, perhaps, if prematurely we dismiss ourselves from this world, all may even have to be suffered through again—the premature birth may not contribute to the production of another being, which must be begun from the beginning. (ST, 2:374)

Using the impersonal pronoun rather than "I" or "you," she rejects simple autobiography and instead creates a mythic, universal quality for "Cassandra," allowing identification with this female prophet by all women. Borrowing from the Judeo-Christian myth, she sees the necessity of prophets and martyrs to serve as precursors for her revised incarnation. Through images of premature births, which she identifies as potential prophets who commit suicide, she notes that suicide's appeal masks the importance of female suffering as well as aborts female advancement by eliminating precursors and consequently delaying the new Christ's arrival.

In her discussion of Milton, Christine Froula has described basic differences in male and female authority. There she distinguishes these two models as: male respect and female questioning of an invisible authority; patriarchal anagogy of history, which invests spiritual authority only in a few; the image of a male creator, which subordinates the visible to the invisible, experience to mediated knowledge, and silence to the word. Froula's paradigm can be applied to Nightingale's revisionist discourse to illuminate the central, defining differences from canonical doctrine as she rewrites Christian doctrine, replacing patriarchal values with feminist ones.[34]

In arguing her theological beliefs, Nightingale points to concrete evidence in the visible world to challenge invisible patriarchal abstractions. This is especially evident in "Cassandra." There she asks: "What *do* we see? . . . We see girls and boys of seventeen, before whose noble ambitions, heroic dreams, and rich endowments we bow our heads, as before *God incarnate in the flesh.* But, ere they are thirty, they are withered, paralyzed, extinguished" (*ST,* 2:387). By comparing seventeen-year-old boys and girls to "God incarnate in the flesh," she empowers "ordinary" people, not an elite group of individuals. Asserting that the "'dreams of youth' have become a proverb" (*ST,* 2:387), she again links human dreams with divine truths and suggests that with the initiation into society, the young lose their spiritual connections and find, instead, a corrupt world. By labeling these repressed dreams proverbs in this way, Nightingale authorizes the dreams, not patriarchal suppression of them. Thus infusing a sacred identity in the seen and experienced as opposed to the invisible and the abstracted, Nightingale extends spiritual authority from a limited segment of believers to virtually all of humanity.

"Cassandra" continues to subvert patriarchal hierarchies, which limit power to a very few, by announcing that prophets were, and can be, abundant in every age. Asserting "it is a privilege to suffer for your race—a privilege not reserved to the Redeemer and martyrs alone, but one enjoyed by numbers in every age" (*ST,* 2:379)—Nightingale associates any who choose to struggle for their race with the Redeemer.[35] Doing so, she extends sacred power to anyone choosing to suffer for spiritual beliefs, contrasting sharply the limits of authority that institutionalized religion demands. Significantly, it is to suffer for this faith, and not to suffer under the restraints of her society, that empowers the individual. With this distinction, Nightingale challenges those who would explain, even condone, oppression in a Christian context: that believers who suffer in the physical world gain their rewards in the next. Instead, while she also recognizes the sacred tradition of suffering, she transfers the spiritual dimension to women and workers; rather than see their suffering as God's plan for them, this revision asserts that they suffer because their exploiters seek to deter God's mission and that the suffering reveals the conflict between worldly and sacred values.

Through this privileged suffering, again linking the common to the sacred, Nightingale raises speech above silence. Recognizing patriarchal culture's ability to silence those under its power, realizing that such enforced silence perpetuates its agenda, Nightingale pleads with women to regain a heightened sensitivity to their suffering: made numb from years of oppression and repressed passion, women become mute; consequently, Nightingale cries for intensified pain. With the epigraph to the second section of "Cassandra," she calls for this resensitivity to oppression's pain: "Yet I would spare no pang, / Would wish no torture less, / The more that anguish racks, / The earlier it will bless" (ST, 2:378). Invoking voice-giving pain to replace silent desensitization, Nightingale claims the martyrs' strength from suffering and rewrites the Christian martyr as female in patriarchal society. Thus she unites female oppression with that of the traditional Christian martyrs and encourages women to find strength, if not authority, through the pain. At the very least, she sees pain as the powerful reminder of their position, one that should help women resist a hegemonic culture.

Nightingale rewrites the Judeo-Christian myth's narrative of prophetic lineage with a feminist version. Using the epigraph "'The Voice of one crying in the' crowd, / 'Prepare ye the way of the Lord'" to begin "Cassandra" (ST, 2:374), Nightingale unites the mythologized "one" with a prophet heralding God's eventual incarnation. She continues to examine women's myopic pleasure in suicide, arguing that the pain and suffering women endure reveal that they are indeed furthering God's intended plan: "Some are only deterred from suicide because it is in the most distinct manner to say to God: 'I will not, I will not do as thou wouldst have me do,' and because it is 'no use'" (ST, 2:394). Rather than fight against worldly values, the suicide victim retreats from the struggle. In charging women to resist suicide, Nightingale extends the traditional view of the sacrilege of suicide: she equates it with female complicity in the patriarchal misreading of God.

Nightingale equates patriarchal suppression of women with the earlier Roman suppression of Christians by pointing to the struggle of women who serve as the necessary prophets of female incarnation. She reminds women of their duty to become those prophets and resist the temptations of silence and suicide, which would make them complicit in patriarchal interpretations of God's plan. She believes that unless women resensitize themselves to their oppression's pain, the new Christ will never be born. Each suffering woman, then, like the unbelieved Cassandras, becomes the new missing "messenger" and quickens the female incarnation.

In this context, Nightingale boldy asserts: "The next Christ will perhaps be a female Christ. But do we see one woman who looks like a female Christ? or even like 'the messenger before' her 'face,' to go before her and prepare the hearts and minds for her?" (ST, 2:408). How, then, will women finally be emancipated from their patriarchal prisons? Who will lead them out of their moral wilderness? These become the crucial questions for Nightingale. Who indeed? Women, like organized religion, need saviors, but again like the Church, "they have no *type* before them," no one to validate their desires (ST, 2:62).[36] The missing saviors, for the Church and for women, would serve the same function—emancipate religion from its antiquated codes and divest patriarchy of its power over women.

Nightingale would return to this belief that Victorian England boasted no prophets or saviors in "A Note of Interrogation"—a distillation of her ideas published in *Fraser's Magazine*—where she asks "Who is to be the founder, who the Bacon, of a method of enquiry into moral service?"[37] Like Carlyle searching for his heroes, Nightingale searches for saviors able to lead the people out of their moral wilderness. Although she admits that most people believe that the "time is past for *individual* saviours (male or female)," Nightingale insists that "the world cannot be saved, except through saviours, at present," and adds, "A saviour means one who saves from error" (ST, 2:201).

By foregrounding in her text the literal meaning of "saviour," Nightingale heightens her readers' consciousness of the corrective element of religion. A savior should be more than an icon for worship that suggests that all evils have been eradicated; instead, a savior should lead the on-going struggle to establish spiritual, as opposed to worldly, values. Nightingale extends this vision of the needed savior beyond the Church and its doctrines to encompass cultural dynamics as well; she adds that "there must be saviours from social, from moral error" (*ST*, 2:202). By including the secular world in her analysis of moral deterioration, Nightingale forces religion out of cathedrals and cloisters to what she sees as its rightful domain—society at large. Just as she believes God wants humanity to serve Him, not lay prostrate before Him, she believes the true motives of religion should be transferred from worship to life. No longer should humanity's morals be divided between secular and religious codes; each individual should shape his or her life with spirituality, as Nightingale believes she will do.

But with society in need of correction and saviors wanting, Nightingale can only lament the current condition: "There is so little religion now that we do not even feel the want of [a Savior]; we need a Saviour now as much as [the Greeks, Romans, and Egyptians] did then" (*ST*, 2:38). "What a hopeless state," she continues, "till some saviour strikes a cord which reveals to man what *is* his proper food by giving him a taste of it, or a consciousness of what that taste should be; for, by God's law, it is the appetite which is to lead to food, to determine *what* food" (*ST*, 2:286). But until a savior comes along to whet humanity's appetite for proper spiritual food, Nightingale fears that savior would be unrecognized. And as she pleads for a savior to herald the coming of God, she, somewhat ironically, becomes that prophet. To her readers Nightingale prophesizes: "Oh! that again someone would cry, in a voice that might reach the human heart, 'Prepare ye the way of the Lord!'" (*ST*, 2:370).

By rewriting the incarnation myth, Nightingale demystifies her patriarchal culture and reenfranchises women into their rightful spirituality. Nightingale subverts the fundamental Western myth—that of God's incarnation as man—by suggesting God's incarnation as woman. Doing so, Nightingale rejects patriarchy as divinely inspired and creates a new model, not matriarchal, but one enfranchising all who use their God-given talents. In this context, her reformed model of nursing, from training to hospital administration, can be understood as an extension of a spiritual vocation: the nurse that Nightingale envisions serves as a type of missionary, spreading a new gospel, a new ethic of care.

Much upon which Nightingale based her reconstructed theology can be found in her own life; because of this, a further examination of her struggle to enact what she believed to be God's plan will help to illuminate her revisionist spirituality. Nightingale's beliefs were shaped by years of suffering, years of tempering her desires while trying to make herself worthier to answer God's calls.[38] During this time, Nightingale read and thought extensively in her attempt to understand those calls. Finding no sanctioned time in her over-orchestrated day to pursue her ethical deliberations, Nightingale established a strict regimen for her "odd moments," studying mathematics, digesting hospital blue books, and recording her thoughts before her "real" day began.[39]

The exhaustion of this schedule and the apparently unswaying attitude of her family propelled Nightingale into a period of deep despair. Her diary for these years reveals her repeated near-suicidal depressions:

> My present life is suicide; in my 31st year I see nothing desirable but death; What am I that their life is not good enough for me? Oh God what am I? The thoughts and feelings that I have now I can remember since I was six years old. It was not I that made them. . . . But why, oh my God, cannot I be satisfied with the life that satisfies so many people?[40]

The frustration so evident here appears in other private writings from the time as well. In her 1847–49 notebook, she laments the need to suppress the thriving desires she cannot ignore:

> There are Private Martyrs as well as burnt or drowned ones. Society . . . does not know them; and the family cannot, because our position to one another in our families is . . . like that of the Moon to the Earth. The Moon revolves around her, moves with her, never leaves her. Yet the Earth never sees but one side of her; the other side remains for ever unknown.[41]

In one of her journals, she writes of her desire for anonymity and hard work to enhance her God-given talents and enable them to "ripen" for "the Glory of His Name."[42] This agony of Nightingale's—caught between her culture's expectations for her and what she believed to be God's—could be neither easily overcome nor dismissed. The unbearable agony of this conflict must have seemed unending as she writes:

> The thoughts and feelings that I have now . . . I can remember since I was six years old. A profession, a trade, a necessary occupation, something to fill and employ all my faculties, I have always felt essential to me, I have always longed for. The first thought I can remember, and last, was nursing work; and in the absence of this, education

work, but more the education of the bad than of the young. . . .
Everything has been tried, foreign travel, kind friends, everything.
My God! What is to become of me?[43]

And, in an 1850 diary entry, Nightingale claims a significant parallel between her life and Christ's, reflecting: "I am 30 . . . the age
of which Christ began His mission. No more childish things, no
more vain things, no more love, no more marriage. Now, Lord,
let me only think of Thy will."[44] By associating her own life with
Christ's, by presuming such a parallel, she reveals the important
aspect of identification with the divine central to her revisionist
theology: rather than operate from a position of deferential worship that would limit her access to sacred authority, she proceeds
from a belief in her own sacred authority through this association.

As this entry also suggests, Nightingale's own life reveals a
striking example of the oppressive position in which Victorian
culture and religion placed nontraditional women, especially
Nightingale, who believed God had called her into His service
but found every opportunity to do so denied her—by family, culture, and organized religion.[45] So with a marriage rejected and a
profession denied, Nightingale nearly suffocated in her mother's
home. She "strove to say to God, 'Behold the handmaid of the
Lord! *not* Behold the handmaid of correspondence, or of music,
or of metaphysics!'"[46] At this point in her life, however, Nightingale had yet to apply to herself the strategies that she would
eventually recommend to other women: suffering redirected into
advancing God's work. Eventually, she would redirect her pain
into the writing of *Suggestions*.

One significant issue in this analysis of Nightingale's spiritual
crisis remains: where did she find the authority to rewrite established doctrine and then to enact her beliefs? Initially, her extensive reading exposed her to what she believed to be scientific
approaches that could facilitate discerning and deciphering God's
laws. Specifically her reading of John Stuart Mill, Edgar Quinet,
and Adolphe Quetelet helped to codify her religious beliefs and
translate them into the theories that *Suggestions* delineates.[47] Mill's
logical assertions, Quinet's radical theological beliefs, and Quetelet's applied statistics provided the foundation for Nightingale's
religion, a religion which thrived, rather than suffered, from con-
temporaneous scientific advances. The discovery of natural laws
only confirmed Nightingale's beliefs; for if there are laws, she
reasoned, then there must be a lawgiver.[48] She wrote that "Law
[was] the basis of [her] new theology" (*ST*, 1:178) since law is the

"volition of God" (*ST*, 3:6). Believing that natural laws—not the Church's preachments—evidenced God's essence, Nightingale, in her first *Fraser's Magazine* article, charged theologians to pursue religious studies with the rigorous inquiry that marked the sciences; they should try to figure out "what *are* the laws that govern the moral world."[49] Experience, research, and analysis, not blind adherence to traditional beliefs, would reveal His moral codes; "His *essence* might remain a mystery," but "the *character* of God was ascertainable" by this careful study.[50]

Applying the statistical methods she learned from Quetelet to discover patterns and correlations of disease and living conditions, Nightingale charged humanity to observe these laws of God, both to ascertain and follow them. The resulting patterns, when carefully studied and understood, could reveal a more advanced understanding of God's will. "In laws," she contended, "are found the means by which man may advance and approximate towards that absolute and perfect moral nature" (*ST*, 3:29). Nightingale's theology professed, then, that from careful study of the world's natural laws, one would discover God's laws, and by understanding His laws one could ascertain the Truth. In this way, she provides access to sacred truths to any who sought after them, any who observed natural patterns, not man-made rules.

The great need for humanity to seek these truths pervades her three volumes. She even concludes *Suggestions:*

> Man has attained much; but as yet man knows not God; man knows not man; man knows not his real satisfaction, though it be essential to him to seek it; man, while unconscious of the depth of his ignorance, is alike unconscious of the height of his ability. (*ST*, 3:126)

Nightingale spends much of the three volumes exposing this moral ignorance by observing its manifestations in her culture. Early in the second volume she asks, "In the last 300 years much has been gained politically, but what has been done for religion? . . . [only] denying and not constructing" (*ST*, 2:189). "Criticism," she asserts, "has stripped Religion of many superstitions. . . . but has it advanced us one step nearer in the study of God's real character, the character which makes us love? . . . May it not rather have killed Religion with the cure of superstition?" (*ST*, 2:36). And although she, like Carlyle, believes Victorian religion is in dire need of revision, Nightingale wants to revitalize it, but not by looking for saviors (or heroes) in traditional, established patterns. She asks: "If religion is lost, what is to become of England? unless one comes to raise up another religion" (*ST*, 2:40). And this, she laments, is unlikely since "there appears to be scarcely anything in England now which bears any resemblance to Christ" (*ST*, 2:189).

Believing that "The spirit of Truth will be our authority, if we will faithfully seek Him" (*ST*, 1:2), Nightingale extends the parameters of sacred authority, limited only by the degree to which the individual desires Truth; doing so, she claims a tremendous amount of authority for herself since, after all, she has dedicated her life to this pursuit. With desire for Truth the only prerequisite for authority, *anyone* can unearth the essence of God's laws, not just theologians, not just leaders of religious communities, not just men. Rather than look heavenward for dictates and rules, Nightingale looks earthward for evidence of God; rather than sanction authority by decree, she turns to experience and motivation.

By investing spiritual authority in any who faithfully seek God, Nightingale lays the groundwork for her mystical spirituality. To demonstrate the need for individual relationships with God rather than salvation through organized religion, Nightingale depicts the life of an individual in the decayed and self-serving society she has already exposed. Frustrated by what organized religion fails to achieve, she puts her faith in the individual member of that community; if sanctioned men of God do not (or will not) work to accomplish God's plan, she believes the individual, through heightened communion with Him, can. In a passage which echoes her own calls from God, Nightingale writes:

> But God does not refuse to answer the longing, devoted spirit, which says, Speak, Lord, for thy loving child heareth. He hears as the Father; He answers as the Son, and as the Holy Spirit. I could not understand God, if He were to speak to me. But the Holy Spirit, the Divine in me, tells me what I am to do. I am conscious of a voice that I can hear, telling me more truth and good than I *am*. As I rise to *be* more truly and more rightly, this voice is ever beyond and above me, calling to more and more good. (*ST*, 2:32)

Nightingale's intense belief in a personal God echoes the earlier Greek and Christian mystics.[51] Significantly, Nightingale's spiritual design also echoes aspects of the Gnostic Gospels. Elaine Pagels's important work on these suppressed texts reveals key parallels: direct access to God, the presence of the divine in the individual believer, and the importance of intuitive insight and the experience of knowing rather than the final knowledge.[52] For Nightingale, the personal connection with God that mysticism provided thoroughly entranced her; here existed a medium through which an individual could better understand God and his or her service to Him. Even if her family and culture prevented one from actively serving God, as was the case with Nightingale, the individual could still develop this personal relationship. In *Suggestions*, Nightingale defines mysticism as the ability to focus on the "unseen" and to "endeavour to partake of the divine nature; that is, of Holiness."[53] Rejecting the notion that mysticism fails to serve community needs because it encourages personal ones, Nightingale believed that a community of believers charged by their own relationship with God would be far more productive than one populated by those told what to do or say by an outdated and misdirected Church. What mysticism offered the faithful, then, she believed, was direct access to God and, subsequently, His truths; mysticism encouraged the individual to serve, to experience, and to understand God, not simply to worship Him. Significantly, mysticism operates between the individual and God in much the same way as that of the semiotic language Kristeva identifies—not as a symbolically systematized abstraction taught or learned, but as a language or form of communication not included in conventional, symbolic constructs. In this, Nightingale reveals another aspect of the revolutionary potential of her revisionist theology: this spirituality would build from experience and connection independent of the exegetical interpretation of symbol enshrined as the foundation of patriarchal Christianity. And, although the Judeo-Christian religion includes a long history of early mystics who would ratify the appropriated religious belief, the authority by which they voiced their faith remained outside the established, hierarchical structure of even the early Church; that is, although incorporated into the myth of Christianity, mystics represented an alternative, independent manner of communicating between their God and fellow believers. Nightingale writes that God desires that we should be "one with Him, not prostrate before Him" (*ST*, 2:22), and thus charges her readers to "Organize then your life to act out your religion" (*ST*, 2:318). In this way, like the earlier Gnostic Gospels, Nightingale's revisionist theology proves extremely threatening to the patriarchal state and its religion; by building its truths upon individual experience and expanding access to the divine to all, these revolutionary tracts stand diametrically opposed to the foundations of the exclusivity of patriarchal authority.

The final section of "Cassandra" reveals the extent to which Nightingale subverts the conventions of her culture by representing a noncomplicitous woman in the dying Cassandra. Although many could read the joy at death as counterproductive to her desires for freedom (as Nightingale herself cautioned against the pleasure of suicide earlier in "Cassandra"), this conscious joy at death must be considered in the contexts of power and power-lessness. In this final section, Nightingale's Cassandra declares: "Let neither name nor date be placed on her grave, still less the expression of regret or of admiration; but simply the words, 'I believe in God'" (ST, 2:411). This dying woman, finding neither joy in this life nor a way to alter that fact, shocks her family by her exhilaration at death. She, and others brave enough to recognize patriarchal oppression of her talents, become messengers an-nouncing the eventual birth of a female Christ, replacing the Judeo-Christian prophets of the male incarnation as new proph-ets of the female incarnation. And, as prophets, these women find divine authority to challenge their culture, regardless of their position in that culture. This Cassandra gains power—regains control over her life (or in this case, death)—by choosing death. Not motivated by complicity in her own subjection, this death refuses even to participate in the patriarchal options life would offer her, refuses even implicitly to validate those choices.[54]

Writing *Suggestions*, Elaine Showalter asserts, was a kind of therapy for Florence Nightingale; this lengthy discourse on reli-gious vision and responsibility "helped her to work through her psychic turmoil."[55] Gaining power and control as author—al-though temporarily—Nightingale could create specific examples of the world as she envisioned it and she believed it could be.[56] With her movement from theory to practice in *Suggestions*, from theological abstractions to Cassandra's story, she produced possi-bilities for her own life—from fictional confrontations to sacrifi-cial deaths.

The writing of *Suggestions*, however, was more than a thera-peutic exercise to emancipate Nightingale; "Cassandra," espe-cially, operated theologically as well.[57] Nightingale gained author-ity—divine authority—through Cassandra's death. Her culture with its outdated, stagnated religion crucified and martyred the victimized Cassandra, and Nightingale symbolically became the resurrected "saviour." Thus, by observing God's laws and re-cording man's misappropriation of them by society, Nightingale was reborn. In Cassandra's death, Nightingale also triumphed over her mother's power (as cultural socializer)—Cassandra (as surrogate for Nightingale) will not participate in her own subjec-tion, and seeing no other alternative completely refuses to live dominated by patriarchal design. This victorious death must be seen in contrast to the seductive attraction Nightingale has earlier condemned: unlike that death which gives up the fight for the sacred truths Nightingale pursues, this death is the culmination of a life victimized by patriarchal oppression. Appropriate for this rejection of patriarchal social codes, Nightingale's production of text parallels that rejection; absent transitions, incomplete sentences, and layered voices mark the final fragment of "Cassandra" in a dialogue with mourners. Here, Nightingale rejects conventional patterns of behavior: celebrating death ("Welcome, beautiful death!" [ST, 2:411]) and calling for "wedding clothes instead of mourning" (ST, 2:411) for this quintessentially Christian interpretation of death as "divine freedom" from the chains of an earthly life (ST, 2:411). Seeing her life as thwarted by cultural restrictions on her talents, a sacrifice causing "a death . . . taken place some years ago" (ST, 2:411), Cassandra becomes a new kind of Christian prophet (identified as such in Nightingale's marginalia)—female in a world ordered not by her God or Christ, but by a patriarchal appropriation of the Judeo-Christian myth.

Earlier in *Suggestions*, Nightingale writes that "Disappointment often costs the woman her life—if by life is meant all spirit, energy, vitality" (ST, 2:214); here, Cassandra has been emotionally, spiritually, and intellectually killed, sacrificed by a patriarchally defined culture. This crucified woman, this female Christ, begins a revolutionary spirituality. In this section, Nightingale—vicariously through Cassandra's death—conquers what has become, in her life, the most restrictive and conservative forces—mother (and "woman's estate" [ST, 2:411]) and mother-church. Again through the association with Christ's crucifixion as well as her previous suggestion that the next Christ will be female, Cassandra's death empowers Nightingale through this symbolic resurrection in her creator.

Suggestions serves still another function for Nightingale. This discourse, especially volume 2 and "Cassandra," revises predominant religious beliefs of her time to include female experience. Elaine Showalter writes that "like other gifted women of her generation, she translated intellectual and vocational drives into the language of religion, the only system that could justify them."[58] In this way, *Suggestions* reveals the theological and cultural issues that Nightingale grappled with—not simply to validate her own desires, but also to reappropriate a religion which shaped her culture's values. That Nightingale chose to frame her own ambitions in a spiritual context, that she empowers herself through a fictive crucifixion and resurrection, cannot be ignored. Although female in a world dominated by men, she can argue and assert with equal, even higher authority. When her culture cites a divine plan to keep her a slave in her parents' home, wasting her talents as a handmaiden to an earthly lord, she can cite divine authority to free herself from that bondage. When her culture quotes scriptures to justify women's oppression, she can cite God's call. She becomes not just a woman critical of her androcentric culture, but a prophet of God.

Through her revisionist theology, Nightingale reappropriates the power associated with religion. Her theological discourse, infused with feminist vision, reveals a doctrine dependent upon women's active participation. By rejecting a patriarchally misconstrued God, Nightingale can challenge her society's controls over women without challenging God. By seeing each woman who struggles as the predecessor to the female incarnation, Nightingale invokes a God who embraces both male *and* female to authorize her criticism of a society that distorts His vision as exclusively male.

By asserting that "The next Christ will perhaps be a female Christ," she radically revises women's place in society. Not only does Nightingale's concept of a female Christ redefine martyr and prophet as female in patriarchal society, but that female divinity also subverts traditional values and images of power. This divinely sanctioned power, harnessed by resisting complicity, celebrating a resensitizing pain, and bearing witness to a greater Truth, shifts the locale of power. This power—both conservative and revolutionary—returns to God for authority while simultaneously revising organized religion and orthodox beliefs.[59] This double power mirrors the two strains of Nightingale's agenda— to participate in theological discourse and revise it. In this way, Nightingale reclaims for women and other marginalized people what she believes to be true religious values and rejects self-serving patriarchal ones that rest on misinterpreted edicts. In asserting the misinterpretation of God's word, Nightingale further conflates the traditional power of the symbolic, the power upon which her culture builds its conventions. Rather than accurately communicate God's word, patriarchal representations distort and misconstrue His meanings and intentions.

Nightingale's revisionist theology, which rejects mother and mother-church and embraces a mystical relationship with God, confounds the gendered associations of God as word/symbol and revises that communication as more like the preverbal that finds parallels in the symbolic and semiotic language distinctions of Kristeva's theory. In Nightingale's discourse, mother and mother-church represent the socializing symbolic; the semiotic, in contrast, is represented by God, traditionally imagined male. Nightingale's mystical relationship with God, however, can be described more like that of the language of the semiotic—associative, fragmented, and representative of a not fully symbolized communication. In this way, Nightingale's spirituality demonstrates the extent to which her Victorian culture has displaced God from their society and religions: if God becomes associated with the nonconventional semiotic even if He has been imagined male, He (or aspects of Him) have become marginalized. The symbolic representation of His word has become too distant, too removed from what it signifies. In addition, God, for Nightingale, is not in concert with patriarchy, is not phallocentric.

Nightingale further conflates the traditional gender distinctions; her next Christ, after all, is female. She is female because women, in her culture, are those in need of a liberating theology. Similarly, she recreates for women a benevolent, nurturing God who sympathizes with women even while men threaten them with His wrath for subversive behavior: "Men say that God punishes for complaining. . . . They take it as a personal offense. To God alone may women complain, without insulting Him" (ST, 2:374). Women can complain because their quarrel is not with God but with man's injustice. In the end, Nightingale turns to God to authorize her desires, not because He is imagined male, but because He can provide her with the necessary authority as God, imagined to have called her to serve. She sees Him rejected even though His name is claimed, and so, even though He may in reality be marginalized, His word still evokes authority, if only, and ironically, because patriarchy has appropriated it.

The impact of these revisionist beliefs in empowering Nightingale can be clarified by returning to her life and considering the events immediately following the completion of Suggestions. After writing this theological treatise and just before her thirty-second birthday, Nightingale received her second call from God, specifically, a "call from God to be a saviour."[60] With her years of waiting and theorizing behind her, Nightingale would act, and act decisively; she would be able to convince her father that she should be financially independent. With her revisionist theology and symbolic resurrection empowering her to act, Nightingale could now become one of those missing types she had looked for; she could attempt to save humanity from its erring ways.

Freed from family dependence, she accepted a job as superintendent of an Establishment for Gentlewomen during Illness, and within two years, she went to the Crimea with her nurses. While the war may have immortalized Nightingale, Strachey, in his biographical sketch of her, describes this experience as only "the fulcrum with which she hoped to move the world. . . . For more than a generation she was to sit in secret, working her lever: her real life began at the very moment when, in the popular imagination, [it] ended."[61] After the Crimean War, Nightingale proceeded to evoke sanitary and poor law reform as well as instigate military reforms by working through Sidney Herbert as commander-in-chief of the little War Office.[62]

Although the popular imagination will remember her as the founder of modern nursing, Nightingale's vision of nursing was not so much that of reforming a profession as answering a sacred call. In a letter to Jowett in 1889, she writes:

> the two thoughts which God has given me all my whole life have been—First, to infuse the mystical religion into the forms of others. . . . especially among women, to make them the "handmaidens of the Lord." Secondly, to give them an organization for their activity in which they could be trained to be the "handmaidens of the Lord". . . . When very many years ago I planned a future, my one idea was not organizing a Hospital, but organizing a Religion.[63]

Nightingale founded her "religion"—a feminist rewriting of the individual's place in her culture—through nursing, not the Church. Abandoning her culture's religious superstructure, she transposed her conception of God and His will into the secular sphere. In her revision, nursing could possibly become the force that would subvert a patriarchal misappropriation of God. A twentieth-century perspective makes it difficult to recognize the polemical impact caused by Nightingale's locating God in nursing: during the Victorian period, nursing was considered a vulgar occupation; nurses, intemperate and immoral women. Because of this, before Nightingale's reform, few respectable women would support themselves in this manner. Nightingale, however, recognized the fundamentally humanitarian, if not, by her vision, Christian, foundation of nursing. From this perspective, she sought to transform this occupation into a respectable and laudable profession.

Stripped of its clerical robes, Nightingale's religion infused what she believed to be God's ethics into the secular world; based on interpersonal care and the alleviation of suffering, this revisionist theology embraced those traditionally marginalized. Even if she rejected organized religion, Nightingale never abandoned her belief in God. For Nightingale, the spiritual crisis of the Victorian era was neither the disappearance of God nor an amoral universe, but rather the patriarchal appropriation of His word that imprisoned women's spirituality. Envisioning herself as a modern prophet of God, Nightingale reclaimed the power of religious myth and wrote her own liberation theology.

3

Radical Protestantism versus Privileged Hermeneutics: The Religion and Romance of Brontë's Spirituality

> when patience has done its utmost and industry its best,
> whether in the case of women or operative, and when both
> are baffled, and pain and want triumph, the sufferer is free,
> is entitled, at last to send up to Heaven any piercing cry for
> relief, if by that cry he can hope to obtain succour.
> —Charlotte Brontë

"What was I created for . . . where is my place in the world?" asks Caroline Helstone in Charlotte Brontë's third novel, *Shirley*.[1] This question, consistently voiced by Brontë's female protagonists from Jane Eyre to Lucy Snowe, preoccupied the author herself and is echoed in her letters:

> life wears away—I shall soon be 30 . . . and I have done nothing yet. . . . I feel as if we were all buried here.

> I know life is passing away and I am doing nothing—earning nothing.

> I shall be 31 next birthday—My youth is gone like a dream—and very little use have I ever made of it—What have I done these last thirty years?—Precious little. (*B*, 2:28, 115, 130)

Discontented, Brontë echoes Nightingale as she also struggled to account for unconventional desires—both her passionate nature and her aspiration to be an author. Despite talent, Brontë faced cultural discouragement against women writing professionally, prohibitions graphically illustrated by a letter written specifically to Brontë by then-poet laureate, Robert Southey[2]:

Literature cannot be the business of a woman's life, and it ought not to be. The more she is engaged in her proper duties, the less leisure will she have for it, even as an accomplishment and a recreation. To those duties you have not yet been called, and when you are you will be less eager for celebrity. You will not seek in imagination for excitement, of which the vicissitudes of this life, and the anxieties from which you must not hope to be exempted, be your state what it may, will bring with them but too much (B, 1:155–56).

In addition to articulating predominant Victorian beliefs in the domestic nature of women's "proper duties," Southey cautions against cultivating imagination when, as a woman, she eventually should fulfill a more "appropriate" female role. As such he also betrays the traditional assumption that marriage and care-taking are the natural, even desired, culmination of a woman's life, that any desire for a profession is simply an adolescent dalliance.

Brontë, however, could not suppress her passionate desire to write. The resulting conflict between talent and passion on the one hand and gender-based codes of behavior on the other produced debilitating crises for Brontë—both as an adolescent and as an adult. And, because she framed her own life and talents within a Christian context, these conflicts became for her nothing less than spiritual crises, crises that would need to be resolved before she could even begin to understand her place in the world. Significantly, Brontë's crisis of faith did not result from the waning belief or growing doubt in God that consumed many of her male contemporaries; in fact she never questioned His existence. Instead, her *unwavering* belief in God precipitated her crisis: how could she reconcile what she believed to be God-given talents with cultural prohibitions (often issued in God's name) against such activities for women?

As this chapter will demonstrate, Brontë would eventually resolve this spiritual crisis by reclaiming sacred authority to defy her culture and justify her writing. Her ardent faith, combined with both the impact of her siblings' deaths and the demystification of clerical authority that came from living in an Anglican parsonage, enabled Brontë to distinguish between God and man and to resolve her spiritual malaise. These significant spiritual crises in Brontë's life, however, have received little critical attention primarily because, like those of the other women in this study, they represent a different relationship between the individual and religion than has characteristically defined the Victorian spiritual crisis.[3] This chapter, however, considers the history of Brontë's spiritual empowerment and the impact it had on her fiction, specifically *Shirley*, by analyzing the closely intertwined roots of her religious and cultural marginalization, her writing and her faith.

To understand fully both her spiritual crises and their resolutions, the social and religious environment in which Brontë grew up and matured, an area marked by its worker unrest and Evangelical heritage, must be analyzed.[4] Although she was the daughter of an Anglican rector, the Calvinistic model of God informed Brontë's youth—both on a personal and public level. West Riding boasted a lengthy Evangelical heritage, one that even filtered into the Low Church Anglicanism preached by her father. In addition to any doctrinal affinities with Evangelicalism, Patrick Brontë shared its muscular attitudes toward Christianity, which although not exclusively Evangelical found vigorous reinforcement through the aggressive and uncompromising aspects of Calvinistic images of God: personifying this, her father, although a rector, carried a loaded pistol and discharged it daily.[5] In both her home and community, then, Brontë experienced this aggressive brand of Christianity, which dictated patriarchally complicit, rigid prescriptions for believers, prescriptions that Brontë felt unable to fulfill.

This Calvinistic model of God produced great despair in her young life: Brontë believed herself already damned because she could not control her passions, the frustration of which can be recognized in letters to her friend Ellen Nussey[6]:

> I am in that state of horrid, gloomy uncertainty, that at this moment I would submit to be old, grey-haired, to have passed all my youthful days of enjoyment and be tottering on the verge of the grave, if I could only thereby ensure the prospect of reconcilement to God and Redemption through His Son's merits. (*B*, 1:140)

Translated into self-hatred, Brontë's attempts to meet the rigid guidelines of these Calvinistic doctrines exaggerated her despair. Shortly after this letter, she would again write: "I abhor myself—I despise myself—if the Doctrine of Calvin be true I am already an outcast" (*B*, 1:143). Brontë later details both her desperate yearning for salvation and her continual failures to achieve the requisite passivity:

> I hope, I trust, I might one day become better, far better, than my evil wandering thoughts, my corrupt heart, cold to the spirit, and warm to the flesh will now permit me to be. . . . If Christian perfections be necessary to Salvation I shall never be saved, my heart is a real hot

bed for sinful thoughts and as to practice, when I decide on an action, I scarcely remember to look to my Redeemer for direction. . . . I acknowledge the truth, the perfection of His word. I adore the purity of the Christian faith, my theory is right, my practice horribly wrong. (B, 1:147–48)

Here under the auspices of a Calvinistic God, Brontë's passions are labeled sinful, just as Southey would imply her desires unnatural. As she matured, Brontë witnessed extensive parallels between these religious doctrines and cultural edicts—both restricting her life and subjecting women. Neither the secular nor the sacred world, when both appeared to embrace a patriarchal image of God, admitted a place for women like her, so until she could liberate herself from this image of God, who anthropomorphized patriarchal values, Brontë suffered extreme mortal anguish.

This vehement desire for salvation combined with the wretched conditions that defined her life—the impossible struggle to tame her desires, her unrecognized talent as writer, the overwhelming loneliness and solitude that came to her with her siblings' deaths, and her unwavering belief in God—forced her either to accept, out of despair, that she was damned and unnatural or to modify her image of God in a way that enabled her to reinterpret her life and her talents in this spiritual context. Revise her beliefs she did: rejecting the vengeful Calvinistic model, Brontë replaced it with one that imaged a merciful, empowering Savior. Through this veritable leap of faith, the God of Brontë's maturity would not only sanction a nonconformist career as a writer but give meaning and focus to her initially directionless life.

Ironically, both her despair and her belief contributed to this leap of faith, to the production of this enabling spirituality. In a letter to her publisher upon Emily's death, Brontë expresses this paradoxical perspective: "Why life is so blank, brief, and bitter I do not know. Why younger and far better than I are snatched from it with projects unfulfilled I cannot comprehend, but I believe God is wise—perfect—merciful" (B, 2:338). In short, watching Anne, Emily, and Branwell all decline and die, Charlotte either had to deny herself (and her siblings' short lives) or reject the damning God of her childhood and culture. Unwilling to accept damnation, Brontë learned to see instances of a merciful God in her siblings' deaths. Considering Branwell's death in the context of his philandering life, she writes:

> If man can thus experience total oblivion of his fellows' imperfec-
> tions—how much more can the Eternal Being who made man, forgive
> his creature! Had his sins been scarlet in their dye—I believe now
> they are white as wool. (B, 2:263)

If peace and succour accompanied her siblings' deaths, then
maybe, Brontë considered, she too might not be already damned,
that possibly "God despises no supplication that is uttered in
sincerity" (B, 1:160). Building upon this belief in a merciful Host,
Brontë wrote that when Emily died, "Had I never believed in a
future life before, my sister's fate would assure me of it. There
must be Heaven or we must despair—for life seems bitter, brief—
blank" (B, 2:339). As witness to both the bleakness of her siblings'
lives and the complete succour of death, Brontë began to believe
that God could only be merciful, not vengeful.

Brontë's faith also evolved in ways which would account for the
increasing loneliness she would have to endure: through this belief in a charitable God, she would eventually recognize that the
restrictions on her life were not of divine but patriarchal design.
When, one by one, Brontë buried each of her siblings, the Haworth parsonage, geographically and intellectually isolated, became more like a suffocating sepulchre than the sanctuary that it
had been in her youth; here she still had to account for *her* life
on earth. Brontë endeavored to understand its bleakness, the op-
pressiveness of which she records in her letters:

> I am a *lonely* woman and likely to be *lonely*. But it cannot be helped
> and therefore *imperatively must be borne*—and borne too with as few
> words about it as may be. (B, 4:6)

> To sit in a lonely room—the clock ticking loud through a still house—
> and to have open before the mind's eye the record of the last years
> with its shocks, sufferings, losses—is a trial. (B, 3:8)

Even with repeated attempts to accept this suffering that might
be God's will, Brontë could not help but question the apparent
inconsistency of the peace she witnessed in her siblings' deaths
with the extensive agony she faced on earth. If God were merciful,
as Brontë now believed she had witnessed, then, it was possible
that her earthly suffering might not be His intention either. If God
had given her talents but her culture limited her opportunities to
develop them simply because she was female, then she might be
able to acknowledge and validate her desires by replacing social
with sacred approval and authority. This belief in an enabling

God, however, produced the spiritual crisis Brontë faced as an adult: how could she enact her faith by increasing her talents—which meant pursuing an unconventional life—in a world that both specifically denied her the opportunity to do so *and* claimed sacred authority to fortify these patriarchal restrictions?

As Brontë's conflict became more clearly one between herself and her culture and not one between herself and God, the "socially insecure" world in which she lived actually contributed to her empowerment, just as it had earlier contributed to her despair.[7] As a parsonage resident, she saw England's state religion as an insider, although powerless because she was female; she witnessed the political, patriarchal underpinnings of the Church, the clerical bickering and the sectarian battles. "I love the Church of England," she wrote, but "Her ministers, indeed, I do not regard as infallible personages. I have seen too much of them for that" (*B*, 2:166). So while she believed in God, Brontë held no illusion about the infallibility of the Church or its clerics, and consequently, Brontë could challenge the "sacred" design of clerical edicts.[8] This marginalization that enables her to distinguish between the Church and God, between patriarchal interests and sacred intentions, informs both Brontë's beliefs and her crises: that is, Brontë believed that even if established *religion,* especially the Evangelical and patriarchal forms, crushed her as an individual, *God* would nonetheless be her savior.[9]

Just as her intense desire for salvation paradoxically enabled Brontë to reinterpret God and her life in a manner commensurate with redemption, so, too, her passionate desire to write induced her to find authority, specifically divine authority, to sanction this as her vocation. The complexity and apparently pardoxical aspects of this nexus between her religious beliefs and her passion for writing can be illuminated by reconsidering her marginality to her culture and its religion. Significantly, these issues—her energy to reconcile the two conflicting models of God, her struggle to determine her purpose in life, and her battle with cultural prohibitions against her being an author—intersect in Brontë's writing: just as her juvenilia had produced an alternative world where she held power, so, too, her mature writing, now infused with biblical allusion, became a form of control and an avenue toward salvation as an adult.[10]

This complex, paradoxical place that writing held in Brontë's spiritual crisis and its resolution cannot be underestimated: as both the stimulus for her despair and the vehicle through which she became empowered, writing is primary to her spiritual malaise and its alleviation. Believing writing to be a *vocational* call in the religious sense, Brontë disintered divine authorization for this activity to counter whatever cultural prohibitions existed. Viewed as a God-given talent that should be nurtured and developed, writing became the mechanism that secured her salvation, liberating her from the despair of her siblings' deaths and giving her life focus and meaning after their deaths.[11] With such sacred association, writing became a channel for and sublimation of the passions and desires that her culture denied her, a vehicle both to diffuse and legitimize her frustrations. In this way, writing provided Brontë access to a limited control over her environment (much the same way that her juvenilia became an alternative visioning of the world) and the opportunity to participate in the cultural dialogues that constructed and interpreted theology that, as female, she could not otherwise enter.

Writing, then, in conjunction with her vision of a nurturing God, became Brontë's salvation.[12] Thomas Wise writes that after Anne, the last of her siblings, died, Brontë "was writing continually" (*B*, 3:1). Brontë herself repeatedly attributes her ability to cope with her siblings' deaths and the resulting solitude to writing:

> Lonely as I am—how should I be if Providence had never given me courage to adopt a career. . . . How should I be with youth past—sisters lost—a resident in a moorland parish where there is not a single educated family? (*B*, 3:6)

> The fact is, my work is my best companion. (*B*, 3:9)

> Whatever now becomes of the work [*Shirley*], the occupation of writing it has been a boon to me. It took me out of dark and desolate reality into an unreal but happier region. (*B*, 3:15)

> The faculty of imagination lifted me when I was sinking, three months ago; its active exercise has kept my head above water since; its results cheer me now, for I feel they have enabled me to give pleasure to others. (*B*, 3:24)

Asserting that "I am thankful to God, who gave me the faculty; it is for me a part of my religion to defend this gift and to profit by its possession," Brontë unequivocally attributes her earthly and spiritual salvation to the act of writing (*B*, 3:24).

To understand fully the impact Brontë's spiritual beliefs had on her writing, the nondidactic, nonpreaching aspect of her aesthetic must be considered.[13] Her aesthetic parallels qualities of her own spiritual liberation: *subjective* interpretation that authorized individual desire. As an author, she would produce, reproduce, what she witnessed and experienced, not an intrinsic Truth, not an allegedly objective representation of life. This nondidactic aesthetic can be further clarified in her persistent and vehement assertions that writing, not teaching, was her talent. Brontë's aesthetic, then, would replicate this distinction. Early in her career she had cautioned her publisher against fiction that propagandized, asserting: "never try to proselytize" (B, 2:267). Later when queried about her "intentions" in fiction, she wrote, "I am no teacher—to look on me in that light is to mistake me—to teach is not my vocation" (B, 3:42). And, to Ellen Nussey, she wrote: "You are not to suppose any of the characters in [*Shirley*] intended as literal portraits. It would not suit the rules of art, nor my own feelings, to write in that style. We only suffer reality to *suggest*, never to *dictate*" (B, 3:37).

One of the fullest definitions that Brontë provides about her nondidactic aesthetic reveals an important junction between the tradition of theological discourse—writing to illuminate God's world—and a nearly pantheistic worship of Nature. "The first duty of an author," she wrote, is "faithful allegiance to Truth and Nature; his second, such a conscientious study of Art as shall enable him to interpret eloquently and effectively any oracles delivered by those two deities" (B, 2:243). This belief in the "duty of the author" to "interpret" nature's "oracles" aligns Brontë's fiction with the typological tradition of religious discourse that sought to reveal God's presence in the natural world. So even if she found herself devoid of a recognized history of women interpreting God's word,[14] Brontë participated in this extant tradition of religious discourse, just as earlier Christians did. In this way, Brontë circumvents to some degree the anxiety of authorship that Gilbert and Gubar argue debilitated many nineteenth-century women writers; rather than believe that the act of writing would isolate or destroy her, Brontë saw writing as a means to enfranchise and empower herself. Charged with a belief that writing was her talent from God, Brontë felt bound to recreate and represent the world as she perceived it, a subjective perspective that would detail female oppression in a patriarchal culture. Her culture may have denied her a female literary tradition, but, by claiming this extant tradition, her God would empower her to write.

With this heritage of exegetes and prophets, Brontë attempted to reproduce reality in her fiction from a female perspective, inevitably transforming this male religious literary tradition.[15] By interpreting God's world through female eyes, she undoes the patriarchal core that has defined both religious and literary interpretation and limited hermeneutical privilege. Written by a woman forced to negotiate cultural restrictions with the aid of her faith, Brontë's fiction reveals the inconsistent agendas of man and God. And, in this way, she used her fiction as feminist parables that would recreate a female, not monolithic, reality. Although to the modern reader, the distinction between preaching and illuminating may seem negligible, this difference defines her aesthetic: rather than articulate *the* truth, her fiction would present one set of experiences.

Brontë grafts this reinterpreted exegetical tradition to the novel and, by doing so, transforms that genre as well. In reproducing the romance plot in her fiction, Brontë's replication exaggerates and mimics those narratives; this rhetorical strategy in turn subverts the patriarchal framework for those literary patterns by emphasizing its restrictive, fictive quality.[16] Her fiction, then, fuses feminist revisions of religious and secular discourse to recreate and represent the realities of female experience.

An analysis of Brontë's novel *Shirley* best illustrates her use of this narrative strategy both to empower herself and to challenge patriarchal standards enforced in God's name. Although one can see similar emphasis given to a woman's search for her place in a patriarchal culture in *Jane Eyre* and *Villette*, it is in *Shirley* that these ideas receive their fullest articulation. At the literal and metaphoric center of *Shirley* is the theme of authority and the interpretive act associated with claiming authority, an act central to religious, sociopolitical, and literary institutions.[17] In addition to revealing female powerlessness in a world circumscribed by fallible, yet authorized, men in clerical positions, Brontë explores the basis of interpretation and the standards used to evoke the requisite authority to do so.[18] Integral to both the spiritual and literary traditions in which Brontë wrote, her feminist reinterpretation of the hermeneutical act points to the traditionally exclusive privilege men held to interpret the natural and supernatural worlds.

In *Shirley* Brontë produces a narrative that foregrounds hermeneutics—both thematically and structurally. As this chapter will demonstrate, a close analysis of how the novel's themes develop as well as how the text provides information reinforces the interpretive aspect of narrative: Brontë achieves this through

the simultaneously buried, yet central assertion of radical protestantism by Caroline Helstone that claims interpretive authority
for women as well as men; the extensive biblical allusions that
redefine the position of women and workers in Victorian society;
the patriarchal models and scripts that are both articulated and
reinterpreted; the inclusion of passages in French, which explicitly heighten the act of translation and interpretation; the self-
referential storytelling; and the recurring incidents where pivotal
information is told and then retold from a different perspective,
altering the "facts."

Understood in this context, the two narrative strategies—the
feminist parable and the subverted romance—intersect. Appropriating the Christian tradition of parable, which uses narratives to instruct the reader/listener about the importance of
distinguishing appearance from reality, Brontë would illuminate
women's restricted lives in patriarchal culture; her use of Christian
allusion in conjunction with an exaggerated adherence to patriarchal plots would recontextualize the oppressive limitations of
those social and clerical scripts.[19] With this intersection of Christian and feminist agendas, Brontë depicts women's lives as limited
and circumscribed by a culture that not only misuses them but
also misappropriates God's word as authority.[20] By paralleling
nineteenth-century women to earlier oppressed Christians,
Brontë both redefines women's lives and challenges traditional
patriarchal authority. And by superimposing a feminist rendering
of Christian narrative onto the romance plot, Brontë is able to
voice her spiritual beliefs without appearing as polemical as she
might, much in the tradition of earlier Christians.[21] Doing so she
shifts the locus of power from the clerics and scribes to the interpretive act itself, away from an exclusive hierarchical group of
interpreters to a radical protestantism that enables the individual
to interpret God's word for herself.

Read in this context, the self-conscious narrative voice and the
inclusion of the curates, Mrs. Pryor, and the worker unrest reveal
Brontë's conscious manipulation of content *and* structure to foreground the act of interpretation—not a "portfolio of sketches,"
not a flawed narrative structure.[22] In *Shirley* Brontë tells the story
of four socially marginalized characters (by nationality, money,
or gender): Robert Moore, foreign, struggling mill owner; his
brother Louis, whose financial dependence limits and disenfran-
chises him; Caroline Helstone, Louis's female counterpart; and
Shirley Kildare, who while initially empowered by financial independence must finally subscribe to patriarchal prescriptions be-

cause of her sex. Brontë develops these characters' stories by juxtaposing realism to a mimicry of the romance plot, the narrative pattern most closely paralleling traditional patriarchal social scripts that subordinate women. This rhetorical strategy serves to illuminate the models of authority subscribed to by her patriarchal culture and those that undermine that structure; doing so, Brontë produces a novel that simultaneously articulates a radical feminist protestantism and recognizes the hegemonic power of the extant Victorian culture. Read in this way, *Shirley* represents a powerful feminist statement, not a failed piece of fiction that regresses into complicity with patriarchal values or standards at its conclusion. In this novel, as I will argue, Brontë submerges the feminist revision (like the mermaid's tale Shirley and Caroline consider in the novel) to present an ending that both exposes women's social limitations and subverts those scripts through the very exaggeration of its presentation.[23]

The architectonics of the novel's three volumes reveal the tensions inherent in Brontë's world—both the traditional patriarchal superstructures and her resistance to them. To accomplish this, Brontë begins by exposing her reader to the stories of her first volume, which delineates the tensions rampant between workers and industrialists (intensified during the period of restricted trade brought about by the Orders of Council during the Napoleonic Wars that historically ground this novel) and the tensions between one young woman, Caroline Helstone, and the debilitating social scripts that deny her power because of her gender. In this story of frustrated individuals, Brontë alternates between presenting worker unrest and the woman question as akin to Christian myth by paralleling Victorian England to biblical history.

Brontë first uses biblical allusions to situate the sociopolitical context of *Shirley* and to reinforce the subjectivity of biblical and political interpretation. While preparing to defend the mill against Luddite violence, the Reverend Helstone asserts allegiance to Wellington, whom he believes to be like God defending the Israelites' flight from Egypt; Moore, however, suggests an alternative version of the events:

> You are right, only you forget the true parallel. France is Israel, and Napoleon is Moses. Europe, with her old over-gorged empires and rotten dynasties is corrupt Egypt; gallant France is the Twelve Tribes, and her fresh and vigorous Usurper the Shepherd of Horeb. (*S*, 39)

Further developing this subjectivity, Brontë depicts workers also claiming divine authority to justify their actions. When they rally at the mill demanding employment, the leaders, significantly named Noah and Moses, assert that they are doing "the Looard's [sic] own purpose" (*S*, 133). Through such examples, Brontë depicts on the larger, public level the impossibility of intrinsic truth and the absurdity of objective interpretation: Helstone (the prowar Anglican), Moore (the antiwar industrialist), and Noah (the leveling Evangelist) *all* claim sacred intent for their mutually incompatible agendas.

This rhetorical strategy also allows Brontë to illustrate the cultural (as opposed to natural) authority that controls interpersonal relationships and the domestic sphere. Frustrated by Moore's inability (because of financial restraints) to profess his love for her, and unable (because of gender-based restrictions) to act herself, Caroline situates and considers her agony, much like Brontë herself, within a spiritual dimension; the narrator reports that "Caroline was a Christian; therefore in trouble she framed many a prayer after the Christian creed" (*S*, 351). With even more highly charged language, the narrator parallels Caroline's romantic disappointment to a Christian metaphor for faith:

> Take the matter as you find it: ask no questions; utter no remonstrances: it is your best wisdom. *You expected bread, and you have got a stone;* break your teeth on it, and don't shriek because the nerves are martyrized. (*S*, 105, emphasis added)[24]

This richly connotative biblical language transforms Caroline's situation from that of a love-sick young woman to that equaling martyred Christians. In a chapter titled "Old Maids," which declares two such women as the most saintly in the novel (*S*, 182), the narrator ties together the two threads of worker unrest and the woman question. Rather than endorse the vision of unmarried women as redundant, a burden, and abnormal in a heterosexual society, this depiction of another degree of female marginalization radically revises both the position and value of these women. In addition, the narrator asserts that "A land ruled by [merchants] alone would too often make ignominious submission [to foreign interests]—not at all from the motives Christ teaches, but rather from those Mammon instills" (*S*, 167). As these examples suggest, Brontë encourages the reader to see the events of Victorian England from a different and emotionally charged perspective by comparing the tensions among the characters—both public and domestic—to sacred myth. With a variety of individuals, from different sociopolitical positions, likened to Christian figures, the text reinforces not only interpretive subjectivity but also the culture's tendency to appropriate the Judeo-Christian myth for its own agenda.

In addition to her use of biblical allusion to foreground the inherent subjectivity of interpretation, Brontë also manipulates narrative scripts for this same end. While the narrative appears to progress to increasing conventionality, the very center of this text erupts with alternative social scripts and interpretive models, a rhetorical feature that I will return to for more extensive analysis. The middle chapter of the second volume, the very center of the novel, voices the most radical challenge to patriarchal models of interpretation even while it is "protected" with a chapter title that warns the readers of its unsavory content—"Which the Genteel Reader is Recommended to Skip, Low Persons Being Here Introduced." As such, the narrative literally pivots on this polemic chapter that is both buried—by place and title—and central to the novel's theme and Brontë's project. From this radical core, the novel develops away from the utopian and alternative vision of myth and life to the appearance of extreme conventionalities and a layered mimicry of such patriarchally inscribed scripts.

In this pivotal chapter, the narratives of the social condition and woman question intertwine: the conflicts between workers and mill owners, women and men, patriarchal social scripts and utopian alternatives, and God's word and its patriarchal misinterpretation all intersect. While the workers rally and the owners enlist military support, the feminist challenge to patriarchal order is explicitly voiced outside a church during services through the confrontational dialogue among Joe Scott, Moore's right-hand man, Caroline, and Shirley. This dialogue among Brontë's characters articulates and debates the very issues central to women's place in Victorian culture and its Church—a dialogue that Brontë, because of her gender, was not given access to. Reinforcing cultural mores that restrict women's social and intellectual freedom, Scott interrupts Caroline and Shirley's political discussion with William Farren, an unemployed worker—all three of whom have been socially marginalized. Scott both dismisses Farren's labor concerns and insists that Caroline and Shirley should go into church because women "had not right to meddle" in politics (*S*, 328). When Shirley asks him if "all the wisdom in the world is lodged in male skulls?" Joe quotes St. Paul's first Epistle to Timothy: "Let the woman learn silence, with all subjection. I suffer not a woman to teach, not to usurp authority over the man; but to be in silence. For Adam was first formed, then Eve" (*S*, 328–29). With Scott's quotation of this biblical verse, one of patriarchy's most cited sources for subjecting women in God's name, Shirley turns the debate on the proper place for women into one about the act of interpretation; she responds, "To confess the honest truth, Joe, I never was easy in my mind concerning that chapter: it puzzles me" (*S*, 328). Revealing a monolithic perspective of language, Scott retorts: "It is very plain, Miss: he that runs may read" (*S*, 328). Significantly it is Caroline who voices the most radical challenge to Scott's, and their culture's, biblical interpretation and hermeneutical privilege—the cultural and clerical double standards for women. Entering this political and theological dialogue for the first time, Caroline questions Scott's uncritical acceptance of the clerical and partriarchal reading of God's word. Doing so, she further refines this discussion specifically to the individual's right to interpret scripture. She begins, asking Joe:

"He may read it in his own fashion. . . . You allow the right of private judgment, I suppose, Joe?"
"My certy, that I do! I allow and claim it for every line of the holy Book."
"Women may exercise it as well as men?"
"Nay: women is to take their husbands' opinion, both in politics and religion: it's wholesomest for them. . . ."
". . . You might as well say men are to take the opinions of their priests without examination. Of what value would a religion so adopted be? It would be mere blind, besotted superstition." (*S*, 329)

Confronted with a theological challenge that would remove gender as a deterrent to interpretive authority, Scott defensively asks Caroline "what [*her*] reading . . . o' them words o' St. Paul's" is (*S*, 328). Here, Caroline voices Brontë's challenge to the patriarchally appropriated privilege to interpret God's word:

I account them in this way: he wrote that chapter for a particular congregation of Christians, under peculiar circumstances; and besides, I dare say, *if I could read the original Greek, I should find that many of the words have been wrongly translated, perhaps misapprehended altogether.* It would be possible, I doubt not, with a little ingenuity, to give the passage quite a contrary turn; to make it say, "Let the woman speak out whenever she sees fit to make an objection;"—"it is permitted to a woman to teach and to exercise authority as much as may be. Man, meantime, cannot do better than hold his peace," and so on. (*S*, 329–30, emphasis added)

Cultural disapproval, however, essentially prevents the training and experience necessary and, therefore, denies interpretive opportunities for women. Consequently this fundamental component of the protestantism that defines England's Church—the individual's unmediated channel with God—excludes women. The hermeneutical privilege rests secure with a very few—educated, predictably wealthy men. What makes Caroline's supposition so subversive, though, is that in addition to exposing the gender- and class-based parameters that circumscribe her culture's Protestantism, she challenges the accuracy of the biblical *interpretation* that her culture cites as evidence of God's intentions. She asserts that God's word has probably been "wrongly translated, perhaps misapprehended altogether." Doing so, Caroline identifies patriarchal misinterpretation and misappropriation of God as the cause of women's and, by extension, workers' powerlessness.

From this literal center of the novel, from this point of interpretive challenge, *Shirley* explores what just such reinterpretation would mean—to women, to their culture, and to their religion—by presenting alternative models of authority and behavior; and, with the novel's conclusion, Brontë subverts the patriarchal models through an exaggerated mimicry of those models. In this central, pivotal volume, Brontë juxtaposes a fantastical quality to the earlier realism she had used: Robert is named both as one of the mythical fairies who once roamed the hollow (*S*, 237) and as Satan (*S*, 238). And just as Robert is associated with these magical and powerful images, Caroline and Shirley fantasize about mermaids that they might encounter at the ocean.[25] Reflecting on these haunting creatures, Shirley tells Caroline:

> Were we men, we should spring at the sign, the cold billow would be dared for the sake of the colder enchantress; being women, we stand safe, though not dreadless. She comprehends our unmoved gaze; she feels herself powerless; anger crosses her front; she cannot charm but she will appal us: she rises high, and glides all revealed, on the dark wave-ridge. Temptress-terror! monstrous likeness of ourselves! Are you not glad, Caroline, when at last, and with a wild shriek, she dives? (*S*, 246).

To this image of woman's lurking powers, Caroline contends: "But . . . she is not like us: we are neither temptresses, nor terrors, nor monsters" (*S*, 246). Shirley, however, understands the predominance of this patriarchal reading of women, telling her: "Some of our kind, it is said, are all three. There are men who ascribe to 'women,' in general, such attributes" (*S*, 246).

Against this image of women's passive manipulation of power, Brontë juxtaposes the overtly muscular tactics available to men in the same culture. Society endorses masculine aggression while demanding female passivity not only in the secular world but in the sacred as well. Brontë vividly depicts this aggressive Christianity when she presents her characters celebrating Whitsuntide. On that Sunday, the Church and the dissenting sects rally independently, but the two groups become engaged in a literal denominational battle, an event that illustrates the earlier banter between the Reverend Helstone, Caroline's uncle, and Robert Moore. When Helstone had asserted that "God defend[s] the right!" Moore retorted: "God often defends the powerful" (*S*, 39). After a physical confrontation brought about because the two parades cannot both simultaneously cross a path, Helstone believes that "The Dissenting and Methodist schools, the Baptists, Independents, and Wesleyans, joined in unholy alliance and turn[ed] purposely into this lane with the intention of obstructing [our] march and driving [us] back" (*S*, 304). He continues, explicitly linking the Church with secular power: "There is not a church woman here but will stand her ground against these folks for the honour of the Establishment" (*S*, 303–4). These Christian sects take on military formation and venture to prove their superiority by trying to drown out each other with song: the dissenting party with a psalm, the Church with "Rule Britannia" (*S*, 304).

What makes this portrayal even more subversive, however, is that Brontë sets this doctrinal competition on Whitsunday or Pentecost. In the Judeo-Christian tradition, it was on this day that the Holy Spirit enabled people of countless nations to *understand* each others' tongues as their own, to communicate although they previously could not, to advance their essentially similar, spiritual goals. Brontë's rendering of this Victorian Pentecost, in contrast, portrays hatred and rigid theological positions, not the unprecedented communication and coalescence of believers that the Christian holiday commemorates. In this way, Brontë demonstrates just how far she believes Victorian religion has diverged from God's intentions, giving additional support to the existence of other misreadings of His word.

After this display of competitive Christianity, and against such a patriarchally constructed religion, Brontë presents an alternative, maternal spirituality. Convincing Caroline not to go into church, Shirley asks her to witness

Nature . . . at her evening prayers. . . . I see her prostrate on the great steps of her altar, praying for a fair night for mariners at sea, for travellers in deserts, for lambs on moors, and unfledged birds in woods. . . . like Eve was when she and Adam stood alone on earth. (S, 319)

Caroline transforms this vision of a maternal diety from the traditional view of nature as passive female (as other) to one that is actively praying, like images of a male God; she insists that this image of Eve and nature conflicts with standard patriarchal renderings, telling Shirley that this Eve "is not Milton's Eve" (S, 319). "Milton's Eve! Milton's Eve!" Shirley responds, "No, by the pure Mother of God, she is not!" (S, 320). At this point, with Shirley's next response, both the text's subversive potential and the real difficulties in achieving that subversion find voice:

we are alone: we may speak what we think. Milton was great; but was he good? His brain was right; how was his heart? He saw Heaven: he looked down on Hell. He saw Satan, and Sin his daughter, and Death their horrible offspring. Angels serried before him their battalions: the long lines of adamantine shields flashed back on his blind eyeballs the unutterable splendor of heaven. Devils gathered their legion in his sight: their dim, discrowned, and tarnished armies passed rank and file before him. Milton tried to see the first woman, but Cary, he saw her not. (S, 320)

Named bold for asserting this by Caroline, Shirley defends herself by claiming divine authority to criticize cultural codes, replying that she is "Not more bold than faithful. It was his cook that he saw" (S, 320). Pointing to the all too secular and patriarchal aspects of religious imaging, Shirley recognizes the human component that shapes that discourse. With this defense of her iconoclastic allusion to Milton, Shirley enacts the radical protestantism that Caroline had earlier articulated and sees that act not simply as privilege but Christian responsibility.

Brontë advances this feminist challenge to patriarchally privileged hermeneutics, which define and unite the religious and secular superstructures, by again foregrounding the inescapable subjectivity of interpretation. This time, however, she does so by exposing the secular agenda presented as sacred, positing a monolithic perspective. As Whitsunday winds down, Shirley and

Caroline discover that the clerics intend to lead the soldiers brought in to crush the workers' revolt, an alliance replicating the harsh and powerful realities of a patriarchal world where might is named right, even if God's word must be appropriated to do so. With the bloody confrontation at the mill paralleling and magnifying the earlier Whitsuntide battle, Brontë strips away any reverential awe for the ordained representatives of God; doing so, actions and people are named as they really are—parsons called soldiers, not of God, but industry. "The Church," the independent Yorke contends, "was in a bonnie pickle now: it was time it came down when parsons took to swaggering among soldiers, blazing away with bullet and gunpowder, taking the lives of far honester men than themselves" (S, 366). This most violent point in the novel also reveals Caroline's most passionate plea for her own emancipation: while the workers attack the mill, she can only plead for activity; while the workers display resistance to their oppression, Caroline must accept restraint.[26] In short, patriarchal scripts, not impotence, limit her. During the attack on Moore's mill, the male characters in *Shirley* assume that they have successfully sequestered the women in safe homes to prevent their knowledge of the night's battle, but Caroline and Shirley sneak out to witness the confrontation. It is there that Shirley restrains Caroline, preventing her from going to the slightly injured Moore; against this literalization of her culture's restrictions, Caroline cries out: "Am I always to be curbed and kept down" (S, 347). Even though she had earlier voiced a radical feminist protestantism that would empower women by authorizing an active life, in reality, Caroline cannot act and must remain within her society's gender-based parameters. It is not that Caroline is incapable of action; it is that she is restricted—metaphorically and literally.

Earlier, explicitly pointing to such cultural restrictions, Caroline and Shirley share their fantasies about being professional women and their wish not to be limited by their gender.[27] Both to herself and to Robert, Caroline repeatedly pleads for the opportunity to work, recognizing that it is precisely her gender that prevents her: "I should like an occupation; and if I were a boy, it would not be so difficult to find one" (S, 71); she "would wish nature had made her a boy instead of a girl, that she might ask Robert to let her be his clerk" (S, 77). Later, Caroline would tell Shirley, "I wish for ["a profession—a trade"] fifty times a day. As it is, I often wonder what I came into the world for. I long to have something absorbing and compulsory to fill my head and hands, and to occupy my thoughts" (S, 229). Caroline longs for a real profession, for genuine activity, not what her culture allows women—such as supplying and circulating the "jew basket," an activity she abhors (S, 112–13). Significantly, these reflections on professional women acknowledge the cultural contention that "hard labour and learned professions . . . make women masculine, coarse, unwomanly" (S, 229). Even with this demonstrated assimilation of patriarchal propaganda, however, Shirley and Caroline refuse to subscribe to these theories completely; Caroline asks, "And what does it signify, whether unmarried and never-to-be married women are unattractive and inelegant, or not?—provided only they are decent, decorous, and neat, it is enough" (S, 229). While they may recognize the inconsistency of their culture's objections to women working, Caroline and Shirley face an even greater paradox: in a culture that defines individual worth through one's vocation, women are not permitted to pursue a career. As such, the culture has incorporated into its superstructure means by which women can neither gain the reigns of sociopolitical power nor actively achieve spiritual worth in ways parallel to their male contemporaries.

Brontë further exposes the link between patriarchal limitations on women and theological issues in the polemical second volume of Shirley. Mr. Hall, the novel's one commendable minister, describes the unmarried Miss Ainley's "life [as] nearer the life of Christ, than that of any other human being he had ever met with" (S, 183); the narrator calls her "a saint" (S, 182). Significantly, it is an unmarried woman—one who does not fulfill the patriarchal romance script—who is identified as the character with the truest Christian life, not any of the clerics, who had *dedicated* their lives to the emulation and advancement of Christianity, especially not any of the young curates who "argued not on politics . . . not even on theology, practical or doctrinal; but on minute points of ecclesiastical discipline, frivolities which seemed empty as bubbles to all save themselves" (S, 9). This conflict between patriarchal and sacred agendas is further emphasized when Caroline, confronted with the belief that Robert Moore will marry Shirley instead of herself, must consider the intent of her life if not for marriage. The attack on the mill graphically illustrates the degree to which her culture circumscribes her behavior: political and social forces contribute to Caroline's inability to marry, and those same forces that do not allow her to participate in cultural codes also prevent her from challenging them. Desiring more from life than darning socks, Caroline wonders what her purpose in life really is: "As far as I know, I have good health: half a century of existence may lie before me. How am I to occupy it? What am I to do to fill the interval of time which spreads between me and the grave?" (S, 173). Caroline cannot conceive of what her life would be like unmarried, so well trained to embrace patriarchal prescriptions that define women by their relationships to men. To remain single, she thinks, would be endless despair since she cannot have a profession:

> God surely did not create us, and cause us to live, with the sole end of wishing always to die. I believe, in my heart, we were intended to prize life and enjoy it, so long as we retain it. Existence never was originally meant to be that useless, blank, pale, slow-trailing thing it often becomes to many, and is becoming to me, among the rest. (S, 390)

Prevented from fulfilling cultural prescriptions and faced with seemingly irreconcilable desires and cultural opportunities, Caroline's despair over her available options (like Brontë's own) propels her to analyze patriarchal scripts. Just as she had earlier claimed the right to a protestantism that genuinely empowered women, Caroline reconsiders patriarchal models for female behavior and, significantly, *reinterprets* them to validate her desires and authorize alternative models. Against the model of the virtuous and subsequently emulatable Lucretia, who upon being raped (and therefore believing herself irrevocably soiled) killed herself, Caroline considers the proverbial good wife. Just as she recontextualizes and reinterprets St. Paul's epistle, she empowers herself through a more historically consistent, less restrictive reading of this proverb, which is traditionally cited as a model for female behavior:

> Lucretia, spinning at midnight in the midst of her maidens, and Solomon's virtuous woman, are often quoted as patterns of what "the sex" (as they say) ought to be. I don't know: Lucretia, I daresay, was a most worthy sort of person, much like my cousin Hortense Moore; but she kept her servants up very late. I should not have liked to be amongst the number of the maidens. . . . The "virtuous woman," again, had her household up in the very middle of the night; she "got breakfast over" . . . before one o'clock A.M.; but *she* had something more to do than spin and give out portions: she was a manufacturer—she made fine linen and sold it: she was an agriculturist—she bought estates and planted vineyards. *That* woman was a manager: she was what the matrons hereabouts call "a clever woman." On the whole I like her better than Lucretia. (S, 392)

Caroline completes this proverb's model of "the virtuous woman" by naming her an agriculturist, and doing so, she exposes the patriarchal abridgment that omits this woman's industry, foregrounding instead her service to her husband. Comparing this rereading to her culture's interpretation of the proverb, Caroline chooses what she believes to be the more complete and therefore more "accurate" biblical version; doing so, she reclaims the divine authority, traditionally used to oppress her, for her own empowerment.

Complementing Caroline's scriptural revision, young Rose Yorke reinterprets the parable of talents, a line of argument that most closely echoes Brontë's own spiritual defense for women's activity. When Mrs. Yorke insists that "solid satisfaction is only to be realized by doing one's duty" (S, 400), Rose questions just what "one's duty" is. Challenging her mother, she asserts that the parable of talents should not simply justify female activity but that women's talents should be identified as one's God-given duty:

> if my Master has given me ten talents, my duty is to trade with them, and make them ten talents more. Not in the dust of household drawers shall the coin be interred. I will *not* deposit it in a broken-spouted tea-pot, and shut it up in a china-closet among tea-things. I will *not* commit it to your work-table to be smothered in piles of woollen hose. I will *not* prison it in the linen-press to find shrouds among the sheets: and least of all, mother—(she got up from the floor)—least of all will I hide it in a tureen of cold potatoes, to be ranged with bread, butter, pastry, and ham on the shelves of the larder. . . . .
>
> Mother, the Lord who gave each of us our talents will come home some day, and will demand from all an account. The teapot, the old stocking-foot, the linen rag, the willow-pattern tureen will yield up their barren deposit in many a house: suffer your daughters at least to put their money to the exchanges, that they may be enabled at the Master's coming to pay him his own with usury. (S, 400–1)

Rose's appropriation of this parable proves to be one that is both a logical defense of women working outside the domestic sphere and one that evokes biblical authority to defy cultural scripts for women. More importantly, however, Rose believes that because women's talents are God's gifts, women do not just have the right to pursue a profession, but a moral duty to use their talents—just as Brontë believed it "part of [her] religion" to "defend" and "profit" by His gifts.

While Rose Yorke and Caroline's reclamation of sacred scripts enables female activity independent of romantic relationships, Shirley's results directly from her resistance to her uncle's attempts to engage her to patriarchally appropriate partners, men she had called "false gods" (*S*, 219). Proclaiming to her uncle that "I disclaim your dictatorship" (*S*, 555), she unequivocally links the patriarchal marriage-partner ritual to a religious misappropriation of God. The following dialogue, which Shirley begins, illustrates this confrontation with her uncle, whom she believes represents a patriarchally distorted ethic:

> "go, offer them a sacrifice to the deity you worship; I'll none of them: I wash my hands of the lot. I walk by another creed, light, faith, and hope than you."
> "Another creed! I believe she is an infidel."
> "An infidel to *your* religion; an atheist to *your* god."
> "*An atheist!!!*"
> "Your god, sir, is the World. In my eyes, you too, if not an infidel, are an idolater: I conceive that you ignorantly worship: in all things you appear to me too superstitious. . . . Your deity is the deity of foreign aristocracies." (*S*, 557)

If Caroline calls for a radical feminist protestantism to allow women equal privilege to interpret both the natural and supernatural worlds, Shirley most boldly charges patriarchal culture with misappropriating sacred allusion for a human agenda.[28] Both characters, however, even with such polemical challenges for their culture, have limited power and cannot totally enact these revised beliefs. As women, they are marginalized, and so by definition cannot easily effect change.

Brontë, nearly as circumscribed as the characters she creates, confronts this conflict between the individual's desires and a society that denies those desires by exaggerating in her narrative the patterns of behavior provided women—the sanctioned patriarchal scripts for female activity. Through this amplification, Brontë subverts these social and narrative scripts in the third volume of *Shirley*—the volume that appears to succumb to conventionality. Here, Brontë illustrates the apotheosis of a patriarchal prescription for women—passivity. Believing that Robert loves Shirley, Caroline abandons herself to absolute passivity and wastes away emotionally and physically. Even Shirley, who had previously defied patriarchal scripts, *appears* to become complicit by choosing to be mastered by a marriage partner, a choice she carries to the extreme by marrying a man who, although her social and financial inferior, appears to be a traditionally masculine partner in interpersonal relationships.

The use of this narrative strategy, which masquerades as a strict adherence to traditional narrative (and social) plots, also explains Mrs. Pryor's function in *Shirley*. With this character, Brontë further challenges a patriarchally privileged interpretation of life and religion. Introduced in the final chapter of volume two, Mrs. Pryor signals the narrative's movement away from the fantastical musings of Shirley and Caroline to the realities of a woman's life. As Shirley's governess and Caroline's mother (a fact not disclosed until Caroline is on the brink of death), she functions in this novel both as an alternative model to male authority—superseding Reverend Helstone in her daughter's life, characterizing values competing with his, and, consequently, undermining the narrative—and as a realistic example of the often unpleasant realities of women in a patriarchal culture—articulating the life of an abused wife and that of a governess. This unenviable position that unmarried, unaffluent women hold in a culture that provides "valued" work by gender had long concerned Brontë; earlier she had written, "the great curse of a single female life is its dependency" (*B*, 3:5). As the sobering voice of a dependent female, Mrs. Pryor tries to check Caroline's plans to become a governess. This check by her mother against entering into a culturally accepted place for single women reinforces the earlier checks against her action: whatever options Victorian society offers young women like Caroline Brontë eliminates for her character—Caroline cannot marry; she is discouraged from being a governess. In this context, Caroline can see no meaning or purpose for her life. Significantly, even though it is Robert's withdrawal from their relationship that precipitates Caroline's physical decline, Mrs. Pryor, not Robert, saves her from wasting away into death precisely because Mrs. Pryor is Caroline's mother; she is the mother for whom Caroline has always longed. Her illness, detailed in a chapter titled "The Valley of the Shadow of Death," enacts the metaphoric principle of the necessity of being reborn to enter the kingdom of heaven (*S*, 421–41).[29] This metaphor takes on added dimension in the feminist context in which it is presented. Denied life by patriarchal scripts, Caroline is given new life, the "strength" she has prayed for, through a reconnection to her mother (*S*, 428). Brontë takes her character to the limits of patriarchal patterns for female behavior and then replaces those values with female ones. If the author ever "succumbs" to convention, then, it is at this point, but in fact she does not: rather, Brontë subverts those conventions by unquestionably identifying Caroline's recovery as a result of her mother's presence. The narrator tells us that the word *mother* "suggested to Caroline's imagination . . . a gentle human form . . . unknown, unloved, but not unlonged-for. 'Oh,' Caroline fantasized, 'that the day would come when she would remember her child! Oh, that I might know her, and knowing, love her!'" (*S,* 321–22). With this description, Caroline's mother is the physical, earthly counterpart to Shirley's maternal creation stories. Once Mrs. Pryor's biological connection to Caroline is known, she not only provides Caroline's salvation but also supersedes Mr. Helstone in Caroline's life, replacing patriarchal codes with maternal ones. Although Caroline does marry Robert in the end, her mother's love, not romance, saves her life—a fundamentally more significant factor in the novel.

Shirley concludes with the narrator telling the readers of two romantic marriages, essentially with the "happy ending" of fairy tales. Marriage is, afterall, what patriarchal society deems the proper role for women, fulfilling the intended order for society. Robert can propose to Caroline when a last minute reprieve of the Orders of Council allows him to anticipate financial success and the ability to marry for love, not money. And Shirley, giving up more affluent marriage partners, marries her former tutor and Robert's brother, Louis Moore. Yet to read this final volume simply as a retreat by Brontë from a radical feminist rendering of culture, or as a rejection of those values, is to miss the narrative cues that Brontë threads into her narrative, to miss the genuinely subversive quality of this feminist fiction. That is, not only does the narrative voice reveal Brontë's *mimicking* of cultural scripts, but the narrative structure itself contributes to the thematic enterprise of hermeneutic privilege and the act of interpretation itself.

The narrative voice of *Shirley* clarifies and explains the map of interpretive choices presented to the reader both through the narrator's comments and through the content itself. In addition to providing a historical context, the narrator prepares the reader for the underlying "truth" of the subverted romance. On the first page, the narrator cautions the reader:

> If you think, from this prelude, that anything like a romance is preparing for you, reader, you never were more mistaken. Do you anticipate sentiment, and poetry, and reverie? Do you expect passion, and stimulus, and melodrama? Calm your expectations; reduce them to a lowly standard. Something real, cool, and solid, lies before you; something unromantic as Monday morning, when all who have work

wake with the consciousness that they must rise and betake themselves thereto. (S, 5)

With such an unequivocal check on the reader who expects romance, why does Brontë seem to disregard this caution and close
her novel with the quintessential happy ending of fairy tales—
not just one marriage, but two? This paradoxical structure is consistent with Brontë's agenda: this reverberation between enacting
and subverting traditional romance scripts reveals the inherent
tensions of negotiating a hegemonic social script and attempting
to challenge it. The narrator cautions the reader that even though
Shirley may appear to be the romance she expects, it is *not*. And,
with this explicit rejection of "romance" for something as "unro-
mantic as Monday morning," Brontë causes her readers to reinterpret the narrative patterns she presents them in *Shirley*.

Significantly, Brontë repeatedly includes in the novel other instances of antiromance, other cautions against applying a roman-
ticized vision to the realism of the narrative. Just as the narrator
begins the narrative with a check against reader expectations, in
the continued description of Mr. Yorke, this "Yorkshire gentleman
. . . par excellence," the narrator schools the reader's expectations
with distinctly similar language: "If you expect to be treated to a
Perfection, reader," the narrator adds, "you are mistaken" (S, 46).
Not many chapters later, the narrator again intrudes, reflecting
on sociological patterns, this time situating her "imperfect characters." Parenthetically, she qualifies their characterization: "though
I have not undertaken to handle degraded or utterly infamous
ones," "every character in this book will be found to be more or
less imperfect, my pen refusing to draw anything in the model
line" (S, 61). Shifting slightly the focus of this caution against a
romantic interpretation of the events in the narrative, she applies
these qualifications directly to Caroline, possibly the most long-
suffering character: "Caroline had, doubtless, her defective side
too: she was human, she must then have been very imperfect"
(S, 131).

Even Caroline, the narrator tells us, tries to school herself
against romantic interpretations of the events. "Her earnest wish
was to see things as they were, and not to be romantic. By dint
of effort she contrived to get a glimpse of the light of truth here
and there, and hoped that scant ray might suffice to guide her"
(S, 172). Later, just before she witnesses Moore and Shirley
walking together one night in the hollow, the narrator tells the
reader: "Miss Helstone was by this time free enough from illu-

sions" (S, 233). The learned reinterpretation of events in the novel continues as both the hollow itself and the concept of a romantic marriage are questioned and redefined. Helstone is shocked that Shirley would call the hollow romantic because it contains the mill, but she responds by restating her assertion: "Romantic with a mill in it" (S, 202). Continuing, she redefines trade as "respected," the tradesman "heroic" (S, 202). Later when Moore tries to figure out whom Shirley will marry and hears that Mrs. Pryor (the least traditionally romantic character in the book) "was charmed," his response is "It can't be romantic then" (S, 605). These instances of challenged interpretations to standard reactions remind the reader to check her own interpretations and question patriarchal, "romantic" scripts for both life and literature.

Written as a revisionist feminist parable, Shirley is structured by a series of narrative patterns that, as I have demonstrated briefly already, foreground the interpretive act. Although readers, when confronted with the romantic ending of Shirley, often discount Brontë's initial caution as evidence of a modified agenda, if one analyzes the novel as a whole, Brontë consistently provides evidence to support this pattern of antiromance. After providing the fairy tale ending of the double wedding, the narrator continues the story, just as Brontë continues the narrative of Jane Eyre beyond Jane and Rochester's "happy" marriage, leaving the reader with an image of patriarchally informed, religious imperialism through St. John River. The final words of Shirley stress the absence of fairies in the hollow and the industrialization of nature: "it is altered now." The narrator concludes this novel as it began—foregrounding the interpretive act:

> The story is told. I think I now see the judicious reader putting on his spectacles to look for the moral. It would be an insult to his sagacity to offer directions. I only say, God speed him in the quest! (S, 646)

While the narrator does frame the story, intruding now and again to qualify or explain meaning in the early chapters of the novel's first volume, by the beginning of the third volume the narrative structure replaces this function, self-consciously highlighting the act of storytelling itself; so this volume, which appears a retreat into conventionality, actually subverts patriarchal prescriptions for romance by challenging the way one knows and interprets life. This exaggerated "storytelling" is produced by Brontë through a variety of ways: the narrator invites the reader to read Louis's journal over his shoulder several times (*S*, 524–26, 610); Louis reads Shirley's school-girl devoir aloud in French, although the narrator *translates* it into English for the reader (*S*, 485–90); the reader discovers the details of Robert's mercenary proposal to Shirley as he *retells* it to Hiram Yorke, who responds that it is a "queer tale" (*S*, 538) when Moore repeats to him Shirley's injunction that they may someday be friends when he has "time to read [her] actions and motives in a true light, and not so horribly to misinterpret them" (*S*, 537–38); and both couples (Shirley and Louis, Robert and Caroline) talk to one another about themselves in the third person (*S*, 514–18, 603). Each of these examples foregrounds the artificiality of narrative plots and social scripts.

The novel provides a kind of legend to this foregrounded storytelling. Just as the act of writing was fundamental to Brontë's own empowerment, so, too, the act of writing is associated with personal relief by Caroline, specifically when she reflects on William Cowper's poem "The Castaway":

> He was nearly broken-hearted when he wrote that poem. . . . But he found relief in writing it—I know he did; and that gift of poetry— the most divine bestowed on man—was, I believe, granted to allay emotions when their strength threatens harm. It seems to me, Shirley, that nobody should write poetry to exhibit intellect or attainment. Who cares for that sort of poetry? Who cares for learning—who cares for fine words in poetry? And who does not care for feeling—real feeling—however simply, even rudely expressed? (*S*, 226–27)

The liberation that writing provides, the ability to manipulate narrative and, by extension, social scripts, is central to this novel. Writing *Shirley*, Brontë, like Cowper, gains emotional relief and empowerment by rendering women's lives, fantastical scripts, and cultural plots—all infused with doctrinal challenges.

The character Louis Moore provides additional understanding of Brontë's purpose for this foregrounded narration. His reflections produce an analogous legend by which the final volume can be interpreted as a subversion of traditional scripts. When the narrator allows us to read Louis Moore's journal directly, both the content and style develop this theme of antiromance. Allowed to *read* the journal unmediated, the reader participates in an act that simultaneously exaggerates (by foregrounding it) and eliminates (by presenting the journal text directly) the *fictive* quality of that journal. We read that for Louis:

It is pleasant to write about what is near and dear as the core of my heart: none can deprive me of this little book, and, through this pencil, I can say to it what I will—say what I dare utter to nothing living—say what I dare not *think* aloud. (*S*, 521)

Just as Shirley can challenge Milton, that great patriarch of religious and narrative scripts, only because she and Caroline "are alone," so, too, Louis can *write* what he cannot even "think."

Brontë repeatedly stresses the contrast between the possibilities of writing and realistic constraints in the third volume. The narrator asserts that Martin Yorke must learn "how many commenced life-romances are doomed never to go beyond the first—or at most—the second chapter" (*S*, 586). And when Shirley proposes a fantastical vision of life, Louis replies that he believes in "nothing Utopian" (*S*, 495). And nothing utopian is exactly what Brontë portrays here when she adheres to patriarchal scripts. Instead, she presents a narrative from which the reader must extract her own moral, to interpret her own truth. No ultimate Truth, no "intellect" or "attainment," is provided for the reader; Brontë both rejects a single truth and demands that her readers interpret their own, keeping within a radical protestant perspective.

Brontë's grafting of Christian imagery onto her secular narrative, then, signals the larger, Christian context in which *Shirley* must be read; with this parable of women's and workers' lives during an unstable period of British history, Brontë provides a "stable" context to inform the narrative and provide crucial context. Patriarchal culture, then, is not *the* standard, but *a* standard, and one that appropriates sacred allusion for its own agenda. Appropriate to a rendering of women's marginal, subjected position, *Shirley* portrays the story of female life enveloped in the male sphere of industry, framed by clerical levitications.[30] *Shirley* is the story of learning to recognize one's vocation, to interpret various models of authority during a period of social and religious upheaval.

The Church does not fair well in this Brontë novel between the curates' hypocrisies and Helstone's muscular tactics. Even so, Brontë does not set out to dismiss religion.[31] "Man, as he now is," Brontë wrote to her publisher, "can no more do without creeds and forms in religion than he can do without laws and rules in social intercourse" (*B*, 2:267). Humanity needs religion, Brontë believes, because God can empower those whom society has marginalized. Her character Caroline, echoing Nightingale's earlier contentions, voices this position:

My consolation is, indeed, that God hears many a groan, and compassionates much grief which man stops his ears against, or frowns on with impotent contempt. I say *impotent*, for I observe that to such grievances as society cannot readily cure, it usually forbids utterance, on pain of its scorn: this scorn being only a sort of tinselled cloak to its deformed weakness. People hate to be reminded of ills they are unable or unwilling to remedy: such reminder, in forcing on them a sense of their own incapacity, or a more painful sense of their obligation to make some unpleasant effort, troubles their ease and shakes their self-complacency. Old maids, like the houseless and unemployed poor, should not ask for a place and an occupation in the world: the demand disturbs the happy and rich. (*S*, 390–91)

In effect, Brontë reclaims the Christian myth to empower society's disenfranchized members so that they can reject their cultural oppression; so long as the "happy and rich" "stop [their] ears," the socially marginalized need to find a higher authority than that of the clerics and politicians, and God provides just *such* authority.

Thus, Brontë presents a radical protestantism that invests each individual—whether male or female, worker or industrialist—with the power to interpret God and His intent, just as she had subjectively reinterpreted her relationship with God to justify her passions and desire to write. Although the popular Evangelicalism of Victorian England also asserted the individual's right to a direct access to God, this right *really* included only men; women remained in a prereformation position to God. Expected to let their husbands and/or fathers mediate the natural and supernatural worlds for them, women were not given the same spiritual privileges as men—even in Evangelical Christianity. By exposing her culture's narrative and social scripts as patriarchal products, Brontë foregrounds the individual's need to actively disinter her own vocation, to look beyond human agendas. Humanity may *need* religion, but Brontë's spiritual vision is not that of the patriarchally complicit religion of her culture. The necessary religion she endorses is a radical protestantism built not upon privileged hermeneutics but upon the individual's relationship to God—one that recognizes the inevitable subjectivity of the interpretive act and one that subsequently nurtures and empowers its various believers.

4

To "Stand with Christ against the World": Gaskell's Sentimental Social Agenda

> "An unfit subject for fiction" is *the* thing to say about [*Ruth*];
> I knew all this before; but I determined notwithstanding to
> speak my mind out about it; only how I shrink with more pain
> than I can tell you from what people are saying, though I wd
> do every jot of it over again to-morrow. . . . In short the only
> comparison I can find for myself is to St Sebastian tied to a
> tree to be shot at with arrows.
> —Elizabeth Gaskell, *LG*, 220–21

Near the end of Elizabeth Gaskell's second novel, *Ruth* (1853), Thurston Benson defends his efforts to help the fallen protagonist work out her salvation, telling Mr. Bradshaw that he intends to "stand with Christ against the world."[1] Although declared late in the novel, this conflict—between Christ and man—permeates the work, shaping the story of Ruth Hilton—her seduction by Bellingham (and the worldly values he represents) and her redemption by Benson's charitable beliefs. Through this dissenting minister's compassion and pronouncements, Gaskell "speak[s] [her] mind out," challenging society. Against this model, she contrasts Bradshaw's moral vengeance: although a member of Benson's Dissenting Chapel, Bradshaw is foremost a capitalist whose dependence on his culture's established practices cause his preachments to echo distinctly those dominant ideological agendas. The extent to which he privileges the symbolic order of that culture—clerical and political—over the values represented by the dissenting minister is revealed when Benson refuses to prosecute Bradshaw's son, Richard, for embezzlement. Even when his son is involved, Bradshaw insists to Benson: "If there were more people like me, and fewer like you, there would be less evil in the world, sir. It's your sentimentalists that nurse up sin" (*R*, 402). Through these confrontational dialogues between Bradshaw and Benson, the novel's main plot about Ruth Hilton and its subplot about Bradshaw's son intersect and illuminate each other. With the nexus of these two narratives, Gaskell can expose her culture's gender-based moral codes and hierarchical agenda and present as an alternative a revolutionary, sentimental model for social reform.[2]

The revolutionary potential of this alternative social vision can best be understood by clarifying the period's dominant social order. At the heart of that order is the complicit dynamic between the political and clerical components of Victorian society. Gaskell believed that the powerful Church of England, with its hierarchical structure and strict dogma, reproduced her culture's ideology: both the sacred and secular spheres separated men and women and subjected women in God's name. Believing such social conditions were man-made and not of divine design, Gaskell charged her culture with appropriating God's word to authorize industrial oppression for greater profit and female subjection for men's vicarious salvation.

Central to Gaskell's conflict with her culture is this appropriation of sacred symbolism for a human enterprise, an appropriation that, she would argue, misconstrues God's word for patriarchal ends. The alternative agenda that she posits would seek to replace her culture's ethical and secular hierarchy with a social vision that recognizes the integral interdependence of humanity—whether worker or master, woman or man. Significantly, by claiming just such authority Gaskell, *re*appropriates sacred imagery to empower and validate those her culture marginalizes.

While Gaskell delineates the tensions between masters and workers inherent in a rapidly industrializing culture more explicitly in *Mary Barton* and *North and South,* no where does she provide such a revolutionary vision for revising gender-based moral codes as she does in *Ruth.*[3] This history of an innocent girl's fall, redemption, temptation, and salvation—a revisionist story of biblical history, replacing Christ's passion as female in patriarchal society—exposes the cultural appropriation of God and His word that Gaskell witnesses. Through this story of social rejection and Christian compassion, Gaskell charges her culture to replace what she sees as a rigid and reductive Old Testament ethic of justice with a charitable and compassionate New Testament ethic of charity. By appropriating the most fundamental myth in Western religion as a narrative strategy to critique and reform Victorian culture, Gaskell challenges her readers to question the doctrines considered sacred and reevaluate standards considered divinely ordained. With her use of religious symbolism in *Ruth*, she challenges her readers to reconsider, like her character Jemima, "Who was true? Who was not? Who was good and pure? Who was not?" (*R*, 322). As with Jemima, "The very foundations of . . . belief [would be] shaken" (*R*, 322). Through this unsettling narrative strategy, Gaskell privileges a New Testament vision built upon a foundation of charity and mercy that grafts what I identify, and will later develop, as the earthly model of mother-love to what she believed to be the sacred law of God the Father.

Gaskell reproduces both the dominant social dynamics of her culture and her competing model in *Ruth;* the tension between these two social patterns not only propels the narrative but also reveals the conservative power Gaskell harnesses to fuel her "sentimental" model. Just as she constructs characters, like Jemima, who must question both their beliefs and the assumptions upon which they rest, Gaskell also foregrounds the anticipated dismissal of this new model by having Bradshaw label it *sentimental.* It is at this self-critical point that Gaskell reveals her text at its most subversive. When Bradshaw names her social vision "sentimental," he uses its pejorative meaning to dismiss Benson and his behavior. Representing the culture's dominant ideology, Bradshaw can only see sentimentalism as negative; Gaskell, however, through Benson and Ruth, reclaims "sentimental" as positive. This reverberation between Bradshaw's negative and Benson's positive naming of sentimental operates in a parallel manner to the text as a whole: not only does Gaskell contrast the dominant social patterns with her radical agenda for human interaction, but she also juxtaposes a reinterpreted symbolic, sacred order to the one appropriated by her patriarchal culture that authorizes the maintenance of established social dynamics.[4]

By reclaiming the power associated with religious imagery to authorize and narrate her story, Gaskell's vision extends beyond the subjection of women or the maltreatment of Victorian workers; Gaskell's revolutionary model is tantamount to collapsing her culture's ideology, replacing it with "sentimental" values. By labeling her own vision sentimental, Gaskell produces two narrative effects. First, because the pharisaical Bradshaw voices this pejorative label, we are forced to question his (and by association the culture's) reliability as an interpreter of either the natural or the supernatural world. Second, with the pejorative connotation of sentimental questioned simply by who voices it, Gaskell subverts the patriarchal energy attempting to disparage and discredit this

alternative model of human interaction. Doing so, Gaskell revalues as positive the behavior pejoratively labeled sentimental, and
more importantly, she reframes it as a model of behavior to be
neither limited to women nor restricted to the domestic sphere.

This chapter will consider in detail the explicit delineation of
the *sentimental* vision found in *Ruth:* how Gaskell appropriates
religious imagery as a narrative strategy to subvert patriarchal
standards and social codes, how she rejects a culturally bifurcated
morality. Jane P. Tompkins has recently argued that sentimental
fiction, what she describes as a political enterprise halfway between a sermon and social theory, attempts to reorganize culture
from a woman's point of view.[5] This revisionist theory of sentimental fiction provides a useful method from which to reconsider
Gaskell's fiction. I argue, however, that to understand Gaskell's
agenda fully, one must recognize that even if Gaskell's culture
domesticated these values, the subculture in which Gaskell lived
did not.[6] These values were propagated by her religion—Unitarianism—regardless of gender. Because of this grounding in her
spiritual beliefs, a brief consideration of the Victorian Unitarian
church is necessary to clarify the extent to which Gaskell's ideology, as it appears in her fiction, reflects not just a woman's perspective, but a social dynamic alternative to that sanctioned and
perpetuated by her culture's dominant ideology.

Elizabeth Gaskell grew up in one of the leading Unitarian families of her day and married into another. Because this dissenting
sect believed in the importance of individual potential, both men
and women were educated. Gaskell, even though raised by her
maternal aunts upon her mother's death, received an extensive
education.[7] The community in which Gaskell grew up, then, challenged not only the Church of England but also, by educating
her, the prevalent gender-based distinctions. The nondoctrinare
history of this faith, its intellectual appetite for multiple perspectives, its disbelief in the Trinity or Christ's divinity, and its powerful philanthropic traditions placed it in firm contradiction to the
patriarchal hierarchy of the established Church; and just as
importantly, it stood in contrast to the prevalent Hebraic and
authoritarian element of Victorian religion by embracing and
practicing a New Testament ethic.[8]

These differences—this ethic of justice represented by the
Church of England and the ethic of Christian charity practiced
by the Unitarian faith—echo important gender distinctions that
Carol Gilligan has identified in her important study of psychological growth. Reexamining patterns of male and female moral devel-

opment, she describes the different developmental paradigms as the ethic of justice (for traditional male development) and the ethic of care (for the female), differences that result from either a perspective of separate (male) or connected (female) object relations.[9] Significantly, though, when considering Gilligan's results against the ethical paradigm illustrated in *Ruth*, the division of justice and mercy is not aligned along gender divisions for Gaskell, just as the "sentimental" values are not relegated to the domestic sphere in her subculture. Instead these ethical models parallel what Gaskell saw as differences between Old and New Testament values, between a Hebraic Church of England and dissent. For this reason, the radicalism of Gaskell's social agenda is underscored when one recognizes that these values of empathy and compassion, traditionally associated with women and the domestic sphere, are put forth as the ethical values through which all humanity should interact in both public and private spheres—men and women alike.

The contrast between the beliefs that the Unitarians held and those they ascribed to the Church of England appears in sermons of William Gaskell, Elizabeth's husband. These sermons reveal the important differences between justice and charity: the fundamental importance of God's mercy, not vengeance, for all; the belief that no sinner is damned to everlasting punishment; the contention that the New Testament offers a system of ethics for everyday life; and finally, the commitment to charitable conduct as a mark of the true Christian.[10] But most significantly, his sermons illuminate the conflict between Gaskell's Unitarian values and the Church of England. Shortly after the Gaskells' marriage, William Gaskell

> preached against intolerance by Protestant theologians, and defended Unitarianism on the principle of liberty of interpretation of the Scriptures and on the grounds that no man can claim infallibility for his views. . . . his view of the Gospel is that: it is simply the highest teacher of humanity. . . . In a still later sermon . . . while reaffirming his view that errors of interpretation need to be fought against, he points out that intelligent artisans reject orthodoxy and religion altogether because of it. . . . He then goes on to attack the popular interpretations which present a religion based on fear.[11]

Living within this religious environment, Gaskell's ethical perspective placed her *outside* her culture's Established Church but still inside a community that significantly defined itself by challenging that church. While many of her contemporaries, when faced with the limitations of organized religion, found themselves crippled with doubt, Gaskell's beliefs provided her with an alternative vision of society and code of behavior. Unitarianism nurtured the values displayed by Benson in *Ruth* and charged the Victorian culture to replace its Old Testament values with those of the new. And, while other sects such as the Evangelicals endeavored as well to make Victorian Christianity a living religion, preferring deeds to doctrine, Gaskell's vision took this idea further: translocating the values associated with the home into the streets, authorizing women as well as men to be spiritual actors.

The importance of Gaskell's religious beliefs and background in shaping her narrative strategies, then, is twofold: 1) because of this heritage, she stands outside the powerful Church, but within an organized body actively working to change cultural values; and 2) because Unitarianism believed in the cultivation of the intellect regardless of sex, she found the religious authority to challenge patriarchal subjection of women, especially those who failed to fulfill their socially defined roles.[12] So, ironically, in a period nearly defined by its theological doubt, Gaskell's spiritual faith authorizes her revolutionary vision.

The nonhierarchical dogma of her faith, her close political ties with Christian socialists,[13] and the numerous industrialist dissenters who attended her husband's chapel contributed to the complexity of Gaskell's vision of industrialism, capitalism, and the workers' plight. Although she believed in the Carlylean doctrine "Do the duty that lies nearest to thee" (*LG*, 117), she could not help but also see the impoverished and dreadful conditions in which the workers lived and often worked. And, just as she could see the workers' exploitation from industrialization, she saw parallel exploitation of women in patriarchal culture.[14]

Many women, especially those from the middle and upper classes, rather than be able to work themselves, became a means of capital for men. Mirroring this condition, Gaskell's character Jemima Bradshaw voices anger and frustration at her father's mercenary attitude that projects her as the future wife of his business partner: she "felt as if she would rather be bought openly, like an Oriental daughter, where no one is degraded in their own eyes by being parties to such a contract" (*R*, 238). The increasing pattern of the overt symbol of purity, yet covert role of monetary status that women were expected to play in maintaining the culture's ideology, fueled the condemnation and ostricization of women who failed to do so. Here, especially, the nexus between the political and clerical appropriation of religious imagery is evident. Any woman who radically rejected her assigned position in culture by defying socially determined sexual mores called forth Milton's image of Satan's expulsion from heaven—the fall—and, like Satan, those fallen women possessed a curious subversive energy with which to threaten the dominant ideology.[15]

It is this energy that Gaskell taps in *Ruth* to reshape personal and social dynamics.[16] If, as Tompkins argues, sentimental fiction is an amalgam of sermon and social theory, then Gaskell's narrative exploited the strengths of both modes of discourse in *Ruth*. Unlike the powerful industrialists who contributed to the domestication of Christianity, Gaskell does not separate the "sermon" from the social theory, the shape of her fiction from her vision.[17] Gaskell, along with her husband, worked and shared common beliefs with the Victorian Christian socialists. This intense interest in a philosophy that sought to explode the Church's pacifying myth of a future, heavenly reward to excuse oppressive conditions on earth provided Gaskell with a political ideology akin to her Unitarian beliefs. And because she lived and worked in the heart of industrial Manchester, Gaskell invested her fiction with vivid details from real life, with an energy born from witnessing real suffering.[18] To this realistic portrait of the poor and fallen, Gaskell fuses religious images and myth, but unlike earlier religious discourse, her narrative would be intimately grounded in the sordid realities of secular life.[19] This grafting in Gaskell's fiction worked two ways. The Victorian reader, in contrast to the modern reader, would quickly respond to even obscure biblical allusions,[20] and because Gaskell secularized biblical myth, her readers would be forced to reexamine cultural beliefs when they failed to concur with these stories made parallel. Like Jemima Bradshaw, they should ask: "Who was true? Who was not? Who was good and pure? Who was not?"

Gaskell's use of religious imagery as a narrative strategy enabled her to subvert patriarchal fictions, to tell a different story from those sanctioned by patriarchal values. In *Ruth*, Gaskell produces a revisionist incarnation story, validating and empowering the ostracized and victimized fallen Ruth Hilton. By creating a character who is first condemned and then revered by her culture, Gaskell calls that culture's values into question; by characterizing Ruth as both a Mary Magdalene and a Madonna figure, Gaskell subverts and explodes her culture's and its sanctioned religion's rigid and reductive dichotomous vision of women.

Gaskell's agenda can best be illustrated by examining the narrative's three sections, each of which culminates in a major turning

point in Ruth Hilton's history: first, the story of her life from
becoming a dressmaker's apprentice until her exposure by Bradshaw as an impostor and fallen woman; the second, her marginalization and ostricization by her culture, her penitence, and
subsequent public salvation; and third, her decision to nurse her
seducer, Bellingham/Donne, through his fever, an act that brings
about her death.[21] Examining Gaskell's choice of narrative structure as well as the importance of the Richard Bradshaw subplot
can demonstrate the full impact of her revolutionary agenda for
the reader.

Significantly, Gaskell spends most of the novel in detailing this
first part of Ruth's story, chronologically carrying the reader
through her character's life, beginning with her first night as an
orphaned apprentice at Mrs. Mason's dress shop. Forcing us to
experience Ruth's life along with her—seeing her world as she
sees it, feeling the isolation and loneliness that she feels—Gaskell
manipulates our values and preconceived notions of fallen
women. The reader sees the naive adolescent, left without mother
or father, forced to manipulate a new and impersonal environment; and so, when Ruth allows herself to be seduced, while the
reader may have the experience to foresee the outcome, we realize
that Ruth does not. Because of this, the reader cannot help seeing
the forces that contribute to this seduction, and should not be as
willing to judge and condemn Ruth.

Not only does Gaskell portray Ruth's fall and redemption in
this first section, but she also tempers the seducer, Bellingham,
by presenting him through Ruth's unworldly eyes. This subjective
rendering, combined with the portrayal of Ruth working out her
salvation through her love for her son, should temper the readers'
cultivated moral reaction. When her past is revealed, then, the
reader *should* see the narrow and reductive reaction of her culture.
Like the Bensons with whom she lives, the reader has made an
investment in Ruth's rehabilitation, has been educated through
Gaskell's characterization of this fallen woman—that, although
Ruth has "sinned," she is not evil.[22]

In this first section of the novel, which traces the history of
Ruth's adolescence, seduction, fall, and redemption, Gaskell pro-
vides a revisionist myth of Christian history: from prelapsarian
Eve to her seduction and fall, Christ's later temptation, his agony
in the garden, and finally his willingness to fulfill prophecy,
Ruth's life reenacts (and reinterprets) Christian myth. Like Eve,
Ruth struggles with seduction, but unlike Eve, she has not re-
ceived God's (or even man's) warnings about evil. With the excep-

tion of confusing and undefined feelings, Ruth is literally without a symbolic code of values; she was, the narrator tells her readers, "too young when her mother died to have received any cautions or words of advice respecting *the* subject of a woman's life" (*R*, 44).

Ruth has neither the living mother, whose behavior would literalize morality for her, nor the ability to translate the vague memories of her mother's actions into an abstracted code of value—whether for sacred or secular agendas. Consequently, she struggles unsuccessfully to reconcile her instinct that meeting Bellingham might be wrong with the genuine pleasure she receives from his companionship and love. The "strange undefined" feelings that she experiences make her question her walks with him (*R*, 39), but after deciding that she had not been "defrauding Mrs. Mason of any of her time," Ruth even concludes that "there must be something wrong in [her] . . . to feel so guilty when [she has] done nothing which is not right" (*R*, 41). Significantly Ruth turns to the memory of her mother's words to reconcile her feelings: since "dear mamma used to say [the ability to thank God] was a sign when pleasures were innocent and good" and Ruth can "thank God for the happiness [she] has had in [the] charming spring walk," she concludes that these walks could not be bad (*R*, 41). Yet on Ruth's fateful journey to her home, the aging family worker fails in his attempts to warn Ruth of her potential seduction. Old Thomas, unable to speak literally to her of this danger, turns to the abstract language of the Bible. Ruth, never having been taught to manipulate this symbolic language, is left baffled, and "never imagined that the grim warning related to the handsome young man who awaited her with a countenance beaming with love" (*R*, 51). Ruth's knowledge of "right" and "wrong," good and evil, exists only on a personal, concrete level; when she encounters new situations, her behavior is guided by the memory of her mother's finite instructions about how to understand those feelings. Much of the following narrative traces Ruth's learning and mastery of the symbolic language that now leaves her baffled with Old Thomas.

This growing consciousness by Ruth of her culture's value system as revealed through its codes of behavior is demonstrated by her attempts to gain control over her fate. When Mrs. Mason spies her and Bellingham arm in arm returning from Milham Grange and dismisses her on the spot, Ruth suddenly "saw how much she had done that was deserving of blame" (*R*, 55); nonetheless, she still struggles to understand the difference between what is "right" and "wrong," between her desires and the cultural prescriptions that deny them. For instance, after her dismissal by Mrs. Mason, Bellingham convinces Ruth that she is friendless and persuades her to go to London with him; but temporarily left alone, she decides that Old Thomas might take her in, attempts to return to him, but discovers she has no money to pay for the tea Bellingham has ordered for her. With her sexual honor in the balance at this moment, it is ironically her social honor that tips the scale and contributes to her fall. So even though she has genuinely attempted to resist complete seduction—not because she recognizes the social impropriety but because she believes in Old Thomas's friendship—circumstances conspire against her. When Bellingham returns with their carriage secured, he "reasons" with Ruth, and the narrator tells us that "She was little accustomed to oppose the wishes of any one—obedient and docile by nature, and unsuspicious and innocent of any harmful consequences" (R, 61). What little socialization she has assimilated into her behavior, her training to be passive finally seals her fate. At this point in her history, then, her understanding of appropriate behavior—albeit incomplete and out of proportion—does her more social harm than good.

The extent to which Ruth remains ignorant of her society's values, even after they live together in London—an unquestionably worldly and sophisticated city—is revealed in the next section of the narrative. While the reader knows she has been seduced, Ruth has neither interpreted nor internalized her culture's moral codes; in fact it is not until a young child refuses her kiss, calls her a "naughty woman," and Ruth sees Benson's sorrowful expression that she begins to comprehend her fallen state as she lives with Bellingham in Wales (R, 71).

More concerned with detailing Ruth's growing consciousness of her fallen state than the fact that she is fallen, Gaskell moves her narrative quickly ahead, jumping over their months in London and focusing in, instead, on Ruth's painful epiphany. It is just this kind of experience with the child—interpersonal, not abstract—that teaches her the abstract code of her culture's value system. Eventually, she will learn to combine her instincts and feelings with the symbolic language used to convey secular and sacred values, but first she will need to repeat this lesson in a variety of forms as she works out her salvation. This obligatory recognition on Ruth's part of the moral impropriety of her life as Bellingham's lover reveals an apparently conservative element in Gaskell's vision; even so, Gaskell subsumes that conservatism to her larger, radical agenda by exposing the harm of the unadulterated social rejection of those individuals who do not conform to society's "moral" codes, by asking "What became of such as Ruth, who had no home and no friends" (R, 34), and by portraying the harsh and uncharitable conditions Ruth must face even while she struggles to enact "Christian" values.

Once Ruth has seen that she is "fallen" in society's eyes, this aspect of her education complete, Gaskell again propels the story to the point of her abandonment by Bellingham and, subsequently, her complete cultural marginalization. Just as Ruth comprehends her social ostricization, Bellingham falls ill with a fever. His physical deterioration mirroring his weak character, he is convinced by his mother to abandon Ruth. This agent of patriarchal law, this phallic mother,[23] completes her son's desertion of Ruth: arranging secretly to quit the inn, Mrs. Bellingham whisks her son away and secures for Ruth a socially appropriate position— totally outcast from society with no apparent hope for reintegration. This function of the partriarchally complicit mother—to reinforce androcentric values—exists as a powerful opponent to Gaskell's social vision, an aspect of the novel to which I will return.

In contrast to predominant cultural scripts concerning fallen women, Gaskell's narrative provides Ruth with the opportunity to master her community's values and to become reintegrated into her society through her character's relationship with Benson, a charitable action on his part that underscores the nongendered ethic of compassion Gaskell found in Unitarianism. Significantly, it is charitable human interaction that saves *both* Benson and Ruth. After finding Ruth crouched behind a hedge taunted by Welsh children, Benson tries to comfort her. Hearing the river, though, she races off to drown herself; when he tries to stop her, Benson slips and aggravates his painfully deformed back.[24] His agonized cry draws Ruth's attention away from herself and suicide, and once she has returned, Benson pleads with her to stay—first unsuccessfully in God's name, then with success in the name of her mother.

This scene, contrasting the power of the earthly mother to a heavenly father (both of whom are absent), reveals an important aspect of Gaskell's vision. As she has already shown, the early death of Ruth's mother (before she could teach her daughter to decipher symbolic social codes) means that Ruth has neither a guide to interpret the symbolic language of the Father nor the skill to interpret it for herself at this time.[25] "For His sake" means little to Ruth at this point, but "In your mother's name" means everything (R, 100).

The important model of mother-love, as opposed to the patriarchally complicit mother, is central to Gaskell's revolutionary vision. Quite the opposite from reinforcing the cultural image of mother as Madonna, Gaskell's vision of mother-love radically subverts those values. The difference also informs the important dissimilarities between the values that Ruth's mother emulated and those endorsed by women complicit in the culture's dominant ideology. At the heart of this difference is the contrast between what Gaskell believed to be God's intentions and her culture's appropriation of His word: Gaskell seeks to differentiate what she believes to be a basic morality from an exaggerated and destructive transformation of that morality into reductive and hegemonic cultural maxims. Whereas the complicit mother reinforces the patriarchal reading of these values, the model of mother-love, in contrast, instructs what Gaskell believes to be the *unappropriated* morality. In this spiritual context, mother-love—human interaction that builds on compassion and care—develops from a communal commitment to Christianity rather than a hierarchical doctrine; traditionally, this model of interaction has been displaced into the home (or to some extent the Church). As long as the behavior identified as mother-love is socially limited to women and the domestic sphere, however, it can be subsumed by the dominant ideology to account for opposing values in a culture without allowing them in the public sphere or even inscribing them with value. By confining this behavior to women, and by extension to the home, a patriarchal culture gains free reign to be competitive and antagonistic in the workplace.

Gaskell's mother-love, however, does not endorse her culture's ideology, even if it appears to enact those patriarchal values sanctioned for women. While the "maternal" qualities were elevated during the Victorian period as the ideal of womanhood, Gaskell's interest in these qualities does not replicate this larger cultural pattern. Rather than advocate the ghettoization of those values to women or the domestic sphere, Gaskell translocates the model of mother-love from an exclusive place in the home out into society at large.[26] In this way, she charges both men and women to embrace the values and behavior represented by Christ, the values and behavior found on earth in mother-love, not in the enshrined Madonna or the phallic mother.

What most distinguishes Gaskell's model of mother-love from the partriarchally complicit model of mother is the differing representations of the values and codes of an absent father: for Gaskell, the model of mother-love represents the Christian Father; that of the phallic mother, the patriarchal. Although bolstered by Established Church doctrine, the patriarchal values that inform her culture's ideology, Gaskell would contend, not only represent oppressive and self-serving policies but also distort and misrepresent God's word. Mother-love, in contrast, replicates the fundamental values of New Testament Christianity—compassion, charity, forgiveness, and, most of all, a vision built on sympathetic projection.[27]

Importantly, it is through Ruth's literal role as mother, the knowledge of her pregnancy, that Ruth's desire to find her own salvation is sparked; until then, she continues to feel that life is hopeless. Although Benson's sister, Faith, cannot quite agree,[28] both Ruth and Benson see this coming child as Ruth's salvation: she must love rather than be loved; she must be both a model and teacher to instruct her child of God's word. Benson tells his sister, "Faith, do you know I rejoice in this child's advent" (R, 118). Through the coming of the child—echoing biblical history of the prophecy—hope is gained; through the coming of one who will allow the sinner to work out his or her sin, Gaskell prepares Ruth for her personal salvation.

At this point the biblical associations that Gaskell creates through her characterizations of Ruth and her son (Eve, Mary Magdalene, the Virgin Mary, Jesus) become conflated. Prior to this, Ruth's character has recreated Eve—the seduction and fall. Now she enacts the second Eve, Mary. Significantly, though, this Mary is not immaculately conceived, let alone virginal. This fallen Mary is more like (and often alluded to as) Mary Magdalene. Yet like the virgin Mary (and Joseph), Ruth is taken into a marginalized place to give birth to her son. And like Christ's, Leonard's birth is seen by Benson as an "advent." Through the birth of the son (named after her mother's father), Ruth will achieve redemption and salvation. Yet from this point in the narrative Ruth's characterization as Eve, or the Virgin Mary, or Mary Magdalene, shifts dramatically to that of Christ Himself—a revolutionary association for a fallen woman. From this point on, the son gains salvation through the mother.

It is through Ruth's ability to turn outward, to project sympathetically, to learn to love more than she may be loved, that she finds her redemption. Through Benson's guidance, Ruth educates herself so that she may teach Leonard; doing so, she learns her God's and her culture's manifestation of symbolic language and codes. Once Ruth has learned the word of the Father through her love for her son, her character is tested, just as the earlier prophets were tested, just as Christ was tempted. For Ruth this temptation takes the form of another encounter with Bellingham: now that she has internalized the symbolic code of law, now that she knows "right" from "wrong," will Ruth have the strength to refuse Bellingham? Indeed, no longer radically naive, will she resist (or be able to resist) Bellingham's temptation? Is the once fallen woman always fallen?

This second temptation and Ruth's ability now to negotiate her culture's codes can best be understood and illustrated by revealing the narrative strategy Gaskell uses to show both Ruth's initial naiveté and her growing assimilation of the law of her spiritual Father. Instead of presenting Bellingham through an omniscient narrator, Gaskell allows readers to see him predominantly through Ruth's eyes, although the readers' experience can foresee what Ruth cannot. Although this presentation of Bellingham's character through Ruth's perspective continues through all three sections of the novel, the vision we see in the first section is especially important in order for readers to project themselves sympathetically into Ruth's naive world. Inexperienced, Ruth sees the world through unsophisticated eyes. Therefore, we see Bellingham's kindness at the ball, offering Ruth a flower in thanks for mending the dress of his condescending partner (R, 16); we even see him ride past her like "lightning" to save a drowning child, a boy whom he would eventually employ (R, 22, 443). Instructing her to, "Tell [me] everything . . . as you would to a brother; let me help you, if I can, in your difficulties," Bellingham appears to Ruth to be nothing if not a loving and compassionate friend, a good and benevolent man (R, 41).

This uncritical presentation of Bellingham through Ruth's eyes is tempered, however, by the narrator's occasional details. Providing another side of Bellingham's character, the narrator reveals the character's thoughts about Ruth's "naïveté, simplicity, and innocence"; he feels "It would be an exquisite delight to attract and tame her wildness, just as he had often allured and tamed the timid fawns in his mother's park" (R, 33). Whether consciously or not, Bellingham sees Ruth, not as a sister, but as a kind of possession, a wild creature for him to control and manipulate. Yet even when we see the limitations of Bellingham's character, we also see him, to his credit, admit to his mother that while Ruth is no "paragon of virtue," he "led her wrong" (R, 88). Still his fever in Wales reveals his moral weakness: rather than fight for the treatment he feels due Ruth, he submits to his mother's socializing forces. He gives in not so much because he agrees with her, but because it will "spare [him] all this worry, while [he] is so weak" (R, 90) and "get rid of [his] uneasiness" (R, 91). Years later, at Eagle's Crag, the Bradshaws' seaside estate, Bellingham, now Mr. Donne, is being wooed by Mr. Bradshaw to be the Eccleston parliamentary candidate. At this point the narrator reveals another aspect of his moral weakness. Struck by the similarity between the Bradshaws' governess, Mrs. Denbigh, and his former lover as they sit across a breakfast table, Bellingham thinks of Ruth "for the first time in several years" but decides that "there was but one thing that could have happened [to her] . . . perhaps it was as well he did not know her end, for most likely it would have made him very uncomfortable" (R, 276).[29]

Significantly, now that Ruth has learned the "Christian" law of the father, her ability to negotiate the patriarchal law will be tested, and she sees Bellingham across that same table with wiser and more critical eyes: "He was changed, she knew not how. In fact, the expression, which had been only occasional formerly, when his worse self predominated, had become permanent. He looked restless and dissatisfied. But he was very handsome still" (R, 277). Seeing both his hardened demeanor and his still handsome face, knowing her past was wrong yet nonetheless attracted to Bellingham, Ruth is primed for her temptation: she now knows the consequences, but she is again attracted to her former lover and the father of her child. Faced by genuine temptation, Ruth, like Christ, must confront it, agonize over sacred and secular codes, and then firmly reject that temptation. Reintroduced into each other's life at Eagle's Crag after years of separation, Ruth and Bellingham face their common past and their potentially different futures. Once convinced that Mrs. Denbigh is his former lover, Bellingham connives and manipulates ways to accost Ruth about their past in the hopes of reestablishing their relationship. For Ruth, this encounter is most dangerous because it is so tempting.

Tortured again by her contradictory feelings for Bellingham, Ruth struggles to act on what she has now learned to be God's word and its translation into societal codes. The great difficulty of this struggle is symbolically demonstrated by Bellingham's literal intervention between her and God's word. Having followed Ruth and the young Bradshaw girls to church, Bellingham enters their pew and sits "just opposite to her; coming between her and the clergyman who was to read out the word of God" (R, 281). In their encounter after church on the heaving sands below Eagle's Crag, Gaskell interweaves allusions to the parable of the house on the rock and the house on the sand when Ruth finds herself confronted and taunted by Bellingham.[30] Here Ruth struggles with confusion over former passion and future salvation (R, 269, 272–73); in contrast, Eagle's Crag, built high on the rocky cliffs, becomes the refuge within which Ruth can regain her strength to resist Bellingham's advances.[31] And like Christ in the Gethsemane Garden, Ruth, wind-swept and rain-soaked from leaning out her room's window into the storm, agonizes over still loving Bellingham; in this blasting storm the words "stormy wind fulfilling his word" (Psalms 148:8) echo in her mind (R, 274). Hearing this causes Ruth to kneel before God and through tears pray: "Oh, my God, help me, for I am very weak. My God! I pray thee be my rock and my strong fortress, for I of myself am nothing. If I ask in His name, thou wilt give it me. In the name of Jesus Christ I pray for strength to do Thy will!" (R, 274). At church she sees her agony as akin to Christ's: "And when they prayed again, Ruth's tongue was unloosed, and she also could pray, in His name, who underwent the agony in the garden" (R, 283). Significantly, the very words that Benson had earlier used without effect to prevent Ruth's suicide attempt are now the words from which she finds strength.

With this renewed strength through divine communion, as she now understands "for His sake," Ruth can resist Bellingham's persistent temptation, even when he condescends to offer marriage. She has learned that "the old time would be as white as snow to what it would be now" (R, 273), and relying on the presence of a poor fisherman to protect her, refuses, telling Bellingham that "The errors of [her] youth would be washed away by [her] tears—it was so once when the gentle, blessed Christ was upon the earth" (R, 301), alluding to Christ's forgiveness of Mary Magdalene. Like the Magdalene, Ruth's past will be forgiven through her penitence, even though, significantly, Bellingham need not go through an equivalent penitence. Here, then, she has won a partial victory over him: she will no longer love Bellingham, and she refuses to be seduced this time.

In this way Gaskell demonstrates what she believes to be Ruth's complete, *personal* redemption: she has learned God's moral code, has taught that code to her son both as a model and through deciphering symbolic word, and has resisted a second temptation. Because of this personal redemption, the story shifts; Gaskell moves from the private to the public sphere. In this arena

Ruth must work out her *public* redemption, and her culture must learn to replace its harsh ethical codes with Christian charity.

The conflict between the new social code of ethics that Gaskell calls for and the prevailing Hebraic justice can be clearly illustrated by the Bensons' interaction with the harsh and judgmental public. While Gaskell presents the Bensons as models of Christian charity, even they fear public admonition enough to misrepresent the truth of Ruth's condition, although out of compassion for the unborn child. In this way, both Ruth and the Bensons are at odds with their culture's ideology: Ruth falls from social grace, failing to fulfill its code for women; the Bensons refuse to comply with their culture's standards for dealing with such women. The narrator, interrupting the story, reflects on the inevitable harm that will result from disguising Ruth as a widow, even if done out of Christian charity:

> Ah, tempter! unconscious tempter! Here was a way of evading the trials for the poor little unborn child, of which Mr Benson had never thought. It was the decision—the pivot, on which the fate of years moved; and he turned it the wrong way. But it was not for his own sake. For himself, he was brave enough to tell the truth; for the little helpless baby, about to enter a cruel, biting world, he was tempted to evade the difficulty. He forgot what he had just said, of the discipline and penance to the mother consisting in strengthening her child to meet, truthfully and bravely, the consequences of her own weakness. (*R*, 122)

Compounding this first deception, Benson does not rectify the original deceit when Bradshaw decides that Ruth should be his daughter's governness. Persuaded by Ruth's penitence, her genuine efforts toward goodness, and her model mother-love for Leonard, Benson gives in to his sister's plan not to tell, and once again the narrator intrudes: "The scroll of Fate was closed, and they could not foresee the Future; and yet, if they could have seen it, though they might have shrunk fearfully at first, they would have smiled and thanked God when all was done and said" (*R*, 200).

When the narrative moves from Ruth's personal penitence to her public shame, Gaskell voices most clearly the values that are at the heart of her ethic of compassion through Benson's confrontation with Bradshaw over Ruth's past. Now recognizing all too clearly the impact of hiding the truth about Ruth's past, now faced with the need to live his faith and beliefs overtly on such a controversial issue, Benson takes his "stand with Christ against

the world." Reacting to Bradshaw's harsh dismissal of any extenu-
ating circumstances in Ruth's past, Benson bears witness to a
higher truth, declaring:

> Now I wish God would give me power to speak out convincingly
> what I believe to be His truth, that not every woman who has fallen
> is depraved; that many—how many the Great Judgment Day will
> reveal to those who have shaken off the poor, sore penitent hearts on
> earth—many, many crave and hunger after a chance for virtue—the
> help which no man gives to them—help—that tender help which
> Jesus gave once to Mary Magdalen. (R, 350–51)

Again voicing his culture's ideology, Bradshaw responds: "The
world has decided how such women are to be treated; and, you
may depend upon it, there is so much practical wisdom in the
world that its way of acting is right in the long run" (R, 351).
Erupting with passion, Benson finally voices his values, this
time unqualified:

> I state my firm belief, that it is God's will that we should not dare to
> trample any of His creatures down to the hopeless dust; that it is
> God's will that the women who have fallen should be numbered
> among those who have broken hearts to be bound up, not cast aside
> as lost beyond recall. If this be God's will, as a thing of God it will
> stand; and he will open a way. (R, 351)

With this exposure of Ruth's past and the harsh realities of
her culture's values made explicit, Gaskell shifts her narrative to
demonstrate her character's efforts to maneuver her way through
this social marginalization and ostricization. This transfer from
domestic to public realms symbolically occurs in the scene where
Bradshaw dismisses Ruth, and Jemima literally "bear[s] witness"
for her (R, 338). Significantly this confrontation occurs in the most
fundamental female place of the domestic sphere—the nursery.
The verbal (and physical) ejection of Ruth—and the mother-love
she has come to represent—out of this female space into the public sphere, traditionally male, sets in motion the translocation of
the "sentimental" values from a secondary sphere of influence to
a confrontation with those of the dominant. Just as significantly,
Bradshaw, who originally labeled these values sentimental, also
forces them out of the nursery and into the public arena. By
shifting her narrative from the personal to the public, Gaskell
impels her readers to see the already penitent Ruth once again
required to work out her redemption, this time for a rigid, Old

Testament public. Although this section of *Ruth* most visibly displays the conflict between God and His human appropriation, Gaskell has prepared us for this conflict throughout the novel. Earlier, the narrator had told the reader of Old Thomas's concern for Ruth, even though he believed that "God judgeth not as man judgeth," and Benson and his sister decide that Ruth "must strengthen her child to look to God, rather than to man's opinion" (*R*, 121). Even Ruth, when telling her son about his illegitimacy, comforts him by saying that "I think God, who knows all, will judge me more tenderly than men" (*R*, 343).

However comforted by her belief in God's mercy, Ruth still must face her earthly judges, must prove her worthiness for redemption within the public sphere. She achieves this by reenacting her mother-love for Leonard; by transforming that love from private to public in nursing the sick and aged, Ruth begins to work out her public salvation.[32] In this way, Ruth must again learn "that it is more blessed to love than to be beloved" (*R*, 248), this time on a larger scale. To do this, she goes to nurse the poor and sick, and when the town is struck by fever, she volunteers at the fever ward.[33] Her impact here brings about public approval of her; witnesses openly voice her goodness like Benson and Jemima have done earlier. Through her example, her community is forced to reconsider the values and standards applied to fallen women like Ruth. Not only do the townspeople gather around outside the fever ward where "many arose and called her blessed" (*R*, 430), but her son, Leonard, can gain his self-respect. Significantly, this public invocation of her holiness erases her sin; her past has been revised. One witness recalls, "They say she has been a great sinner, and that this is her penance"; but another person insists, "Such a one as her has never been a great sinner; nor does she do her work as a penance, but for the love of God, and of the blessed Jesus" (*R*, 429).[34] This public witness is especially important because it challenges a reading of *Ruth* that simplistically reduces her behavior as solely motivated by penitence; instead, this witness suggests an alternative, possibly complementary motivation—mother-love, Christian love.

The profound reversal of opinion displayed by the previously Hebraic public and its powerful subversion of dominant ideology can be more fully illuminated by examining Gaskell's application of biblical text to Ruth. When the narrator reports that "many arose and called her blessed," Gaskell subverts her culture's patriarchal appropriation of the Old Testament proverb of the good wife; instead of reinforcing her culture's vision of the good wife, or even echoing texts about Mary Magdalene, Gaskell here applies these words of honor to a fallen woman.[35] Gaskell's narrator praises Ruth's compassion and mother-love, and she portrays a public that has learned through this fallen woman to reinterpret God's words, not to accept uncritically the patriarchal appropriation of them. When the worst of the fever abates, Ruth is sent home with proclamations from the town council and doctors about her worthiness. And just as her sin has been revised and eradicated, so is her literal shame—her son—accepted and acknowledged: genuine offers to educate Leonard arise from Mr. Farquhar and Mr. Davis.

If Gaskell had only wanted to demonstrate Ruth's penitence and salvation, the novel could end here. And many readers believe that it should have. Gaskell's agenda, however, is more extensive than redeeming *a* fallen woman. By including the final section of Ruth Hilton's story (as well as the Richard Bradshaw subplot), Gaskell creates a truly revolutionary tract for social revision. It is in this next section that Gaskell takes her narrative beyond just a critique of her culture's treatment of fallen women, as subversive as that would be.[36] Instead Gaskell presents a radical vision of her culture's need to replace Old Testament values and religion with New Testament charity by her representation of Ruth's death.

Here Gaskell most clearly and boldly presents Ruth as a Christ or prophet figure.[37] Having gained public approval and absolution for her past, Ruth does not need to nurse Bellingham, who has contracted the fever; she does not need to perform this act from which she will eventually die herself. In fact, rather than endorse this self-sacrificial act, both Benson (as spiritual advisor) and Mr. Davis (as social spokesperson) attempt to keep her from going— she has been both morally and socially redeemed. And contrary to what most critics believe (both Gaskell's contemporaries and modern), Gaskell sends Ruth to her inevitable death to portray a radical sentimentalism through the model of mother-love, not to punish Ruth further because her sins cannot be absolved on earth.[38]

Gaskell has Ruth nurse Bellingham to demonstrate the most revolutionary aspect of her social tract: Ruth gains the final victory over her seducer; like Christ, this sacrifice infuses her with a greater power than Bellingham had over her.[39] This embrace with death is neither punishment for her sins nor a variation of her suicide attempt in Wales. While Ruth has too often in the past lived and thought only about her present, looking neither forward nor back (R, 420), here she enacts a radical version of her mother-love, putting others before herself because she sees the intricate web of human connectedness. Bellingham's fever is potentially fatal for him, not just morally weakening, and this time he is no longer nursed by his patriarchally complicit mother. (She, like general public sentiment about Ruth, has died [R, 320].) With this fever, Bellingham is nursed to health by Ruth, and then she leaves. She no longer waits outside his door, passive and dependent on him for strength or direction.

Having given life to her seducer, Ruth completes the Passion story. In these final pages, Gaskell includes two important images about Ruth's death that solidify her association with Christ. As Mr. Davis and Benson watch over her, Gaskell alludes to the song of Cymbeline, writing that Ruth "home must go, and take her wages" (R, 447). To the Victorian reader, who would know this allusion, the significance that Imogen is not dead would evoke important Christian parallels; to that Christian, death would not mean dying, but life everlasting.[40] As if this first allusion to Ruth's resurrection and affinity with Christ is not sufficient, Gaskell unquestionably invokes the crucified Christ by Ruth's death: "'I see the Light coming. . . . The Light is coming,' she said. And raising herself slowly, she stretched out her arms, and then fell back, very still for evermore" (R, 448). Gaskell emphasizes this parallel to Christ even further by having Bellingham go to Ruth on the third day after her death—the day of Christ's resurrection. Here Ruth gains her final victory over Bellingham: he is exposed as her seducer, and he and his values are finally and completely rejected by Benson, a triumphant rejection of the culture's ideologies for the new "sentimental" ones.

This final visit of Bellingham foregrounds the revolutionary component of Gaskell's sentimental agenda by revealing that Bellingham has misunderstood Ruth's motives when she nursed him to health. Standing over Ruth's laid out body, Bellingham tells Benson: "I cannot tell you how I regret that she should have died in consequence of her love of me" (R, 453). By this he discloses his belief that romantic love, not Christian love, had motivated Ruth's sacrificial act. Significantly, Gaskell has earlier prepared the reader to reject this misinterpretation of Ruth's actions by including the chapter aptly titled "Sally tells of her Sweethearts and Discourses on the Duties of Life." In addition to voicing a challenge to the notion that married life is always preferable to single life for women, Sally dispels the idea that one can die of romantic love by telling the story of Dixon's proposal of marriage to her. Upon rejecting him, she believes "he'd die for love for [her]," influenced by the romantic "old song of Barbary Allen" (*R*, 169). But, less than three weeks later, Sally hears, via the church bells, of Dixon's wedding. Reinforcing this tale of anti-romance, Gaskell juxtaposes this with an image of Ruth "peaceful as death," foreshadowing the actual event (*R*, 170). It is the difference between earthly and religious love that clarifies how Ruth's death is a victory over Bellingham and not punishment for her earlier love for him. Unlike Richardson's Clarissa, who after her rape eventually dies of her integrity, Ruth dies from an active working out of her beliefs and principles. Not a passive victim of patriarchal values, Ruth becomes a victim, like Christ, a female martyr in her male culture as a prophet of God's word, as a model of mother-love.[41]

But if Gaskell so thoroughly calls for society to revise its values through the story of Ruth Hilton, why does she include the subplot of Richard Bradshaw's embezzlement of Benson's money? First, this subplot serves as a supplement to extend further Ruth's story from the female and private spheres to the male and public. The sexual double standard that existed in Gaskell's culture presented different codes for men and women: Ruth, not Bellingham, is punished for their relationship. So to explore a male fall from grace in her culture, Gaskell writes Richard Bradshaw's subplot about the male equivalent of a moral fall—not living by the established codes of business. Through Benson and Farquhar's compassionate treatment of Richard, the reader sees Gaskell's new code of behavior extended into and enacted in the public arena. Gaskell charges her culture to replace completely its values with those associated with the domestic sphere. And with those concrete domestic values, she forces the rigid Old Testament values so clearly exemplified by Mr. Bradshaw to be replaced by the ethic of care—displayed here both by Benson and Farquhar when faced with Richard's fall.

In this story, the unwavering adherence to a Hebraic God by the father at the expense of his son inverts the thwarted sacrifice of Isaac by Abraham found in the Old Testament. There, the degree of Abraham's faith is tested, and it is his blind faith in God's principles that allows his son to live. Here Gaskell presents a Victorian Abraham, Mr. Bradshaw, whose faith is too blindly obedient to those abstract, impersonal principles; it is this unwavering commitment that nearly causes, not reprieves, his son's death. Although Bradshaw fully intends to sacrifice his son for what he believes to be God's and culture's laws, when he fears that Richard is dead in a coach accident, Bradshaw can no longer operate on that abstract level. Only when faced with the actual loss of his son does Bradshaw begin to understand New Testament compassion. For Gaskell, it is the importance of this interpersonal love, the interdependence of all humanity, that gains power over the abstract code of behavior.

While Richard's fall parallels Ruth's, unlike her, he does not die. Why? He does not need to die in Gaskell's narrative because of the differing codes of his culture for the male crime of abstract principle and the female crime of sexual indiscretion. His sin is not as much a crime against his culture's ideology as Ruth's is; hers is a more subversive rejection of its values because female chastity is the foundation of political and clerical patriarchy.

The main plot and the subplot are also tied together by the concept of salvation through the son, a clear allusion to Christ's sacrifice for humanity. Richard's crime and near death challenge Bradshaw's reductive morality; the very real possibility that Richard has died in a coach accident enables Bradshaw to return to a human, not abstract, level of interaction. Similarly Leonard proves the initial and important focal point for Ruth's redemption; it is his coming birth and his need to be educated as to God's and man's codes that spark Ruth's penitence. But with Leonard and Ruth, the biblical roles blur. He is her salvation, but so she is his. His birth is considered an "advent" by Benson, and Leonard mourns her the way Mary Magdalene mourns Christ. Finally through Leonard, the two stories connect. Bradshaw achieves his greatest salvation through this son of a fallen woman: finding Leonard crying upon his mother's grave, Bradshaw takes him home to the Bensons; this act not only reestablishes ties between Benson and Bradshaw, but also causes Bradshaw to cry, bringing the novel full circle to the motto from which it began—with the image of sin washed away through repentant tears.

With *Ruth*, Gaskell provides a revolutionary model to reform her culture; in the process of doing so, she empowers its marginalized members by asserting a diametrically opposed ideology to that which dominates Victorian society. She gives voice to new social codes by reclaiming the law of the Father through the model of the Son (Christ) and the daughter (as symbolized by mother-love).

Throughout her oeuvre Gaskell rejects an equation of God's words with her culture's ideological vision; she rejects an appropriation of Christianity that serves man and not God. Whether she explicitly uses biblical allusions as she does in her early fiction or veils those values by historical settings or even simply presents this ethic characterized by communities of women enacting mother-love, Gaskell challenges a patriarchal appropriation of God.[42] God the Father may be in heaven, but on earth, his saving words are represented by the mother's love. Seeing a society where both God and mother-love are absent in the power-wielding public domain, where both—under a guise of deferential worship—have been marginalized, Gaskell subverts her culture's values and produces a competing vision that replaces Old Testament justice with New Testament mercy. By reclaiming the Judeo-Christian myth from patriarchal misinterpretation, Gaskell reappropriates Christian symbolism to empower those the Victorian Church has rejected and reenfranchise those the culture has marginalized.

5

The "Hidden Heroism" of "Social Sympathy": George Eliot's Ethic of Humanity

> For my part, I wish to be among the ranks of that glorious crusade that is seeking to set Truth's Holy Sepulchre free from a usurped domination. We shall then see her resurrection!
> —George Eliot

"Who that cares much to know the history of man," asks George Eliot in her "Prelude" to *Middlemarch*, "has not dwelt, at least briefly, on the life of Saint Theresa."[1] With this opening question and the ensuing narrative, Eliot challenges the patriarchal standards that measure an individual's worth and limit the boundaries of that life. This question, often misread as an ironic deflation of Saint Theresa's significance (and subsequently Dorothea's as a "modern Saint Theresa"), instead rejects canonical and clerical values, emphasizes gender-based limitations on women endorsed by the Church and state, and sanctions the revaluation of the criteria used to determine individual significance.[2]

Eliot, however, dwells more than briefly upon Theresa, presenting her as a model of human potential against which Middlemarch's modern Saint Theresa may be considered.[3] In establishing this model, she does not simply detail Theresa's feats; rather, Eliot tempers them with the story of Theresa's aborted child-pilgrimage.[4] Eliot includes this symbolic episode to illustrate the perennial conflict between the individual and society; yet, for Theresa, even formidable societal restraints could be circumvented because her ardor would eventually be acknowledged as part of God's grand plan.[5] For Theresa the church became the sanctioned ministry through which she could channel her "passionate, ideal nature": it allowed her respectability to remain unmarried, and through her conventual reform, Theresa found the "epic life" her nature "demanded" (*M*, 25).

This allusion provides Eliot with the vehicle to contrast the life available to Theresa's spiritual daughters: "Many Theresas have been born," she asserts, "who found for themselves no epic life" (*M*, 25). As early as 1855, this missing epic life for women concerned Eliot. In her essay "Margaret Fuller and Mary Wollstonecraft," she quotes Fuller's condemnation of cultural attempts at "absolute definitions of woman's nature and absolute demarcations of woman's mission."[6] Eliot continues the Fuller quote, which distinctly resonates with her own beliefs: "I think women need, especially at this juncture, a much greater range of occupation than they have, to rouse their latent powers" (*GEE*, 204). This "greater range of occupation," however, is not available for Theresa's descendants because no "coherent social faith or order [exists] which could perform the function of knowledge," so these women find only restrictions, never the opportunities for an "epic" life (*M*, 25). Without this external, recognized "faith" or "order," the modern Theresa will never defeat her cultural uncles; instead, like Dorothea, she will desperately seek for that "coherent faith and order," and mistakenly see authority and wisdom where only greater constraints exist. Quite simply, no life like Theresa's is now possible:

> Here and there a cygnet is reared uneasily among the ducklings in the brown pond, and never finds the living stream in fellowship with its own oary-footed kind. Here and there is born a Saint Theresa, foundress of nothing, whose loving heart-beats and sobs after an unattained goodness tremble off and are dispersed among hindrances, instead of centering in on some long-recognizable deed.[7] (*M*, 26)

Paralleling its musical counterpart, this literary prelude introduces the subsequent narrative's theme—a revaluation of historical significance and consequently what constitutes an "epic life" and "long-recognizable deed[s]." Developing this through the life of a modern Theresa, Eliot schools her readers in the virtue of Dorothea's passions and the values of her Middlemarch uncles.

While the "Prelude" contextualizes Dorothea's life, the "Finale" provides commentary on modern life: Eliot revalues historical significance by redefining epic. Here, she explicitly demarcates the prescribed boundaries of a "modern" woman's life—marriage, the realm of which has not traditionally been considered epic.

Eliot writes that "Marriage . . . is still a great beginning to the *home* epic" (*M*, 890, emphasis added). If the home epic begins with marriage, then the private sphere frames and interpersonal relationships compose *this* epic life. In the place of armies clashing or gods interfering, Eliot portrays the painful discoveries—both personal and interpersonal—that marriage engenders as the ideal gives way to the real. Doing so, Eliot extends the traditional narrative of a woman's life from the wedding to the marriage itself.[8]

Expanding on this alternative epic, Eliot further subverts canonical standards by explaining the revised components of this genre: "Some set out, like Crusaders of old, with a glorious equipment of hope and enthusiasm, and get broken by the way, wanting patience with each other and the world" (*M*, 890). With spiritual and epic simile, Eliot transforms both the genre (epic, novel as epic, novel) and the significance of the domestic sphere.[9] Circumscribed by this sphere, the life associated with this revisioned genre forces—by comparison to traditional epic—a revaluation of historic acts as well as women's lives. Eliot explicitly focuses on this revaluation not just in the opening question of her "Prelude," but throughout the narrative as well. As such, she transfers the historically established criteria for the epic to its modern equivalent—fiction. Contrasting the modern writer to his/her predecessors, in this case Fielding, Eliot again redefines significance through her narrative focus; here she begins the chapter that reveals Lydgate's own history:

> We belated historians must not linger after his example; and if we did so, it is probable that our chat would be thin and eager, as if delivered from a camp-stool in a parrot-house. I at least have so much to do in unravelling certain human lots, and seeing how they were woven and interwoven, that all the light I can command must be concentrated on this particular web, and not dispersed over that tempting range of relevancies called the universe. (*M*, 170)

Identifying herself, not with Homer, but Penelope, Eliot's narrator reconstructs the epic's locus. Like Penelope whose worth is measured implicitly by the weaving—an act inherently domestic and in contrast to a "long-recognizable deed"—and significantly the *unweaving* of the shroud, Eliot valorizes "unhistoric acts" and defines the home epic as domestic.[10]

Eliot's belief in the inescapable influence of environment—historical and spiritual—on an individual life must be recognized to understand fully this revaluation in her fiction.[11] For Dorothea, the "determining acts" of her life "were the mixed result of a young and noble impulse struggling amidst the conditions of an imperfect social state, in which great feelings will often take the aspect of error, and great faith the aspect of illusion" (*M*, 896). Sympathizing with Dorothea, Eliot continues, "there is no creature whose inward being is so strong that it is not greatly determined by what lies outside it" (*M*, 896). In addition to this inescapable cultural web, Eliot points to one crucial difference between Dorothea and Theresa's worlds—"the medium in which [Theresa's] ardent deeds took shape is forever gone." Because of this, "A new Theresa will hardly have the opportunity of reforming a conventual life, any more than a new Antigone will spend her heroic piety in daring all for the sake of a brother's burial" (*M*, 896).[12] Thus the focus of "epic" must change; the criteria for individual worth must change as well.

Acknowledging the missing "medium" or "coherent social faith or order," Eliot brings her novel full circle with a final subversion of the traditional criteria for worth, positing instead the importance of the unsung, uncanonized individual:

> But we *insignificant* people with our daily words and acts are preparing the lives of many Dorotheas, some of which may present a far sadder sacrifice than that of the Dorothea whose story we know.
>
> Her finely-touched spirit had still its fine issues, though they were not widely visible. Her full nature, like that river of which Cyrus broke the strength, spent itself in channels which had no great name on the earth. But the effect of her being on those around her was incalculably diffusive: for the growing good of the world is partly dependent on *unhistoric* acts; and that things are not so ill with you and me as they might have been, is half owing to the number who lived faithfully a *hidden* life, and rest in *unvisited* tombs (*M*, 896, emphasis added).

In this concluding commentary, Eliot conflates Theresa, Antigone, and Christ; contrasting these transfigured images to the modern Theresa, she emphasizes the individual's struggle against an imperfect state. All three, motivated by moral passion, confronted social opposition—whether it be in the form of an uncle, an uncle who represented the state, or the state and its religion.

Eliot awards significant emphasis to religious myth in her "study of provincial life" by framing it with allusions to Saint Theresa, which expand to include both Christ and Antigone. Eliot grafts religious imagery onto the secular world of Middlemarch. Doing so, she sets in relief Dorothea's character and life against the pre-Christian Antigone, the Catholic Saint Theresa, and Christ, and their relative worlds to that of Middlemarch. In Middlemarch, religion (let alone ethical passion) is subordinated to business and title. The state religion—the Church of England—is considered a respectable profession for an educated young man of good family (like Fred Vincy), not a channel through which to funnel passionate energies for humanity's reform. Essentially secularized as a profession, the Church hierarchy is seldom, if ever, a vehicle for ethical or social change; consecrated with power via secular sanction, the Church, far from sparring with society, has an investment in its perpetuation. Eliot compounds the presence of the religious allusions by placing *Middlemarch* within the larger tradition of epic; a religious superstructure frames the epic hero's journey and life while he confronts earthly adversaries and obstacles. The importance of these "sacred" components and allusions to the larger project of redefining significance—the grafting of ethically charged imagery to this decidedly secular story—can neither be ignored nor minimalized to fully understand the narrative of Dorothea Brooke.

Yet why does George Eliot, one of the nineteenth century's great unbelievers, frame *Middlemarch* with and develop its theme through religious allusion?[13] Why, throughout her canon, does she present individuals either with religious callings (Dinah Morris, Sarvanarola, Daniel Deronda) or comparable secular passions (Felix Holt, Maggie Tulliver, Romola, Dorothea)? Why, when she found organized religion ineffective and God untenable, does Eliot infuse religious allusion in her fiction? Her ethical beliefs must be considered in order to understand this paradoxical grafting of sacred to secular.

In January of 1842 Marian Evans (then twenty-one years old) shocked and angered her family by refusing to attend church. Later that month, she wrote: "For my part, I wish to be among the ranks of that glorious crusade that is seeking to set Truth's Holy Sepulchre free from a usurped domination. We shall then see her resurrection!" (*GEL*, 1:125). With this radical assertion, she (like the other writers considered) situates her values against traditional doctrine, differentiating between Truth and organized religion. While Evans did not believe in "vengeance eternal," "predestined salvation," or the "reward" of "future glories," she "fully participate[d] in the belief that the only heaven here or hereafter is to be found in conformity with the will of the Supreme; a continual aiming at the attainment of that perfect ideal, the true Logos that dwells in the bosom of the One Father" (*GEL*,

1:125–26).[14] This earth-bound "religion," this reach for the "perfect ideal," permeates her fiction and becomes—in tandem with sympathetic identification—the basis of her ethical and moral beliefs.

As her early abandonment of the Church demonstrates, Evans's late adolescence found her (eventually quite deliberately) searching for what she would later call a "coherent social faith" (the same superstructure needed by her characters) that she could embrace. Raised in the Church of England, she remained there until her complete rejection of organized religion.[15] Still, she aligned herself with various doctrinal degrees within that church; through the influences of her schooling at Nuneaton with Maria Lewis's Evangelicalism and her Aunt Samuel, a Methodist preacher, Evans experienced a period of charismatic fervor. She explains her beliefs at this time: "I was then strongly under the influence of Evangelical belief, and earnestly endeavouring to shape this anomalous English-Christian life of ours into some consistency with the spirit and simple verbal tenor of the New Testament" (GEL, 3:174). But Evans would not discover the "consistency" she struggled so hard to find: instead, she would see only hypocrisy, superstition, and man's appropriation of God.[16]

With equal fervor, Evans left the Church.[17] She details her reasons for this controversial step in a letter to her father[18]:

> I regard [the Christian Scriptures] as histories consisting of mingled truth and fiction, and while I admire and cherish much of what I believe to have been the moral teaching of Jesus himself, I consider the system of doctrines built upon the facts of his life and drawn as to its materials from Jewish notions to be most dishonourable to God and most pernicious in its influence on individual and social happiness. In thus viewing this important subject I am in unison with some of the finest minds in Christendom in past ages, and with the majority of such in the present. . . . Such being my very strong convictions, it cannot be a question with any mind of strict integrity, whatever judgment may be passed on their truth, that I could not without vile hypocrisy and a miserable truckling to the smile of the world for the sake of my supposed interests, profess to join in worship which I wholly disapprove. (GEL, 1:128–29)

Two important aspects appear early in Evans's ethical history—the inconsistency of organized religion with what she perceives as the will of God and the inherent suffering of individuals who participate in these doctrines. She writes that:

I have faith in the working-out of higher possibilities than the Catholic or any other church has presented, and those who have strength to wait and endure, are bound to accept no formula which their whole souls—their intellect as well as their emotions—do not embrace with entire reverence. The highest "calling and election" is to *do without opium* and live through all our pain with conscious, clear-eyed endurance. (*GEL*, 3:366)

She strikingly echoes Nightingale, who also believed that man had appropriated religion, so that the sanctioned, codified beliefs stymied individual development and fostered individual pain. But where Nightingale would look above this world to God for a direct channel to authorize individual belief, Evans concentrated on an earth where she saw no relief from suffering except through sympathetic human interaction, writing that "It seems to me the soul of Christianity lies not at all in the facts of an individual life, but in the ideas of which that life was the meeting-point and the new starting-point" (*GEL*, 4:95).

At the heart of her ethic, then, is the entwined dynamic of individual suffering alleviated by sympathetic human interaction. Although this analysis of Evans's beliefs complements the critical dialogue that studies how her ethical beliefs inform her fiction, my project diverges from this scholarship because I consider the interrelationship within a feminist context.[19] This context is crucial to recognizing the full impact of her ethics on her fiction; read from this perspective, her novels detail the inherent suffering of marginalized individuals when artificially limited and restricted by gender, position, or religion. Thus the pain of the individual— trapped in a culture that does not recognize his or her passion or needs—becomes the focal point of her ethical beliefs and the common thread that runs throughout her fiction. "My own experience and development deepen every day my conviction that our moral progress may be measured by the degree in which we sympathize with individual suffering and individual joy" (*GEL*, 2:403). She would later describe this sympathetic projection as "what I mean by a chief act of religion" (*GEL*, 5:325).[20]

Eliot clarifies her concept of sympathetic identification by redefining the individual life as that of a hero or heroine. Meditating on the impact of an individual life, she asks: "who has not more or less need of that stoical resignation which is often a hidden heroism, or who, in considering his or her past history, is not aware that it has been cruelly affected by the ignorant or selfish action of some fellow-being in a more or less close relation of life"

(*GEL*, 6:99). She continues, explaining the "hidden heroism" that would become both a key motif in *Middlemarch* and also the crux of her belief for moral advancement: "to my mind, there can be no stronger motive, than this perception, to an energetic effort that the lives nearest to us shall not suffer in a like manner from *us*. The progress of the world—which you say can only come at the right time—can certainly never come at all save by the modified action of the individual beings who compose the world" (*GEL*, 6:99). Writing this during the early stages of *Daniel Deronda*, Eliot distinctly echoes her "Finale" to *Middlemarch*, composed nearly five years earlier (*GEL*, 6:97).[21] Here, as in both of these novels, she defines "religion" as individual effort directed toward a larger human good, not egoistic concerns.

Knoepflmacher sees Evans's beliefs as consistent with the Victorian religion/science milieu in which she placed herself and a natural result of her own intellectual makeup. She "attempted to conserve a Christian 'essence' that would be ethical as well as empirical, 'natural,' or 'scientific.'"[22] To this scientific context, Knoepflmacher points to the "multiple perspective" she gained from being a novelist, poet, reviewer, and essayist as well as her immersion in Hennell's, Strauss's, and Feuerbach's Higher Criticism as making her "eminently fitted for the role of Victorian authoress-sage."[23] These features, Knoepflmacher asserts, produce what he defines as her religious humanism.

But to see Evans's ethical beliefs as a standard religious humanism replacing the Established Church (or organized religion) rather than a critique also of the patriarchal foundation of that church is to miss the fundamental connections between her ethics, feminism, and cultural criticism. Although never naming herself a feminist, Evans, in her life and her fiction, protests the patriarchal order that limits and restricts an individual—especially women. Her understanding of the interrelation between the subjection of the individual and a patriarchal appropriation of a culture's values, not the individual religion, originated in Evans's own experiences, as revealed in a letter written by Mrs. Charles Bray to her sister Sara Sophia Hennell:

It seems that [Evans's] brother Isaac with real fraternal kindness thinks that his sister has no chance of getting the one thing needful— i.e. a husband and a settlement, unless she mixes more in society, and complains that since she has known us she has hardly been anywhere else; and that Mr. Bray, being only a leader of mobs, can only introduce her to Chartists and Radicals, and that such only will ever fall in love with her if she does not belong to the Church. (*GEL*, 1:156–57)

Evans's life exemplifies, like Nightingale's, that of the suffering individual who finds herself at odds with her culture, by virtue of both gender and beliefs.

Evans herself unites her cultural and religious criticisms, writing that she "hardly know[s] whether [she is] ranting after the fashion of one of the Primitive Methodist prophetesses" (*GEL*, 1:126). Her prophetic "ranting"—both in fiction and nonfiction— reveals not only her ethical speculations and beliefs but also her attempt to understand women's place in her culture. She rejects a patriarchally appropriated religion and constructs instead an alternative vision, stressing the importance of the individual and the individual act in the advancement of common good. Evans found no place suited for herself in either the secular or sacred world; she found no life appropriate for her needs. Without the spiritual history of Dissent that could provide her with a nonconformist community, she could see no place within any organized religion for individuals like herself. Because of this, Evans did not see the efficacy of *any* organized religious body—the extant patriarchal or a revisionist alternative. The Church functioned, she believed, as debilitating oppressor or pacifying drug to its congregations, unmotivated for addressing individual needs inconsistent with patriarchy's. While Elizabeth Gaskell could lead a relatively conventional private life because her spirituality found authority within a coherent nonconformist community, Evans had to defy both her culture and the Church of England to emancipate her potential. In short, she had to abandon her culture's codes—religious and secular—to write fiction.[24]

Organized religion rejected, she saw her fiction as a vehicle for moral progress in much the same way an earlier Christianity had taught through parables: "If Art does not enlarge men's sympathies, it does nothing morally" (*GEL*, 3:111).[25] Eliot reiterates this belief in the moral component of art nearly twenty years later: "It is my function as an artist to act (if possible) for good on the emotions and conceptions of my fellow-men" (*GEL*, 6:289).

Fiction, for Eliot, does not replace the Sunday sermon as a means to disseminate doctrine; it is not mere didacticism replicating the patriarchal model in another form. Instead, fiction is an opportunity for experiencing alternative perspectives and subsequently better understanding lives other than one's own.[26] She identifies this important difference between preaching and sharing experience as that between a *"profession"* and a *"confession"* (*GEL*, 1:163). Eliot further clarifies this distinction: "I think aesthetic teaching is the highest of all teaching because it deals with life in its highest complexity. But if it ceases to be purely aesthetic—if it lapses anywhere from the picture to the diagram—it becomes the most offensive of all teaching" (*GEL*, 4:300). This distinction reveals that she saw her role *not* as sage but illustrator:

> My function is that of the *aesthetic*, not the doctrinal teacher—the rousing of the nobler emotions, which make mankind desire the social right, not the prescribing of special measures, concerning which the artistic mind, however strongly moved by social sympathy, is often not the best judge. It is one thing to feel keenly for one's fellow-beings; another to say, "This step, and this alone, will be the best to take for the removal of particular calamities." (*GEL*, 7:44)

Because she sees her art as instructive only through the illustration of lives different from the readers', Eliot insists, in a letter to her publisher John Blackwood, on portraying not simply "eminently irreproachable characters, but . . . the presentation of mixed human beings in such a way as to call forth tolerant judgment, pity, and sympathy" (*GEL*, 2:299).

Fiction then, not religion, serves for Eliot as the means through which to train the individual in moral behavior. Why then does she infuse theological and biblical allusions throughout her fiction? Specifically, why does she frame *Middlemarch* with the allusions to Saint Theresa? Why does she implicitly parallel Dorothea's spiritual journey to that of Bunyan's pilgrim, Christian?

Religious allusion in Eliot's fiction serves two paradoxical functions. First, by likening the modern individual's struggle against an imperfect social state to Christian figures who also faced earthly opposition, Eliot invests that struggle, here Dorothea's, with a comparable moral worth; therefore, Dorothea's passionate ardor is elevated in value by a culturally recognized religious symbol, even if hers is not acknowledged as such. If the modern ethical prophet must struggle in a decidedly secular world, Eliot transforms that struggle to a nonetheless moral one by comparison with biblical imagery. While Eliot's contemporary readers may find themselves in a world that also appears devoid of an overarching moral code, these religious allusions tap a richly moral and easily recognized antecedent.

Second, although evoking this moral context, these allusions function as any other literary allusion, illuminating the novel's world through forced comparison to that which is alluded. So, although Victorian organized religion may be ineffectual, the allusions attest to an earlier "coherent social order and faith" that could credit individual passion and recognize an ethical vocation. These specifically religious allusions in *Middlemarch*, however, are especially charged: while their modern equivalents (the Church, its voices) may be in Eliot's view unproductive, religious allusion would still produce a greater impact on the average reader than a parallel literary allusion. As a narrative technique, these allusions contrast a nineteenth-century British religion appropriated by patriarchal imperialism (a "usurped domination") with an earlier efficacious system of belief. Rather than deflate Dorothea and her passionate ideals, these allusions elevate her and her beliefs and deflate her community's values, which fail to recognize her real worth.

From *relative* historical obscurity, Eliot disinters Saint Theresa and religious ardor: this saint, through her idealistic passion and religious reform, becomes the model for ethical behavior, not the Victorian Church. Eliot bestows authority on Dorothea's passions as a modern Saint Theresa; and, through Dorothea's subsequent connection to a larger moral web, Eliot exposes the disintegration of Middlemarch's (and Victorian England's) ethical web. Dorothea's patronized, thwarted, and seemingly insignificant acts and efforts become epic in such a community, providing the thread with which Eliot unites her novel, framed with religious allusion.[27]

In this context an analysis of the "religious" characters in *Middlemarch* reveals the corruption and ineffectualness of organized religion, both theologically and politically. Eliot portrays three men, each of whom represents a particular religious or ethical position: Bulstrode, the Dissenter; Farebrother, the gentle rector; and Casaubon, the learned theologian. Although fueled in his youth by a belief "that God intended him for special instrumentality" (*M*, 664), Bulstrode realizes only failure and shame at the end of the novel. Rather than advance the moral or ethical good of humanity, Bulstrode advances his wealth and position through participation in an illegal business and immoral inheritance. It is precisely his inability to reject material concerns that makes him legally corrupt in his youth and morally bankrupt in his maturity. Like the Church, in Eliot's view, Bulstrode may have "aimed at being an eminent Christian" (*M*, 570) and even appeared to many too consciously pious, but in reality his motivations are self-serving. Essentially Bulstrode operates from a moral perspective exactly opposite from that which Eliot proposes as truly religious; rather than directing his actions by a sympathetic understanding of those affected by his deeds, he acts for his own self-interest regardless of how it will affect another. Whether in loaning Lydgate one thousand pounds or providing an annuity to Will Ladislaw (even while claiming, as he does to Will, that it is his conscience, not legal compulsion, which motivates him [*M*, 669]), Bulstrode operates from egotism.

At the other end of Middlemarch's religious spectrum from Bulstrode is the Reverend Farebrother. Whereas Bulstrode's ambition seduced him away from a ministry, Farebrother's lack of political savvy prevents him from obtaining a better living. Although motivated by an admirable morality, Farebrother's inability to play society's politics prevents him from the much deserved and needed hospital chaplainship. In the Victorian world where public and private spheres separate genders, where the tactics of mammon translate into muscular Christianity, Farebrother lives quietly and gently in a household of women—his sister, mother, and aunt—all of whom he supports.[28]

While clearly the most positive representative of the Church in *Middlemarch*, Farebrother lacks the religious passion (that even Bulstrode once had) to consider his ministry a true calling; he tells Lydgate: "Ah! you are a happy fellow. . . . You don't know what it is to want spiritual tobacco" (*M*, 202). Like the narrator, Farebrother points to the contrasts between past and current religion, implicitly identifying the sectarian controversies which impede moral instruction and diffuse moral energy. His mother tells Lydgate: "When I was young . . . there never was any question about right and wrong. We knew our catechism, and that was enough; we learned our creed and our duty. Every respectable Church person had the same opinions. But now if you speak out of the Prayer-book itself, you are liable to be contradicted" (*M*, 199–200).[29] These theological changes function two ways: if they dilute religious energy through moral debate, they also, by virtue of those debates, introduce new voices into religion. While this explosion of challenging positions rejects the closed hierarchy of the Church, it too often still reveals tendentious agendas superseding real moral instruction. Even ministers like Farebrother, who are less doctrinairely aggressive, cannot completely escape the effects of these holy wars, as his comments to Lydgate suggest. Nonetheless, he does serve his parishioners well. Motivated by a sympathetic understanding of those around him rather than by his own self-interests, Farebrother performs significant acts of kindness, that although "unhistoric," do change people's lives for the better. In addition to serving as a moral sounding board for Lydgate, he offers to aid him financially when he can ill afford to do so. With Fred Vincy, Farebrother not only acts as intermediary with Mary Garth, but also as a moral prod: although he, too, loves Mary, Farebrother reminds Fred of his promised reform, when to leave Fred unchecked could have advanced his own position with her. In this manner, even if he may be politically naive, Farebrother does embody through his actions what Eliot called "the chief act of religion." Significantly, though, by Middlemarch standards, those "unhistoric acts" of kindness advance his place neither in Church hierarchy nor in social importance, so while Farebrother may be morally admirable, this very fact prevents him from being in a position to wield power and effect *historic* changes.

In striking contrast to Farebrother's gentle, noncompetitive, and content demeanor is Casaubon, the character who best symbolizes the Established Church: he is antiquated, impotent, and egoistic. Although his parish, Lowick, even by Dorothea's accounts, does not need humanitarian reform, Casaubon is seldom seen ministering to his parishioners; instead, with the exception of two Sunday services, he spends the majority of his time as scholar. Described as a "mummy" by Mrs. Cadawaller (*M*, 81), Casaubon himself tells Brooke: "I feed too much on the inward sources; I live too much with the dead. My mind is something like the ghost of an ancient, wandering about the world and trying mentally to construct it as it used to be, in spite of ruin and confusing changes" (*M*, 40). In his search for the "key to all mythologies," he represents both the anachronistic condition and ineffectual energy of the church. As Will Ladislaw reveals to Dorothea, Casaubon's inability to read German, and therefore enter into a dialogue with Higher Criticism, prevents his "key" from being anything but useless before its completion.[30] In this way, any religious energy becomes diffused, spent either on an antiquated codification of theological beliefs or the denial of this major failing of his life.

Like the Church, Casaubon is self-serving. The self-consciousness of his scholastic failings prevents him from understanding the motivation behind Dorothea's interest in and desire to help compile his "key," and again he misspends his energy defensively rather than sympathetically. Echoing Bulstrode more than Farebrother, he defines his financial support of his second-cousin Will Ladislaw (whose paternal inheritance Casaubon gained through familial squabbling) as a "duty"—sparked not by Christian compassion, but by obligation (*M*, 258). Jealous of and threatened by Ladislaw, Casaubon adds a codicil to his will, prohibiting Dorothea from inheriting his monies if she should marry him. This act not only replicates the earlier generational folly, but guarantees, out of self-interest, that the earlier error will never be rectified.

As representative of organized religion, Casaubon portrays little that is inviting; and, as theoretician of theological scholarship, he is, as we have seen, equally inept. This act, quite the opposite of advancing (and thereby improving) theological scholarship, reveals a conservatism which clings (either out of ignorance or fear) to the outdated. Quite early, Eliot criticized this kind of scholarly pursuit; in a letter to Maria Lewis, she quotes from "Woman's Mission": "Learning is only so far valuable as it serves to enlarge and enlighten the bounds of conscience" (*GEL*, 1:107).

Casaubon's "learning," however, does neither. With her portrayal of her character's scholarship—both an escape from and denial of life, which only intensifies his injustice toward Ladislaw—Eliot reinforces the paucity of moral energy for human development found in Middlemarch's "religion." Just as Eliot creates an implicit contrast to the past potential efficacy of religion through allusion to Saint Theresa, she also uses this allusion to demonstrate the absence of reform in Middlemarch. Aside from Casaubon with his travesty of reform, seeking to identify religion's fundamental key, two other men turn their energies toward reform: Lydgate in medicine and, eventually, Ladislaw in politics.

Like Casaubon, Lydgate fails to achieve his intended goal. Although he cannot maintain Casaubon's singleness of purpose, Lydgate does possess both a greater passion and capability for his reform than Casaubon does for his. Lydgate's desire to modernize medicine is fueled by what he sees as "the most direct alliance between intellectual conquest and social good. [His] nature demanded this combination: he was an emotional creature, with a flesh-and-blood sense of fellowship which withstood all the abstractions of special study" (*M*, 174). In Lydgate's search for the "primitive tissue" he intends "from diligent application, not only of the scalpel, but of the microscope" to "do good small work for Middlemarch, and great work for the world" (*M*, 178). But the world is too much for him: just as he failed to learn the potentially deadly seduction of society from his first love in Paris, so medical reform in Middlemarch soon becomes subsumed to maintaining Rosamond's materialistic passions; and, while innocent of any immoral or illegal activities, his alignments with Bulstrode bring him as much public shame and retribution as if he had been complicit in Raffle's death.

In contrast to both Lydgate and his cousin, Casaubon, Will Ladislaw does eventually succeed at political reform through his election to Parliament. It is because he achieves this reform, when Casaubon and Lydgate do not, that a closer analysis of Will is in order. Critical appraisal of Will has traditionally been divided: he is either considered unmanly and effeminate or the fantastical ideal man.[31] He is, in a sense, a triple outcast from Middlemarch society: although he is male, he is the son of a disinherited father (and therefore as dependent on Casaubon's financial support as if he had been female); he has foreign blood; and he appears dilettantish as he searches for a profession in a time when work determined one's social (as well as moral) position. In this nineteenth-century Middlemarch, where a morally fueled vocation is held as frivolous, if not in contempt, an individual like Will (or Dorothea) faces ridicule in their search for a vocation.

In the patriarchal, secular world of Victorian England, gender determines vocation: this becomes especially evident through the complementary characters of Will and Dorothea. Men must—if they are not independently wealthy—have a profession, maybe a vocation. (Consider the degree to which society tolerates Fred Vincy's extravagant and dilettantish behavior as long as he is believed to be the primary heir to Peter Featherstone's estate.) In this context, Will's inability to choose a profession is disgraceful. Only Dorothea voices a tolerant and empathetic understanding of Will's search; she tells Casaubon that his continued financial support of Will is "noble. After all, people may really have in them some vocation which is not quite plain to themselves. . . . They may seem idle and weak because they are growing" (*M*, 107–8).

While Dorothea may recognize this individual need for a vocation even when at odds with community standards, the same community that condemns Will's idleness criticizes her vocational passion.[32] Part of that community's gentle (and not so gentle) consternation over Dorothea's passion to perform good works, to find a vehicle to funnel her idealism, is that she is female. As a woman—especially with her looks and station—she should not, according to cultural prescriptions, have a profession, let alone a vocation.[33] These social restrictions placed on women, which reflect a patriarchally appropriated religion, are voiced much earlier by Eliot in *Adam Bede* (1859) through Dinah Morris's justification of her preaching: "It isn't for men to make channels for God's Spirit, as they make channels for the water-courses, and say, 'Flow here, but flow not there.'"[34] Man's imperialistic drive, however, does just that, deciding that men should have vocations and women should not. Dorothea and Will have subverted their culture's gender distinction: Dorothea acts as Will should, and he as she. (The ultimate fruitfulness of their nonconformity will be returned to later in this chapter.)

It is these gender-based distinctions that, while certainly not productive for Will, severely limit Dorothea's opportunities and contribute to her misdirected efforts to find her vocation—whether planning cottages or marrying to be helpmeet. Throughout her oeuvre Eliot illustrates the restrictions placed on women, which Maggie Tulliver succinctly explains to her brother: "you are a man, Tom, and have power, and can do something in the world."[35] Just as recurrent is Eliot's use of religious allusion to clarify these patriarchal limitations. Felix Holt assumes that Esther, as a woman, will not understand what he believes to be his calling and tells her that "women, unless they are Saint Theresas or Elizabeth Frys, generally think this sort of thing madness, unless when they read of it in the Bible"; but like Maggie, Esther understands a woman's life much more clearly, retorting: "A woman can hardly ever choose in that way; she is dependent on what happens to her. She must take meaner things, because only meaner things are within her reach" (FH, 367). Eliot returns again to this theme in her final novel, Daniel Deronda; here, Daniel's mother, Princess Leonora Halm-Eberstein, checks his condemnation of her rejection of the even more overtly patriarchal religion Judaism:

> You are not a woman. You may try—but you can never imagine what it is to have a man's force of genius in you, and yet to suffer the slavery of being a girl. To have a pattern cut out—"this is the Jewish woman; this is what you must be; this is what you are wanted for; a woman's heart must be of such a size and no larger, else it must be pressed small, like Chinese feet; her happiness is to be made as cakes are, by a fixed receipt."[36]

Narrating Dorothea Brooke's life, Eliot develops this theme. She introduces Dorothea and the novel's text in Middlemarch with an epigraph from Beaumont's and Fletcher's The Maid's Tragedy: "Since I can do no good because a woman, / Reach constantly at something that is near it" (M, 29). Doing so, Eliot restates once more the theme of the absent epic life, this limited sphere in which women find themselves. Like Esther Lyon, Dorothea must recognize that "After all, she was a woman, and could not make her own lot. . . . 'A woman must choose meaner things, because only meaner things are offered to her'" (*FH*, 524–25).

Against this patriarchal constraint women must face, Eliot's first description of Dorothea, as fitting this modern Saint Theresa, portrays the extreme ardent religious nature that puts her at odds with her community. In her own way, Dorothea is as much a cultural enigma as Casaubon's "key"; but unlike her first husband, her culture provides her with neither approved scholastic nor theological channels through which to harness and direct her yearnings, and, unlike Casaubon, she strives to understand how she can advance moral good in the present, not how to codify the past:

> Dorothea knew many passages of Pascal's *Pensees* and of Jeremy Taylor by heart; and to her the destinies of mankind, seen by the light of Christianity, made the solicitudes of feminine fashion appear an occupation for Bedlam. She could not reconcile the anxieties of a spiritual life involving eternal consequences, with a keen interest in guimp and artificial protrusions of drapery. Her mind was theoretic, and yearned by its nature after some lofty conception of the world which might frankly include the parish of Tipton and her own rule of conduct there; she was enamoured of intensity and greatness, and rash in embracing whatever seemed to her to have those aspects; likely to seek martyrdom, to make retractions, and then to incur martyrdom after all in a quarter where she had not sought it. Certainly such elements in the character of a marriageable girl tended to interfere with her lot, and hinder it from being decided according to custom, by good looks, vanity, and merely canine affections. (*M*, 30)

Although Dorothea's character and priorities are continually at odds with what her community values in a woman—searching for martyrdom instead of lace, contemplating eternity instead of dance partners—she does not totally reject the social codes of her world. Whether because she recognizes that there are no viable alternatives for her or she has simply internalized those codes too well, Dorothea does not entirely defy cultural prescriptions for women.[37] In Protestant nineteenth-century England, life held few options for any ideal and passionate Dorothea Brooke. As female, she cannot enter the Church, so her passionate ideals must be channeled through a secular medium—marriage.

If Dorothea acknowledges marriage as her only opportunity to channel her dreams and ideals (which she does), she does not, however, see marriage in the manner that her community prescribes it. Unlike her sister Celia, Dorothea will not embrace the role of angel-in-the-house. Rather than dream romantically of a future husband's gestures, Dorothea meditates on doing good works. Later she would tell Will that since she was a small child "it always seemed to me that the use I should like to make of my life would be to help someone who did great works, so that his burthen might be lighter" (M, 399). With marriage her only entree to independence (limited though it would be), Dorothea recognizes that she must marry a man not necessarily deemed a good match by society, but one with similar passions to her own. With this motivation and no real experience to see otherwise, Dorothea finds the scholarly and serious Casaubon the perfect potential husband:

> The intensity of her religious disposition, the coercion it exercised over her life, was but one aspect of a nature altogether ardent, theoretic, and intellectually consequent: and with such a nature, struggling in the bands of a narrow teaching, hemmed in by a social life which seemed nothing but a labyrinth of petty courses, a walled-in maze of small paths that led no whither, the outcome was sure to strike others as at once exaggeration and inconsistency. The thing which seemed to her best, she wanted to justify by the completest knowledge; and not to live in a pretended admission of rules which were never acted on. Into this soul-hunger as yet all her youthful passion was poured; the union which attracted her was one that would deliver her from her girlish subjection to her own ignorance, and give her the freedom of voluntary submission to a guide who would take her along the grandest path. (M, 51)

With the proper guide, Dorothea saw marriage akin to a religious experience; finally, she would find her vocation in serving a great man and, simultaneously, become privy to a world previously closed to her as a woman:

> Dorothea, with all her eagerness to know the truths of life, retained very childlike ideas about marriage. She felt sure that she would have accepted the judicious Hooker, if she had been born in time to save him from that wretched mistake he made in matrimony; or John Milton when his blindness had come on; or any of the other great men whose odd habits it would have been glorious piety to endure. . . . The really delightful marriage must be that where your husband was a sort of father, and could teach you even Hebrew, if you wished it. (M, 32)

Dorothea's analogy between the perfect husband and "a sort of father" betrays the extent to which a patriarchal ideology informs her culture: made dependent, like a child, first on fathers and then on husbands, women like Dorothea, who wish access to the language and scholarship that orders and defines her world, must acquire that knowledge indirectly, their intent obscured as helpers and aids to men. Through helping Casaubon, she would know for herself what was right, what was good; as her spiritual guide, Casaubon would provide that otherwise lacking "coherent social order" which would "perform the function of knowledge":

> I should learn everything then. . . . It would be my duty to study that I might help him the better in his great works. There would be nothing trivial about our lives. Everyday-things with us would mean the greatest things. It would be like marrying Pascal. I should learn to see the truth by the same light as great men have seen it by. And then I should know what to do, when I got older: I should see how it was possible to lead a grand life here—now—in England. I don't feel sure about doing good in any way now: everything seems like going on a mission to a people whose language I don't know. (*M*, 51)

Key to Dorothea's passions, quite simply, is her desire "to see the truth by the same light as great men have seen it by" because then she "should know what to do . . . [she would] see how it was possible to lead a grand life here—now—in England" (*M*, 51). Through Dorothea, Eliot points to both the need for some kind of medium by which the "truth" could be seen and the relativity of that medium; the operative phrase—"here—now—in England"—reveals the cultural grounding that Dorothea recognizes as essential for obtaining the truth, something that Casaubon fails to see.

This genuine quest for knowledge ("she had not reached the point of renunciation at which she would have been satisfied with having a wise husband; she wished, poor child, to be wise herself" [*M*, 88]) prompts Dorothea to suggest to Casaubon that she might "learn to read Latin and Greek aloud . . . as Milton's daughters did to their father, without understanding what they read" (*M*, 87–88). In reality, however, rather than be one of Milton's daughters, Dorothea wanted to be like Milton himself: revealing Dorothea's real motivation to learn Latin and Greek, the narrator asserts that she believed that "Those provinces of masculine knowledge seemed to her a standing-ground from which all truth could be seen more truly. As it was, she constantly doubted her own conclusions, because she felt her own ignorance" (*M*, 88). It is precisely this self-doubt that drives Dorothea's search for the truth; in contrast, Casaubon begins from a position of authority (social, theological, scholarly). His "self-doubt" cannot be acknowledged personally or publicly; Dorothea begins from a culturally determined position of ignorance and powerlessness, holding neither presumptions to her grasp of Truth nor fear in confronting it. She seeks knowledge in an attempt to reconcile her beliefs with what might be a larger Truth: "how could she be confident that one-roomed cottages were not for the glory of God, when men who knew the classics appeared to conciliate indifference to the cottages with zeal for the glory? Perhaps even Hebrew might be necessary—at least the alphabet and a few roots—in order to arrive at the core of things, and judge soundly on the social duties of the Christian" (*M*, 88). The narrator stresses that Dorothea's quest for knowledge, this time explicitly paralleling Saint Theresa, again evokes the inefficacy of Victorian religion in Dorothea's world:

> She did not want to deck herself with knowledge—to wear it loose from the nerves and blood that fed her action; and if she had written a book she must have done it as Saint Theresa did, under the command of an authority that constrained her conscience. But something she yearned for by which her life might be filled with action at once rational and ardent; and since the time was gone by for guiding visions and spiritual directors, since prayer heightened yearning but not instruction, what lamp was there but knowledge? Surely learned men kept the only oil; and who more learned than Mr. Casaubon? (*M*, 112–13)[38]

Eliot reinforces the connection between Dorothea's quest for knowledge and her religious passions through this explicit allusion to the oils that fuel Christ's power in *Pilgrim's Progress*.[39] In her feminist revision of that work, Eliot has her pilgrim, Dorothea, contend not just with a Victorian Vanity Fair but also with a patriarchy that holds the key to learning. Bunyan's pilgrim learns that the holy flame is fueled by Christ with the oils of grace, oils that perpetuate God's flame even while Satan continually attempts to extinguish it. Dorothea must learn that she is mistaken in her belief that "learned men kept the *only* oil" (emphasis added); she must eventually recognize that the oil that fuels her moral flame will not come from scholars like Casaubon but from sociological relationships.

Dorothea suffers, however, from a twin hamartia: she finds that marriage to Casaubon cannot "perform the function of knowledge" for her, and she must learn to look to human interaction (specifically sympathetic identification), not classical scholarship, for the "coherent social order and faith" appropriate for England "here—now."[40] The narrator informs the reader that Dorothea discovered that "Marriage, which was to bring guidance into worthy and imperative occupation, had not yet freed her from the gentlewoman's oppressive liberty"; in fact, "it had not even filled her leisure with the ruminant joy of unchecked tenderness" (M, 307).

If her marriage fails to satiate Dorothea's religious yearnings, it does provide the first step of her growing understanding of sympathetic projection—that ability which will become the new ethic and supersede the Church. Casaubon's scholastic insecurities extinguish the flame of Dorothea's intentions of being a helpmeet, but this initial disappointment simply enlarges her perspective and causes her religious energies to shift course: "in Dorothea's mind there was a current into which all thought and feeling were apt sooner or later to flow—the reaching forward of the whole consciousness towards the fullest truth, the least partial good. There was clearly something better than anger and despondency" (M, 235). Dorothea's ability to overcome her own pain and return to Rosamond in an attempt to clear Lydgate's name echoes this first struggle to transcend personal suffering for a larger good: "She yearned towards the perfect Right, that it might make a throne within her, and rule her errant will. 'What should I do—how should I act now, this very day if I could clutch my own pain, and compel it to silence, and think of those three!'" (M, 846).

Still searching for some body of knowledge to guide her, Dorothea learns that the "something better" is sympathetic identification. In *Romola* (1863) Eliot had earlier explored this theme of marriage as a vehicle through which an individual learns sympathetic identification. There Eliot portrays Romola's disillusionment in her own marriage to Tito and her growing consciousness of other women's suffering. Romola reflects that "Perhaps all women had to suffer the disappointment of ignorant hopes"; and, craving the reciprocity of sympathetic identification, she realizes that "if she only knew their experience," that common bond would ease both their suffering.[41] Like Romola, Dorothea finds in her marriage the context in which her perspective is enlarged; she realizes that Casaubon has "an equivalent centre of self" (M, 243) and that Julia, Will's grandmother, shared with her a common experience in marriage: "What breadths of experience Dorothea seemed to have passed over since she first looked at this miniature! She felt a new companionship with it" (*M*, 308).

With this heightened "social sympathy," Dorothea begins to articulate her spirituality and its evolution. She tells Will "That by desiring what is perfectly good, even when we don't quite know what it is and cannot do what we would, we are part of the divine power against evil—widening the skirts of light and making the struggle with darkness narrower" (*M*, 427). When Will describes it as a "beautiful mysticism," she stops him short, asking him not to name it because, as she tells him: "It is my life. I have found it out, and cannot part with it. I have always been finding out my religion since I was a little girl. I used to pray so much—now I hardly ever pray. I try not to have desires merely for myself, because they may not be good for others, and I have too much already" (*M*, 427). Refusing Will's codification, Dorothea rejects likening it to any organized religion or system of belief, and echoes her own earlier acknowledgment that "prayer heightened yearning but not instruction." She expands on this rejection of a church (or The Church) in the stead of a compassionate ethic based on individual needs, later telling Lydgate:

> I have always been thinking of the different ways in which Christianity is taught, and whenever I find one way that makes it a wider blessing than any other, I cling to that as the truest—I mean that which takes in the most good of all kinds, and brings in the most people as sharers in it. It is surely better to pardon too much, than to condemn too much. (*M*, 538)

For Eliot, the truly religious figures in the modern world—the figures akin to Saint Theresa—are those who shed their societal skins, those who advance humanity by working through a passionate ideal. The real saviors of England ("here—now"), however, will not be recognized; they will "live faithfully a hidden life, and rest in unvisited tombs." Eliot reflects on the importance of these unrecognized individuals and their "insignificant" actions to modern fiction:

> Artistic power seems to me to resemble dramatic power—to be an intuitive perception of the varied states of which the human mind is susceptible with ability to give them out anew in intensified expression. It is true that the older the world gets, originality becomes less possible. Great subjects are used up, and civilization tends evermore to repress individual predominance, highly-wrought agony or ecstatic

joy. But all the gentler emotions will be ever new—ever wrought up into more and more lovely combinations, and genius will probably take their direction. (*GEL*, 1:247–48)

These real saviors with culturally repressed expression will perform "unhistoric acts" prompted by sympathetic identification. As a modern Theresa, Dorothea's "unhistoric" acts do indeed achieve watershed results in people's lives. She brings the Lydgate narrative to its most positive conclusion by counseling Rosamond. As Gwendolyn Harcourt will tell Daniel Deronda, "it shall be better with me because I have known you," so Rosamond's interaction with Dorothea will profoundly affect her life (*DD*, 510). The final line about Rosamond in *Middlemarch* confirms the significance of Dorothea's act of kindness: Rosamond "never uttered a word in depreciation of Dorothea, keeping in religious remembrance the generosity which had come to her aid in the sharpest crisis of her life" (*MM*, 893).

Just as *Middlemarch* is framed by the "Prelude" and "Finale" with allusions to Saint Theresa (evoking the disintegrated state of Victorian religion), so the narrative is framed with allusions to political reform—the Reform Act of 1832. In this way, the novel parallels the domestic/private reforms to the public/political ones. Writing in her essay "Margaret Fuller and Mary Wollstonecraft," Eliot asserts that "There is a perpetual action and reaction between individuals and institutions; we must try and mend both by little and little—the only way in which human things can be mended" (*GEE*, 205). This "action and reaction" occurs not through a hierarchical institution, but through human interaction—thus the home epic, not the traditional epic, records the modern world's saviors.

Because Eliot circumscribes this epic with marriage, it becomes a metaphor for all human interaction; as such, marriage becomes the medium through which humanity measures its ability to interrelate on a sympathetic level.[42] Although he and Rosamond fail to achieve it fully, Lydgate points to this interpersonal potential between men and women when he tells his future wife: "Happily, there is a common language between women and men" (*M*, 189). Forcing interpersonal relationships from ideal to real, marriage, for both men and women, has the potential, through this "common language," to reveal another as he or she really is—for men not to see women as merely potential mates or little birds (as Sir James and Lydgate initially perceive women) and for women not to see men as earthly lords as Dorothea sees Casaubon. Even with this potential, marriage, because traditionally built upon ste-reotyped gender relations, often becomes, as Eliot portrays it, the disillusioning reality, rather than an opportunity to understand the partner and his or her needs. A couple's inability to find the other's "equivalent centre of self" destroys the relationship: Casaubon's failure to understand Dorothea creates the unreconcil-able breach in their marriage; Rosamond and Lydgate's inability really to understand the other (both before and after the wedding) taints their life together.[43]

Just as Dorothea enables Rosamond to understand Lydgate bet-ter, she also contributes to his and Sir James's expanded perspec-tive of women; both learn to see a woman not simply as an object of romance or marriage. For Sir James, once Dorothea is no longer his potential future wife, he was "gradually discovering the de-light there is in frank kindness and companionship between a man and a woman who have no passion to hide or confess" (M, 97); for Lydgate, reflecting on Dorothea's financial kindness re-veals that "She seems to have what I never saw in any woman before—a fountain of friendship towards men—a man can make a friend of her" (M, 826). It is all these "unhistoric acts" by Doro-thea that make Middlemarch the better, advancing the level of human interaction.

The individual through unhistoric acts, like Dorothea, becomes the instrument to achieve moral progress. Like Bunyan's pilgrim, Christian, Victorian individuals find themselves in a secular world that undervalues vocation unless it contributes to financial gain. The individual must fight a materialistic culture, propped up with a facade of *the* Church, masking a war of sectarian squabbles. It is the individual, the solitary pilgrim, who must confront culture if he or she is to succeed in a calling or a vocation which serves a higher good. It is often the outsider—cut off in one way or another from culture—who confronts those secular values. Doro-thea by gender, Will by class and nationality, are outsiders. Nei-ther is seduced by secular values (financial or rationalized morality like Bulstrode). Will refuses the doubly tainted money offered by Bulstrode (his maternal inheritance), and Dorothea refuses to comply with Casaubon's codicil and instead relin-quishes her title to vast properties (his paternal inheritance). For Eliot the modern savior finds meaning not in social success or personal satisfaction, but through human sympathy. As Deronda tells Gwendolyn:

life *would* be worth more to you: some real knowledge would give you an interest in the world beyond the small drama of personal desires. It is the curse of your life—forgive me—of so many lives, that all passion is spent in that narrow round, for want of ideas and sympathies to make a larger home for it. (*DD*, 507)

Just as the characters Esther Lyon before them and Daniel Deronda after them, Dorothea and Will choose to reject their culture's gender-based prescriptions and be modern-day martyrs—martyrs both in a historical, religious sense and in their community's eyes. Will and Dorothea choose to work for humanity's advancement, unhampered by material constraints, and because they relinquish financial independence and position for a "fanatical" pursuit, their community is dismayed.

It is important in understanding Eliot's ethical agenda, however, to recognize the dynamics of this "martyred" individual in his or her culture, a recurrent theme of her fiction. Although the individual must embrace renunciation on some level, she or he does not (as many critics mistakenly suggest) thrive on this act: it is not renunciation that ennobles the individual, but rather what is renounced.[44] While "on each side there [is] renunciation," as Esther Lyon contemplates in *Felix Holt*, the best path involves renouncing materialistic, not human concerns (*FH*, 590). Philip Wakem criticizes Maggie for what Eliot would consider inappropriate renunciation—suppressing her own needs for those of the patriarchy. "Stupefaction," he tells her, "is not resignation." Thus Eliot's modern, religious renunciation is not a

> shutting [one's] self up in a narrow self-delusive fanaticism, which is only a way of escaping pain by starving into dulness all the highest powers of your nature. Joy and peace are not resignation; resignation is the willing endurance of a pain that is not allayed, that you don't expect to be allayed. (*MF*, 344)

The modern-day saint for Eliot (echoing Nightingale) advances humanity neither through negation nor through a numbing dose of the opiate of organized religion. Instead the proper renunciation is achieved through sympathetic identification and acting upon the belief that "the lives nearest to us shall not suffer in a like manner from *us*." As Maggie Tulliver tells Stephen Guest: "Faithfulness and constancy mean something else besides doing what is easiest and pleasantest to ourselves. They mean renouncing whatever is opposed to the reliance others have in us, whatever would cause misery to those whom the course of our lives has made dependent on us" (*MF*, 499). Echoing Elizabeth Gaskell's belief in sympathetic identification as the key to human progress, Eliot identifies the supreme human act as understanding and empathizing with another human being, not self-sacrifice or embracing a restrictive life.

Eliot's theory of renunciation, a fundamental component of her ethic of human sympathy, can be further clarified by considering it, as she does, in relation to religion. Early in her career, Eliot, in a critical analysis of Hebraic Evangelicalism, asserted that "the best minds that accept Christianity as a divinely inspired system, believe that the great end of the Gospel is not merely the saving but the educating of men's souls, the creating within them of holy dispositions, the subduing of egoistical pretensions" (*GEE*, 181). She would later return to this relationship between the best of religion and negated egoism: "The test of a higher religion might be, that it should enable the believer to do without the consolations which his egoism would demand" (*GEL*, 5:69).

Eliot contrasts these demands of egoism as opposed to sympathetic interaction through her fiction. In *Middlemarch* she explicitly reflects on the pervasiveness of egoism amongst the characters, how each "was the centre of his own world" (*M*, 111). The narrator explains this phenomenon and reveals the disillusion and social unproductivity of such self-centered perspectives in this often-quoted passage:

> An eminent philosopher among my friends, who can dignify even your ugly furniture by lifting it into the serene light of science, has shown me this pregnant little fact. Your pier-glass or extensive surface of polished steel made to be rubbed by a housemaid, will be minutely and multitudinously scratched in all directions; but place now against it a lighted candle as a centre of illumination, and lo! the scratches will seem to arrange themselves in a fine series of concentric circles round that little sun. It is demonstrable that the scratches are going everywhere impartially, and it is only your candle which produces the flattering illusion of a concentric arrangement, its light falling with an exclusive optical selection. These things are a parable. The scratches are events, and the candle is the egoism of any person now absent. (*M*, 297).

It is in reaction to such egoism that Eliot endorses a renunciation that contributes toward a human interaction similar to that for which Gaskell calls. But where Gaskell would liken the appropriate behavior of an individual to that of Christ, Eliot moves one step closer to humanity; she rejects the attribution of a supernatural quality to humanity precisely because it misdirects the appropriate focus of attention away from earth and toward a stupefying religion or a nonexistent God. Eliot writes: "the fellowship between man and man which has been the principle of development, social and moral, is not dependent on conceptions of what is not man: and that the idea of God, so far as it has been a high spiritual influence, is the ideal of a goodness entirely human (i.e., an exaltation of the human)" (*GEL*, 6:98). Christ may embody the personal renunciation necessary for ethical progress, but, for Eliot, his modern equivalent does not exist: no single person or act will save all humanity; no Carlylean natural supernaturalism will propel human moral progress; no discipleship will develop—the modern saviors rest in "unvisited tombs." The day for heroes and hero-worship, Eliot would argue, is gone; modern individuals must look to the common experience of humanity for their direction.

It is this redirected focus that informs the revised scope of epic. Through Dorothea's life—her first unsuccessful marriage (which nonetheless taught her human sympathy) and her fruitful second marriage to Will—Eliot depicts the range of a modern Theresa's life. Marriage and human interaction, not traditional heroics, define significant acts. Thus Eliot diffuses the hierarchy of patriarchal religion and egoistic politics and instead posits an interpersonal, interconnected web of humanity.

Eliot brings the appropriation of religious imagery considered in this study to its secular extreme. Shifting the ethical locus, Eliot turns away from the heavens and even the lofty clerical heights and focuses instead on humanity for her moral foundation, an appropriate act in her agenda of reevaluating significant and individual acts. She subverts patriarchal hierarchy by valorizing individual experience, not classical intellect and scholarship. The clerical elite no longer holds exclusive "rites" to morality; knowledge of Latin, Greek, or Hebrew is no longer a prerequisite to obtaining the Truth. Any and each individual who struggles against injustice participates, Eliot argues, in that Truth. Writing of society's "oppressive narrowness" for such an individual in *The Mill on the Floss*, Eliot acknowledges the multitude of suffering individuals who contribute to moral progress:

> The suffering, whether of martyr or victim, which belongs to every historical advance of mankind is represented in this way in every town and by hundreds of obscure hearths; and we need not shrink

from this comparison of small things with great, for does not science tell us that its highest striving is after the ascertainment of a unity which shall bind the smallest thing with the greatest? In natural science, I have understood, there is nothing petty to the mind that has a large vision of relations and to which every single object suggests a vast sum of conditions. It is surely the same with the observation of human life. (*MF*, 287)

Eliot's "coherent" ethical agenda, then, is that of "social sympathy" accomplished through a multitude of unegoistical acts. The religious and epic imagery and allusions she uses serve to demonstrate the extent to which organized religion fails to advance humanity and the necessity for its replacement with this social sympathy.

Throughout her oeuvre Eliot, the great unbeliever, portrays her culture's inefficacious religion and demonstrates an alternative kind of "knowledge" to provide the missing yet crucial coherence for individual lives.[45] In her final and only contemporaneously set novel, *Daniel Deronda*, Eliot returns to this theme. Here she explores both the individual life given over to egoism and the life dedicated to eradicating that egoism by working toward the rebuilding of a coherent moral order. Appropriately, then, in this novel, Eliot returns to the same question of historical significance that framed *Middlemarch*. Here she explicitly compares individual, "unhistoric" "martyrdom" with poetic energy:

the fervour of sympathy with which we contemplate a grandiose martyrdom is feeble compared with the enthusiasm that keeps unslacked where there is no danger, no challenge—nothing but impartial midday falling on commonplace, perhaps half-repulsive, objects which are really the beloved ideas made flesh. Here undoubtedly lies the chief poetic energy:—in the force of imagination that pierces or exalts the solid fact, instead of floating among cloud-pictures. To glory in a prophetic vision of knowledge covering the earth, is an easier exercise of believing imagination than to see its beginning in newspaper placards, staring at you from a bridge beyond the cornfields; and it might well happen to most of us dainty people that we were in the thick of the battle of Armageddon without being aware of anything more than the annoyance of a little explosive smoke and struggling on the ground immediately about us. (*DD*, 431)

The patriarchally appropriated politics and religion with their oppressive and numbing doctrines divert attention away from the crucial focal point—humanity itself. Not God the Father in heaven, not the hierarchical social structures which stratify communities, not the public sphere of mammon where competitive tactics dominate, but interpersonal relationships based solely on sympathetic identification and understanding will induce moral progress.

Through this intricately interconnected web of "human sympathy," the "hidden heroism" of the modern Saint Theresas and the new epic heroes and heroines replace the enshrined and worshipped saviors of the past. As such Eliot abandons religion as enigmatic and anachronistic in the modern world. Instead she sees a human fellowship unhampered by sectarian or political ends, joined simply by the recognition of another's "individual suffering and individual joy."

Eliot's ethical vision, then, transcends religion to reach a secular extreme, infusing each individual not with a part of God, but with his or her ability to empathize with one another. In this way, Eliot is both the most conservative and most radical of these women studied: it is her very belief in the past efficacy of religion as a means to advance human potential and morality that insists on its modern impossibility. While she may not believe in the supernatural Christ, she does believe in the past power of organized Christians (or other organized religions) to effect moral progress. The modern world, she believes, has evolved beyond religion, really beyond any abstract system. The individual, therefore, must face life head on, without the benefit of a grand plan or the comfort of future reward: individuals must take responsibility both for their own lives and the lives of their fellow humans—"here—now—in England."

6

Afterword: Women Writers and the Victorian Spiritual Crisis

Florence Nightingale and Charlotte Brontë ardently believed in a radical feminist Protestantism that afforded them unmediated access to God and enabled their secular empowerment and spiritual salvation. Elizabeth Gaskell and Marian Evans embraced ethical visions built upon individual recognition of community responsibility, sympathetic projection, and compassion. Regardless of their varying degrees of traditional faith or classic doubt, each experienced a spiritual crisis that became central to their individually evolving ethical visions. None, however, have been considered in detail in studies of the Victorian spiritual crisis; what attention they have received in this context has failed to take into account gender, that they were *women* writers.

This scholarly gap may have resulted from the specific spiritual crises these women experienced, crises that did not fit neatly into traditional definitions of faith and doubt. It may also be the result of a tacit assumption that men and women responded in parallel ways to the sociohistorical forces that produced the traditionally identified spiritual crises.

This reading of Victorian women's responses as similar to those of their male contemporaries could be supported by a number of prominent women whose beliefs and attitudes were consonant with those reflected in the dominant ideology of their culture. That is, not all women felt the need to challenge the patriarchal hegemony of their culture; in fact, not all women even believed that patriarchal hegemony existed. So, just as not all Victorians experienced a spiritual crisis, not all women responded to their patriarchal culture in a singular way. This can be illustrated through a figure like Sarah Ellis, a woman who produced countless manuals for Victorian England's wives and daughters detailing their duties and their place—both within a distinctly Christian context.

Significantly, Ellis asks what proves to be the key question pre-occupying Bunyan's Christian and the four women considered in detail in this study: What is my place in this world? In *The Daughters of England,* she queries: "What is my position in society? what do I aim at? and what means do I employ for the accomplishment of my purpose?" (7). Maybe even more interesting, however, is that while Ellis reaches the same conclusion as Nightingale and Brontë, that "the profession of Christianity as the religion of the Bible, involves responsibility for every talent [women] possess" (*D*, 12), she applies this deduction to women differently than did these two women: Ellis's interpretation of Christian duty and talent operates within a predetermined paradigm of gender. In this way, rather than see Christianity as a means for the oppressed individual believer, in this case female, to pursue her talents regardless of cultural restrictions, Ellis finds in this faith a means by which secular mores can be intensified, reinforced, and justified. Especially interesting, in this context, is her analysis of what could be conflicting aims of God and humanity. While she cautions young women to look to God and not man[1] and warns especially of the dangers of a woman being converted or disillusioned by a disbelieving husband (*D*, 229), her vision of God's plan does not contradict that of a patriarchal culture; instead her concern is with those whom she perceives to be atheistic—those who would challenge the institutionalized sacred and secular doctrines. Consequently, Ellis gives voice to values of the dominant Victorian ideology; complicit with a patriarchal agenda, she entwines their sacred and secular ideologies in her edicts for women.

Further complicating any analysis of women's relationship to the period's spiritual crisis is the impact of Mary Augusta Ward's *Robert Elsmere.* This immediate bestseller captivated the imagination of a generation by reproducing the ethical struggles and moral agony that so preoccupied many Victorians. Considered to be the fin de siècle version of the earlier *Sartor Resartus* or the mid-century *In Memoriam* or *Apology*,[2] *Robert Elsmere* provides a provocative text for any study of the Victorian spiritual crisis. Unlike the works just mentioned, this exploration of faith and doubt was written by a woman, although, like theirs, it is primarily concerned with the crisis of doubt experienced by a male protagonist. The novel Ward writes expresses an ideology somewhere between the conservative vision of Sarah Ellis and the radical perspectives of Nightingale, Brontë, Gaskell, and Eliot. And while Ward's "conservative morality and revolutionary theology" are not necessarily unusual during the period,[3] the way in which she explores her topic, this revisionist melding of conservative and polemical agendas, makes the novel especially interesting for this study.

Robert Elsmere represents the position adopted by many of the period's Christian socialists and Unitarians—applying the morality and ethics of Christianity to a secular community. In other words, he, like many of the period's great thinkers, cannot escape the intellectual challenge that German Higher Criticism presents to his earlier beliefs; the result, that Christianity as a metaphor for life can thrive, but the literal and/or historical foundation of the faith inevitably crumbles. Complicating Elsmere's moral agony further is his ascetic wife, often called St. Catherine, who embodies, for the most part, the ideal of Victorian womanhood.[4] In scenes that would make Sarah Ellis proud, Catherine Elsmere triumphs in her stuggle against the loss of her own faith that loving a disbelieving husband could effect. And, in an ending that partially reflects Ward's own vision of a new spirituality, Catherine, while not losing her fervent belief in mainstream Christianity, does temper it as she comes to accept her husband's beliefs as an alternative morality—one that complements, not invalidates, her faith.

This novel provides a number of opportunities against which the writings of Nightingale, Brontë, Gaskell, and Eliot can be considered. Significantly, Ward's narrative, like those traditionally considered in reference to the Victorian spiritual crisis, is about a *man's* spiritual doubt. In striking contrast, the women examined in this study all write about *women's* stories, *women's* spiritual crises. Key passages from Ward's novel also underscore the different visions of these women. For instance, while Elsmere's inspirational work among London's poor could find easy parallels with the selfless nursing of the sick performed by Gaskell's character Ruth, Elsmere's actions, as a man, do not overtly challenge his culture's edicts for gender-based activities and vocations—Ruth's do. Not only does she transfer "women's work" from the domestic to the public sphere, but she also does this through the then questionable profession of nursing. Similarly, Elsmere's death by tuberculosis, brought on by saving a drowning man and aggravated by his relentless work among the poor, can be compared to Ruth's death, but hers is directly produced by her nursing the sick, not one that results from several contributing factors like Elsmere's. His death and earlier doubt also provide significant parallels to Eliot's *Middlemarch*.[5] In an ironic reversal of Casaubon's fruitless search for the key to all mythologies, Elsmere discusses with the Squire the key to beliefs and mythologies that unlocks the historical context for each age's manifestation of faith; and, significantly, in Elsmere's case, this discovered key literally demystifies Christianity for him and initiates his consuming doubts. Further echoing Eliot's novel, the narrative commentary on Elsmere's death, that "His effort was but a fraction of the race," unmistakenly recalls the "Finale" of *Middlemarch*.[6] But, unlike Dorothea Brooke, whose energies go unrecognized, Elsmere's are acknowledged: the Brotherhood he establishes grows and thrives. Additionally, Ward's vision, as demonstrated in Catherine's accommodation of her husband's beliefs, allows for traditional Christianity to continue alongside the New Brotherhood; the women in this study, in contrast, either completely dismiss the viability of organized religion or revolutionize its makeup. Ellis and Ward, then, represent two Victorian women whose writings and perspectives can be accommodated into the prevailing thesis of the period's spiritual crisis. Both, in short, represent a variation not inconsistent with the visions of their male contemporaries.

Perhaps, women writers like Gaskell, Brontë, Nightingale, and Eliot have not been included in earlier analyses of the Victorian spiritual crisis because, although all four women experience conflicts and all engage in their period's ethical dialogue, no spiritual crisis seems to have occurred when the experiences of the period's male writers are used as the standard. In Gaskell's case, her spiritual beliefs have been easily categorized as that of a dissenter because of her Unitarianism and association with Christian socialists. Brontë's life, because of her unequivocal faith in God, has been described as "singularly free from the religious conflict that tormented so many of her contemporaries."[7] And Nightingale (if she is considered at all) is described and defined as "the St. Clara or Theresa of Protestant England."[8] The beliefs of Marian Evans, as unbeliever, have generally been described simply as a kind of religious or liberal humanism.[9] Because these women's spiritual crises differ so distinctly from that of doubt, they continue to be overlooked, even though many of the male writers traditionally included in such studies were also members of a church, had clerical fathers, or were unbelievers; for these women, however, such associations (with the exception of Evans) appear to be the result of a crisis-free spirituality.

Another possibility for this oversight that excludes women from analyses of this Victorian phenomenon is the polemical nature of these women's crises: Nightingale, Brontë, Gaskell, and Evans all describe a complicitous relationship between the institutions of Church and state in limiting female potential and restricting women's lives; all use sacred imagery and allusion to criticize a patriarchally misappropriated institutionalized religion. Even when the progressive theological perspectives of the male Victorians are considered with those of the women in this study, differences are evident. For instance, those who sought to *reform* Victorian religion—as in the case of Charles Kingsley (who endorsed Christian socialism but, becoming increasingly conservative, called for slower, less radical change) or with Arnold (who wanted to reinject Christian dogma with feeling—did not discard the patriarchal economy of their organized religion. Their intended reforms did not revolutionize the institutions by challenging the fundamental structure and ideology upon which they rested. In contrast, the radical reformation of these women's spirituality did. Rather than simply modifying the outward manifestations of the Victorian Church's central tenets, these women questioned the veracity upon which they were based. These differing agendas can be seen in the issues of biblical misinterpretations or mistranslations—topics increasingly debated during the Victorian period. Charles Kingsley, for instance, asserts that any biblical misinterpretation would be of little importance when considered against the message of the whole, since the Bible was "inspired and divine."[10] In addition, Sarah Ellis, addressing women's desire to learn Greek or Latin to enable them to read the Bible in the original, contends that the existing translations should more than serve everyone's needs (*D*, 51). "[F]ar be it from me," she continues, "to wish to put the slightest obstacle in their way . . . [but] it does appear to me a little strange, that any young woman, of moderate abilities . . . [should] hope of attaining a nearer approach to the truth" (*D*, 52). In short, "take the Bible as it is" (*D*, 52). In striking contrast to these views, Brontë's character Caroline Helstone challenges her male detractor:

> if I could read the original Greek, I should find that many of the words [of the Bible] have been wrongly translated, perhaps misapprehended altogether. It would be possible, I doubt not, with a little ingenuity, to give the passage quite a contrary turn; to make it say, "Let the woman speak out whenever she sees fit to make an objection;"—"it is permitted to a woman to teach and to exercise authority as much as may be. Man, meantime, cannot do better than hold his peace," and so on. (*S*, 329–30)

Not only does Brontë endorse the possibility of grievous mistranslations in the standardized Bible, but she unequivocably ties those inaccuracies to patriarchal oppression of women's voice, action, and authority.

Just as the writings of Nightingale, Brontë, and Gaskell could be shrouded by a devotional appearance, other women's texts, especially hymns, appeared less challenging to standard theology because of an inherently spiritual content. The Victorian period, in fact, experienced an increase in the number of women writing hymns—one of the few remaining opportunities for women to find a voice in religion. Significantly, many of the hymns written by women present an alternative vision of God and an individual's relationship to the divine, reflecting differences present in male and female spirituality, especially when housed within a patriarchal institution. Even when one allows for liturgical differences found between the High and Low Churches, Establishment and Dissent, an interesting pattern can be seen in Victorian hymns written by women. Margaret Maison analyzes the curious role that hymns written by women played in Church doctrine. While these hymns, which reflected female concerns and not clerical edicts, were incorporated into the church service, they were often differentiated from the sanctioned dogma.[11] Helsinger, who also considers this phenomena, writes that "the hymn encroaches upon the sermon in Protestant liturgy, as more than one minister realized: Rev. Joel Hawes used to announce caustically after a hymn that 'divine service would now recommence.' "[12] In addition to this division, women's hymns were also often segregated by category; paralleling their duties in secular culture, women were the primary authors of hymns for children, often reworking the tone of the doctrinal messages from "terror" to "tenderness."[13]

This quality of "tenderness" associated with hymns written by women can be demonstrated by a closer look at some of their lyrics.[14] For instance, Dorothy Frances Gurney's hymn "Great King of nations, hear our prayer, while at thy feet we fall" depicts a loving relationship between the believer and his or her God. She describes God as giving "grace" (l. 3) and "help" (ll. 4, 8), embodying "goodness" (l. 6), and "With pitying eye behold[ing] our need" (l. 11). Significantly she presents an image of a compassionate God, who would "Correct us with thy judgments . . . then let thy mercy spare" (l. 12). Similarly, Charlotte Elliott speaks of God not as a vengeful judge but as "the contrite sinners' Friend," in her hymn of the same name (l. 1), and the source of "strength . . . renew'd" (l. 13); this loving God also enables her "sins . . . [to be] forgiven" (l. 14) in "My God, is any hour so sweet." In addition to this imaging of God as beneficent, He is presented as a source whose power provides the believer with strength, not fear of His supremacy unloosed. Elliott, in "O Holy Saviour, Friend unseen," suggests that souls are "safe . . . calm . . . [and] satisfied" that "cling to thee" (ll. 23–24), and her savior is "my strength, my rock, my all" (l. 31). Not only does the believer gain strength from God, but she also becomes likened to Him; thus, significantly, the individual is empowered through an identification with, as opposed to worship of, her God. This can be seen in Gurney's hymn "Lord, as to thy dear cross we flee," where she suggests "let thy life our pattern be" (l. 3) as each has his or her "daily cross to bear" (l. 6). She continues with this association of the earthly life with the sacred: "We, in our turn, would meekly cry, / Father, thy will be done" (ll. 15–16). Interestingly, Gurney distinguishes in these lyrics the differences between humanity's and God's goals and puts forth "love," not power, as the triumphant force of the divine:

> Should friends misjudge, or foes defame,
> Or brethren faithless prove,
> Then, like thine own, be all our aim
> To conquer them by love. (ll. 17–20)

These lyrics present a significant parallel to the relationship of women to their God that Nightingale, Brontë, and especially Gaskell articulate in their writing: the conflict between God and humanity, the association of the female with the divine, and the unsurpassed power of love.

In this way, the hymns written by women, regardless of church affiliation, tended to parallel the characteristics of those written from an Evangelical perspective. More personal, subjective, and concrete than the rather abstract, allegedly objective ones utilized by the Oxford movement, women's hymns concerned the individual's relationship with God, not simply symbolic dogma.[15] While not surprising, the similar emphasis on experience found in both hymns written by women and those by Evangelicals reveals an interesting correlative in their respective positions in organized Christianity.[16] As I have already discussed, the religious revival of the Low Church expanded sacred enfranchisement—transferring access to the divine from the exclusive control of the clerics to any who believed. While the reality of this movement empowered men, not women, the basic tenets of this belief—the personal, unmediated communion with God—inspired and, to a degree, authorized many women's nonconformist desires. Charlotte Brontë, for instance, claimed strength from a radical Protestantism to critique and re-envision cultural appropriations of sacred ideals. Extending the doctrine of Protestantism to incorporate her desires in this way, Brontë, like the women hymn writers, engaged in theological debate—although cloaked in a kind of clerical robe, giving their challenging voices the appearance of devotion. Whether because of this acceptable appearance or because of their differing perspectives, this aspect of women's spirituality has been disregarded or overlooked in discussions of the period's spiritual crises.[17]

Florence Nightingale, paralleling the women who wrote hymns, framed her own spiritual exploration in the context of a revisionist theology, which voiced both her belief in God and her conviction that man had appropriated Him for self-interested ends. *Suggestions* became the vehicle through which Nightingale claimed authority to found modern nursing, defying her family and her culture. Believing God had charged her with the vocation of social reform, Nightingale exposes in this document her culture's inappropriate gender-based limitations of an individual's talents. The seemingly contradictory place theology had in her life can be revealed by juxtaposing Nightingale's life and writing: if organized religion oppressed the individual, God liberated her.

As with Nightingale, writing played a pivotal role in Charlotte Brontë's life. Paradoxically, her passion to write both provoked Brontë's spiritual crisis and enabled its resolution: discouraged from pursuing this career because of gender-based cultural restrictions, she eventually claimed divine authority to defy those restrictions, asserting that writing was her God-given talent and, therefore, sinful to neglect. With feminist parables and subverted romance plots, Brontë mimics androcentric narratives and challenges the social and spiritual scripts available to women in Victorian culture.

Just as living in an Anglican parsonage allowed Brontë to see clerical fallibility, Unitarianism enabled Elizabeth Gaskell to reject the social values propagated by her culture's established Church. Through a revolutionary "sentimental" social vision, Gaskell proposes a compassionate New Testament ethic to replace what she sees as the Hebraic character of the Church of England. Doing so, Gaskell attempts to revise radically her culture's bifurcation of public and private spheres as the respective arenas of competition and charity, justice and mercy. Through this "sentimental" agenda, Gaskell rejects a domesticated Christianity that would enshrine women for men's vicarious salvation. Instead she charges her entire culture with the responsibilities of a self-proclaimed Christian community.

Like Nightingale and Brontë, Marian Evans faced societal restrictions because of gender; unlike either of these two or Gaskell, however, she would look not to God but to humanity to empower those marginalized by her culture. Paradoxically, then, Evans represents the most conservative and the most radical of the women studied: she rejects modern religion largely because she believes in the past efficacy of a "coherent social order or faith" that could advance human potential, just as Nightingale believed in an earlier living ethic. Evans's complex and apparently contradictory belief explains why she, although disbelieving in God or the social usefulness of organized religion, repeatedly makes use of religious allusion in her fiction. No mere abstract system of belief, Evans's ethical vision focuses on the concrete "hidden heroism" of an individual act of kindness as the key to any moral progress in the modern world.

Foregrounding Christian imagery and allusion, Nightingale, Brontë, Gaskell, and Eliot all subvert patriarchal scripts. Claiming divine inspiration, Nightingale ignores gender limitations and theorizes her own theology; Brontë mimics narrative patterns to expose androcentric, not divine, ideologies in interpreting the world; Gaskell creates a "fallen" woman as a Christ-like protagonist; and Eliot infuses female experience into her psychologically enhanced realism.

Nightingale, Brontë, Gaskell, and Evans—each situated differently in relation to the Established Church, each with varying degrees of faith and doubt—experienced spiritual crises that, unlike those of their male contemporaries, grew out of their culture's political and clerical complicity in women's subjection. These writers produced discourse which asserts that their culture's moral progress depended on an antihierarchical, antipatriarchal structure. In this sense, they redefined the spiritual and secular hero and heroine in female terms, and unlike Carlyle, who lamented the absence of heroes and hero-worship, these writers all saw humanity's salvation in the unrecognized, individual act—not of heroic dimensions but, as Eliot would name it, "unheroic" ones.

Significantly, two patterns exist in the larger alternative ethic that these women produce: one built upon a radical feminist Protestantism that explicitly affords women unmediated access to God; the second defined by human interaction. For Nightingale and Brontë, the individual's right to belief—free from patriarchal design—was the cornerstone of their secular empowerment and spiritual salvation; the act of writing for both of these women authorized the nonconformist aspects of their lives. For Gaskell and Eliot, the ethical vision they endorse involves an individual's interrelationship with her community, based on sympathetic projection and identification; both writers construct an alternative morality built upon "insignificant acts of kindness" and a pure "Christian" sense of socialism. All four writers, however, advocate an enacted ethic—one delineated through individual acts—rather than an abstracted doctrine. Translated into their aesthetics, this preference reveals itself in the reproduction of individual, subjective experiences rather than allegedly universalized ones.

Nightingale, Brontë, Gaskell, and Evans all point to the patriarchally complicitous relationship between their culture's sacred and secular institutions, a dynamic that divests women of power and authority. By analyzing the neglected spiritual crises that these women experienced as well as their discourse in this context, this study begins the long-overdue project of reexamining the Victorian spiritual crisis in order to reveal a more complex, problematic, and polemical dialogue than has been believed previously.

Notes

CHAPTER 1. INTRODUCTION: RECLAIMING THE WORD

1. For a detailed analysis of the complexities of Victorian religious movements and institutions, see L. E. Binn's *Religion in the Victorian Era* (1936; reprint, London: Lutterworth Press, 1964).

2. Catherine M. Prelinger points to the cultural advantages that resulted from sanctioning a limited role for women in the Church—a place to cloister this disproportionate number of women to men ("The Female Diaconate in the Anglican Church: What Kind of Ministry for Women?" in *Religion in the Lives of English Women, 1760–1930*, ed. Gail Malmgreen, 161–92 [Bloomington: Indiana University Press, 1986], 161). See also Susan P. Casteras' article "Virgin Vows: The Early Victorian Artists' Portrayal of Nuns and Novices," in *Religion in the Lives of English Women*, ed. Malmgreen, 131.

3. Barbara Taylor, *Eve and the New Jerusalem: Socialism and Feminism in the Nineteenth Century* (New York: Pantheon, 1983), 124.

4. See Elizabeth Helsinger, Robin Lauterbach Sheets, and William Veeders, eds., *The Woman Question: Society and Literature in Britain and America, 1837–1883*, 2 vols. (New York: Garland, 1983), 175. See also Olive Anderson's "Women Preachers in Mid-Victorian Britain: Some Reflexions on Feminism, Popular Religion and Social Change," *The Historical Journal* 12, no. 3 (1969): 467–84.

5. Sarah Stickney Ellis, *The Daughters of England: Their Position in Society, Characters, and Responsibilities* (New York: D. Appleton, 1842), 8. Subsequent quotations from this work are cited in the text as *D*.

6. Ellis reveals a Carlylesque bias in her suggestions for England's daughters as she, to her credit, acknowledges that some women must support themselves: she instructs that "a woman, by any process of education, can be made to feel that all honest work is noble just so far as it is pursued faithfully and with worthy motives, that work need not necessarily and in itself be vulgar or mean, that idleness is infinitely more vulgar" (*The Education of the Heart* [London: Hodder & Stroughton, 1869], 19–20). Yet Ellis also undercuts the Carlylean mandate to "nurse no extravagant hope" in a manner that betrays her complicity in a patriarchal culture's prescriptions for women—to direct their time and attention toward others in a way that produces an "active" passivity rather than laziness. In *Daughters*, she cautions young women *not* to reduce their expectations, "that when we bring down our good intentions to a lower scale, it is a certain symptom of some failure either in our moral, intellectual, or physical power" (30). In other words, whether or not one accepts one's fate depends on what is to be endured; when the act reinforces cultural values, one should not settle for less, but when one's desires challenge standard mores, do not expect personal satisfaction.

7. Judith Ochshorn, *The Female Experience and the Nature of the Divine* (Bloomington: Indiana University Press, 1981), 241.

8. Walter E. Houghton, *The Victorian Frame of Mind, 1830–1870* (New Haven: Yale University Press, 1957), 126.

9. In *Eve and the New Jerusalem,* Barbara Taylor provides an important historical analysis of the interrelationship between industrialization and the domestication of Christian values; see esp. 126–27.

10. Sheila Rowbotham, *Women, Resistance, and Revolution* (New York: Random, 1972), 29.

11. Sarah Ellis would address this distinction in *The Education of the Heart.* There, she writes: "It is not the actual work, it is the stigma attaching to work that is done in the way of business, it is the looking down of friends and acquaintances upon the *poor relation* who has to provide her own maintenance" (14–15).

12. Marian Evans's lengthy struggle to fix her own place in relation to her culture is mirrored in the fragmentary identity produced by the many names with which she referred to herself. She was baptised Mary Anne Evans, and her "Christian" name would evolve through Mary Ann, the French Marian, and the charged Pollian (pet for Apollyan) to her *nom de plume,* George Eliot. During her twenty-five-year relationship with Lewes, Evans insisted, to the frustration of her feminist friends, on being called Mrs. Lewes. Because of this complex and complicated issue, I will refer to her as George Eliot when discussing her as a writer; Marian Evans when considering her life.

13. Alfred Lord Tennyson, *In Memoriam, A. H. H.,* in *Tennyson's Poetry,* ed. Robert W. Hill, Jr. (New York: Norton, 1971), 119; Houghton, *Victorian Frame of Mind,* 18.

14. Matthew Arnold, *Poetry and Criticism of Matthew Arnold,* ed. A. Dwight Culler (Boston: Houghton Mifflin, 1961), 162; Tennyson, *In Memoriam,* 148, 147; Thomas Carlyle, *Sartor Resartus,* ed. Charles Frederick Harrold (New York: Odyssey, 1937), 127; John Stuart Mill, *The Autobiography of John Stuart Mill* (New York: Columbia University Press, 1924), 94.

15. *The Woman Question,* ed. Helsinger, Sheets, and Veeders, includes a brief study of the short-lived rise, with evangelicalism, of women's voices in theological issues during the Victorian period, and asserts that one way women could "preach" was through fiction (183). Although no scholarship has heretofore examined the issue of gender in the Victorian spiritual crisis, much work by feminist literary and theological scholars has explored the revision of patriarchal evaluative standards. For studies of women's reclamation of female religious figures, see Clarissa W. Atkinson, Constance H. Buchanan, and Margaret R. Miles, eds., *Immaculate and Powerful: The Female in Sacred Image and Social Reality* (Boston: Beacon, 1985); Carol Christ, *Diving Deep and Surfacing: Women Writers on a Spiritual Quest* (Boston: Beacon, 1980); Mary Daly, *Beyond God the Father: Toward a Philosophy of Women's Liberation* (Boston: Beacon, 1975); and Rita M. Gross, ed., *Beyond Androcentrism: New Essays on Women and Religion* (Missoula, Mont.: Scholars Press, 1977). For a reexamination of the Gnostic Gospels and a delineation of how their suppression contributes to the monovocal concepts of a patriarchal culture, see Judith Ochshorn's *The Female Experience and the Nature of the Divine* and Elaine Pagels's *The Gnostic Gospels* (New York: Random House, 1979). For studies that trace the evolution of Judeo-Christianity from polytheistic beliefs, which incorporated both female and male deities, to monotheistic ones, see Rosemary Radford Ruether's *Womanguides: Readings Toward a Feminist Theology* (Boston: Beacon, 1985) and Merlin Stone's *When God Was a Woman* (New York: Dial, 1976).

16. Thomas Sheehan, *The First Coming: How the Kingdom of God Became Christianity* (New York: Random House, 1986), 11.

17. Houghton, *Victorian Frame of Mind*, 61.

18. Charles Kingsley, *His Letters and Memories of His Life*, ed. Mrs. Kingsley (London: Macmillan, 1901), 3:219. See also Houghton, *Victorian Frame of Mind*, 204, 206.

19. Houghton, *Victorian Frame of Mind*, 346.

20. Kingsley, *Letters and Memories*, 4:65.

21. Ibid., 1:71. It is interesting that, just the opposite of Kingsley, Eliot would preference Teresa, the unmarried saint. These choices seem especially revealing in what they suggest about the writers' relationship to the dominant culture: Kingsley presents women with the model of marriage for fulfillment, sacred and secular; Eliot, in contrast, puts forth an unmarried woman and suggests that women might find their salvation independently of men and patriarchal ideals.

22. Taylor, *Eve and the New Jerusalem*, 126–27.

23. Catherine Gallagher, *The Industrial Reformation of English Fiction: Social Discourse and Narrative Form, 1832–1867* (Chicago: University of Chicago Press, 1985), 119; Sarah Stickney Ellis, *Education*, 17. Subsequent quotations from this work are cited in the text as *E*.

24. Kingsley, *Letters and Memories* 4:12, 4:65.

25. Houghton, *Victorian Frame of Mind*, 355, 389.

26. Julia Kristeva, *Desire in Language: A Semiotic Approach to Literature and Art*, trans. Thomas Gora, Alice Jardine, and Leon Roudiez, ed. Leon Roudiez (New York: Columbia University Press, 1980), 237.

27. Daly, *Beyond God*, 81.

28. Ruether, *Womanguides*, 106.

29. John Ruskin, "Of Queens' Gardens," in *The Works of John Ruskin*, vol. 18 (London: George Allen, 1905), 127.

30. One way in which women gain this distorted power is through patriarchal complicity whereby they act in the capacity of a phallic mother, as an instrument to perpetuate an androcentric agenda. Although failing to provide women authentic power, the role of the phallic mother is "more dangerous" to women's emancipation "because less obviously phallic" (Jane Gallop, *The Daughter's Seduction: Feminism and Psychoanalysis* [Ithaca: Cornell University Press, 1982], 118). Nina Auerbach's *Woman and the Demon: The Life of a Victorian Myth* (Cambridge: Harvard University Press, 1982) identifies another way in which patriarchal imaging invests women with a kind of perverse power—by representing them as serpents and demons.

31. Yvonne Yazbeck Haddad and Ellison Banks Findly, eds., *Women, Religion, and Social Change* (Albany: State University of New York Press, 1985), xvii.

32. Elizabeth Schussler Fiorenza, "Interpreting Patriarchal Traditions," in *The Liberating Word: A Guide to Nonsexist Interpretation of the Bible*, ed. Letty M. Russell (Philadelphia: Westminster Press, 1976), 55. Merlin Stone, in *When God Was a Woman*, considers a similar example of the patriarchal, cultural forces affecting the suppression of the female divinity. Writing about the Neolithic societies in the Middle East, she asserts: "It was upon the appearance of the invading northerners, who from all accounts had established patrilineal, patriarchal customs and the worship of a supreme male deity sometime before their arrival in the Goddess-worshiping areas, that the greatest changes in religious beliefs and social customs appear to have taken place" (61).

33. "The Goddess, the original supreme deity of the people conquered and

ruled by the invading Indo-European," Stone writes in *When God Was a Woman*, "was not ignored, but was symbolically included" (67). Expanding on this, she writes: "Despite the insistent, perhaps hopeful, assumption that the serpent must have been regarded as a phallic symbol, it appears to have been primarily revered as a female in the Near and Middle East and generally linked to wisdom and prophetic counsel rather than fertility and growth as is so often suggested. . . . The actual association of the serpent with the female deity, all through the texts and inscriptions of Sumer and Babylon, was probably the very reason this symbolism was used in the Indo-European myths . . . and, the tree of knowledge, the *ficus sicomorus*, was believed to bear the fruit of the goddesses" (199, 200, 214–16).

34. Stone, *When God Was a Woman*, 66–67.

35. This project to reconstruct the female aspects of the deity is also analyzed in the scholarship of Rachel Jacoff and Christine Froula. Jacoff details Julian of Norwich's mystical revelations that describe God as possessing the "female" quality of love, not wrath, in "God as Mother: Julian of Norwich's Theology of Love," *Denver Quarterly* 18, no. 4 (1984): 134–39. Froula asserts that the repression of maternity in the Judeo-Christian myth enables a patriarchal monopoly in formulating God's word in "When Eve Reads Milton: Undoing Canonical Economy," *PMLA* 10 (1983): 321–47.

36. Pagels expands on this process-oriented aspect of Gnosticism, writing that "As the gnostics use the term, we could translate it as 'insight,' for *gnosis* involves an intuitive process of knowing oneself" (*Gnostic Gospels*, xix).

37. Reuther, *Womanguides*, 110.

38. Pagels, *Gnostic Gospels*, 95, 11.

39. Ibid., 6–7, 10.

40. Ochshorn, *Female Experience and the Nature of the Divine*, 14.

41. Pagels, *Gnostic Gospels*, 27.

42. Sharon H. Ringe, "Biblical Authority and Interpretation," in *The Liberating Word: A Guide to Nonsexist Interpretation of the Bible*, ed. Letty M. Russell (Philadelphia: Westminster Press, 1976), 27.

43. Both Northrop Frye and Barry Qualls study this transformation of sacred into secular literature: Frye calls romance the "secular scripture" in his *The Secular Scripture: A Study of the Structure of Romance* (Cambridge: Harvard University Press, 1976), 60; Qualls, "biblical romance" in his *The Secular Pilgrims of Victorian Fiction: The Novel as Book of Life* (Cambridge: Cambridge University Press, 1982), 14. For an analysis of the effects of male dominance over language in canon formation, see Adrienne Auslander Munich's "Notorious signs, feminist criticism and literary tradition," in *Making a Difference: Feminist Literary Criticism*, ed. Coppélia Kahn and Gayle Greene (London: Methuen, 1985), 238–59.

44. Providing a useful overview of nineteenth-century American women in her *Religious Issues in Nineteenth-Century Feminism* (Troy: Whitson, 1982), Donna Behnke reveals a similar phenomenon:

> If woman's chief enemy was tradition and the men and women who upheld it, her chief weapons were faith, reason, and the finest arguments the democratic mind could muster. Reason and justice, they charged, were antithetical to claims demanding half of the human race's submission to the dictates of the other half. Such reasoning was similarly opposed to the spirit of the Christian gospel and the Judeo-Christian testimony that God was a god of love and all persons children of that love. (3)

45. Taylor, in *Eve and the New Jerusalem*, provides a detailed account of this phenomenon (118–82); similarly, Ruether, writing about the Shakers, asserts

that "the female Christ is the theological expression of the androgyny of God and of God's image . . . which must be expressed in a redeemer from both the male and female orders of humanity" (*Womanguides*, 111). For a useful analysis of this "privilege of oppression," see Lee Cormie's "The Hermeneutical Privilege of the Oppressed: Liberation Theologies, Biblical Faith, and Marxist Sociology of Knowledge," *Proceedings of the Annual Convention of Catholic Theological Society of America* 32 (1978): 155–81. Rosemary Ruether also considers this aspect of Christianity, focusing on the role of prophets: "By servanthood Jesus did not mean simply an acceptance of the servile status of the human in present society. . . . Rather he used the term servant in the prophetic sense of a relationship to God that freed one from servitude to all human masters" (*Womanguides*, 108).

46. Rowbotham, *Women, Resistance, and Revolution*, 34.

47. See Elaine Showalter's *A Literature of Their Own: British Women Novelists from Brontë to Lessing* (Princeton: Princeton University Press, 1977) for a detailed analysis of this missing literary heritage.

48. Sandra M. Gilbert and Susan Gubar, *The Madwoman in the Attic: The Woman Writer and the Nineteenth-Century Literary Imagination* (New Haven: Yale University Press, 1979), 49.

49. Michael Wheeler, *The Art of Allusion in Victorian Fiction* (London: Macmillan, 1979), ix.

50. Qualls, *Secular Pilgrims*, 14.

51. Margaret Maison, *The Victorian Vision: Studies in the Religious Novel* (New York: Sheed & Ward, 1961), 1; Elizabeth Jay, *The Religion of the Heart: Anglican Evangelicalism and the Nineteenth-Century Novel* (Oxford: Clarendon Press, 1979), 53–54.

52. Qualls, *Secular Pilgrims*, 12, 13–14.

53. R. K. Webb, "The Victorian Reading Public" in *From Dickens to Hardy*, vol. 6 of *The New Pelican Guide to English Literature*, ed. Boris Ford (Harmondsworth: Penguin, 1982), 199.

54. Gilbert and Gubar, *Madwoman*, 189. They add that "For whatever Milton is to the male imagination, to the female imagination Milton and the inhibiting Father—the Patriarch of patriarchs—are one" (192).

55. Rachel Blau duPlessis, *Writing Beyond the Ending: Narrative Strategies of Twentieth-Century Women Writers* (Bloomington: Indiana University Press, 1985), 4–5.

56. Luce Irigaray, *Speculum of the Other Woman*, trans. Gillian C. Gill (Ithaca: Cornell University Press, 1985); duPlessis, *Writing Beyond the Ending*; Nancy K. Miller, "Emphasis Added: Plots and Plausibility in Women's Fiction," *PMLA* 96 (1981): 36–48; Margaret Homans, *Bearing the Word: Language and Female Experience in Nineteenth-Century Women's Writing* (Chicago: University of Chicago Press, 1986); Miller, "Emphasis Added," 46.

57. Jane P. Tompkins's "Sentimental Power: *Uncle Tom's Cabin* and the Politics of Literary History," in *The New Feminist Criticism: Essays on Women, Literature and Theory*, ed. Elaine Showalter (New York: Pantheon, 1985), 81–104.

CHAPTER 2. FLORENCE NIGHTINGLE'S REVISIONIST THEOLOGY: "THAT WOMAN WILL BE THE SAVIOUR OF HER RACE"

J. A. V. Chapple and Arthur Pollard, eds. *The Letters of Mrs. Gaskell* (Cambridge: Harvard University Press, 1967), 307. Subsequent quotations from this work are cited in the text as *LG*.

1. Florence Nightingale, *Suggestions for Thought to Searchers After Religious Truth* (London: Eyre and Spottiswoode, 1860), 2:374, 405. Subsequent quotations from this work are cited in the text as *ST*.

2. Although the Anglican church did provide a limited number of Protestant convents for women, Nightingale felt her calling was to serve God in a public, less cloistered domain.

3. Sir Edward Cook, *The Life of Florence Nightingale* (New York: Macmillan, 1942), 1:5, 7, 246; William George Tarrant, *Florence Nightingale as a Religious Thinker* (London: British and Foreign Unitarian Association, 1917), 8, 9. L. E. Elliott-Binns provides a useful explanation of the limited rights of Unitarians as well as the effects of the repeal of the Corporation and Test Acts (*Religion in the Victorian Era* [1936; reprint, London: Lutterworth Press, 1964], 31).

4. Significantly these tensions between Nightingale and her mother continued throughout her life. Even after she returned from the Crimea a national figure, Florence felt so oppressed by her mother's influence that she developed an invalidism that enabled an escape from social obligations. These debilitating bouts lasted until her mother's death at which time she rose from bed cured.

5. Cook, *Life of Nightingale* 1:6, 13, 122–23, 130.

6. Donald R. Allen, "Florence Nightingale: Toward a Psychohistorical Interpretation," *Journal of Interdisciplinary History* 6, no. 1 (1975): 31.

7. Cook, *Life of Nightingale* 1:14.

8. Lytton Strachey, *Eminent Victorians: Cardinal Manning, Florence Nightingale, Dr. Arnold, and General Gordon* (New York: Capricorn, 1963), 131. Despite the fact that enforced passivity nearly drove Nightingale insane, Benjamin Jowett, who for years acted as her spiritual advisor, told her, "I sometimes think . . . that you ought seriously to consider how your work may be carried on, not with less energy, but in a calmer spirit" (Strachey, 190).

9. The forced patience and the passing of time is one of the extraordinary features that Cecil Woodham-Smith notes about Nightingale's life; eight years would pass between her first call from God and Nightingale's knowledge that nursing was to be her vocation, another eight years before she could pursue her work. "Sixteen years in all, sixteen years during which the eager susceptible girl was slowly hammered into the steely powerful woman of genius. The last eight years . . . were years in which suffering piled on suffering, frustration followed frustration, until she was brought to the verge of madness" (*Florence Nightingale* [New York: McGraw-Hill, 1951], 42).

10. Woodham-Smith lists these four occasions: 7 February 1837; in 1853 prior to working at the Hospital for Poor Gentlewomen in Harley Street; in 1854 before going to the Crimea; and in 1861 after the death of Sidney Herbert (*Florence Nightingale,* 13). Nightingale believed that these calls were not "inward revelation" but an actual, external voice like that heard by Joan of Arc (12). In "Florence Nightingale: Toward a Psychohistorical Interpretation," Donald R. Allen asserts that "All of these experiences with 'voices' occurred after periods marked by personal disappointment, strong feelings of self-doubt, deep depression, and a sense of failure. In turn, all were followed by a strong desire to accomplish something, a devotion to work, and some kind of fulfillment" (33).

11. Cook, *Life of Nightingale* 1:14.

12. Ibid., 1:15.

13. Woodham-Smith, *Florence Nightingale,* 42. From our modern perspective, nursing is not considered an immoral profession, nor is the only qualification to be a woman, but our sense of nursing is largely the result of Nightingale's reform. In fact, ironically, nursing has become synonymous with "good" female

characteristics; this results partly because the popular imagination remembers Florence Nightingale not as the "Commander-in-Chief" of the "little War Office," but as the "Lady with the lamp." For a detailed analysis of this, see my manuscript "The Lady with the Lamp Refracted by Patriarchy: The Image of Florence Nightingale in Popular Consciousness and Historical Memory." It is also significant that what most worried Fanny Nightingale was the fear that her daughter was involved in a questionable relationship with a surgeon. Her concern reflects in a significant way just how radical Nightingale's desires were and the extent to which patriarchally prescribed heterosexuality saturates women's lives: an interclass liaison, while feared and frowned upon, would nonetheless be more comprehensible than a woman challenging cultural values for her own needs. The assumption presumes women act in relation to men, not independently. That Nightingale's desires existed outside this paradigm made them both more threatening and less understandable to those operating within it.

14. Cook, *Life of Nightingale* 1:44–45. Mary Poovey also notes analogies between Nightingale and Christ (*Uneven Developments: The Ideological Work of Gender in Mid-Victorian England* [Chicago: University of Chicago Press, 1988], 239). See also Martha Vicinus's *Independent Women: Work and Community for Single Women, 1850–1920* (Chicago: University of Chicago Press, 1985), esp. "Church Communities: Sisterhoods and Deaconesses' Houses" (46–84), for a useful analysis of the role religious communities played in Victorian women's spirituality.

15. Elaine Showalter describes Nightingale's three-volume discourse as an attempt to "justify the laws of God to men—especially working men—and, most important, to women" ("Florence Nightingale's Feminist Complaint: Women, Religion, and *Suggestions for Thought*," *Signs* 6 [1981]: 399). Cook describes the three-volume work as "ostensibly one of Reconstruction; it was in fact very largely one of Revolt" (*Life of Nightingale* 1:475). See also Mary Poovey's insightful "Introduction" to her recent edition of *Cassandra and Other Selections from Suggestions for Thought* (New York: New York University Press, 1992) for a consideration of Nightingale's desire to write *Suggestions*.

16. Showalter, "Nightingale's Feminist Complaint," 400.

17. Kristeva, *Desire in Language*, 6.

18. Toril Moi, *Sexual/Textual Politics: Feminist Literary Theory* (London: Methuen, 1985), 166.

19. Ibid., 170, 11. In her analysis of Kristeva's revolutionary subject, Moi raises important questions about the relationship between agency and subversion. See pages 170–71 for an expanded discussion of Kristeva in a political context.

20. Although *Suggestions* was only printed privately, the religious speculation that Nightingale pursued in it eventually reached the public forum through two articles—"A Note of Interrogation" (*Fraser's Magazine*, n.s., 7 [1873]: 567–77) and "A Sub-Note of Interrogation: What Will Be Our Religion in 1999?" (*Fraser's Magazine*, n.s., 8 [1873]: 25–36). Revising her ideas for these publications—focusing primarily on loss of faith and inadequate religious inquiry—Nightingale diluted the potency of the original text. With the militant challenges to patriarchy removed, the ideas become lost in the many voices of religious debate prevalent during the Victorian period. These two articles, however diluted, did elicit response: Carlyle described her second article as "a lost sheep bleating on the mountain," and Cook records that many prayed for Nightingale's conversion (*Life of Nightingale*, 1:219). *Suggestions* is available on microfiche as part of the Adelaide Nutting Historical Nursing Collection, and selections from the three-

volume treatise have been published in Mary Poovey's recent edition, *Cassandra and other Selections from Suggestions for Thought.*

21. Cook, *Life of Nightingale* 1:469.

22. Ibid. 1:472, 475.

23. Ibid. 1:477.

24. The structure that Nightingale uses in *Suggestions,* framing her most radical discourse with more traditional analysis (and that Brontë reproduces in *Shirley* to a lesser degree), anticipates that of Irigaray's *Speculum of the Other Woman.*

25. Nightingale's decision not to convert was not entirely her own. On the brink of converting to Catholicism, Nightingale gave Cardinal Manning, then a priest, the manuscript of *Suggestions;* when he read her manuscript, Manning concluded that she was not in the "requisite state of mind for admission into the Church of Rome" (Woodham-Smith, *Florence Nightingale,* 65).

26. Taylor, *Eve and the New Jerusalem,* 126.

27. For an informative study of the interrelationship between religious and capitalistic politics in the shaping of Victorian values, see Taylor's *Eve and the New Jerusalem.*

28. Nightingale, "Sub-Note," 28.

29. In considering what society has done for women, Nightingale deliberately includes "fallen" women in her question; society treats these women, she contends, as if they are beyond redemption, with no claims to humanity (*ST,* 2:209). Like Gaskell, Nightingale sees the systemic cause of these women's problems, and in "Cassandra" she goes so far as to suggest that women who marry are just another kind of prostitute.

30. Nightingale expands on this in a private note written in 1851: "Women don't consider themselves as human beings at all. There is absolutely no God, no country, no duty to them at all, except family. . . . I have known a good deal of convents. And of course everyone has talked of the petty grinding tyrannies supposed to be exercised there. But I know nothing like the petty grinding tyranny of a good English family. And the only alleviation is that the tyrannized submits with a heart full of affection" (Woodham-Smith, *Florence Nightingale,* 62).

31. Woodham-Smith, *Florence Nightingale,* 51.

32. Cook, *Life of Nightingale* 1:102.

33. Taylor, *Eve and the New Jerusalem,* 126, 137.

34. Froula, "When Eve Reads Milton," 321–47.

35. In a 26 September 1863 letter to her father, Nightingale wrote: "*God* does hang on the Cross *every day* in *every one* of us" (Cook, *Life of Nightingale,* 1:485).

36. She does add, however, that "it is perhaps incorrect to say that they have no type, England has the type of making money" (*ST,* 2:73). With this assertion, she once again echoes Carlyle's belief that their culture's values had shifted from spiritual to materialistic ones.

37. Nightingale, "Note," 577.

38. Woodham-Smith notes that at the end of 1845 Nightingale "spent her nights sleepless, wrestling with her soul, seeking with tears and prayers to make herself worthy to receive the kindness of God; she spent her days performing the duties of the daughter at home" (*Florence Nightingale,* 42).

39. Nightingale began studying blue books and hospital reports at Lord Ashley's suggestion; just a few years earlier the first of these government reports dealing with public health had been published (Woodham-Smith, *Florence Nightingale,* 43).

40. Showalter, "Nightingale's Feminist Complaint," 399.

41. Cook, *Life of Nightingale* 1:59.
42. Ibid., 1:43.
43. Strachey, *Eminent Victorians*, 134–35.
44. Cook, *Life of Nightingale*, 1:101.
45. Allen divides Nightingale's life into five periods, which he identifies as turning points, each "marked by an internal crisis, that led to a new stage in her development." In chronological order they are: her childhood to around age 7; her call from God that she experienced when 16; her decision to reject marriage and follow what she believed to be God's call, a decision which Allen asserts "resolved her long crisis of identity"; her political alliance with Sidney Herbert after the Crimean War; and, finally, the death of her parents and sister, which, Allen contends, "freed her from a lifelong conflict and permitted her to enter a long period at the end of her life when, her fury abated, she enjoyed the fruits of her labors and contributions" ("Florence Nightingale," 28).
46. Cook, *Life of Nightingale* 1:94.
47. According to Clough, Nightingale regarded Quinet and Mill as "the two men who had the true belief about God's laws. She referred in particular to two chapters in Mill's *Logic* about Free Will and Necessity, which seemed to her to be the beginning of the true religious belief" (Cook, *Life of Nightingale* 1:469).
48. Tarrant, *Florence Nightingale*, 18.
49. Nightingale, "Note," 577.
50. Cook, *Life of Nightingale* 1:480.
51. Ibid., xv.
52. Pagels, *Gnostic Gospels*, 27, 95, xix.
53. Cook, *Life of Nightingale* 1:480.
54. See Barbara Bellow Watson's extremely useful "On Power and the Literary Text" (*Signs* 1 [1975]: 111–18) for an examination of these issues in Chopin, Woolf, and Lessing. See also Elaine Showalter's *The Female Malady*, where she asserts, "The ending of *Cassandra* dramatizes the despair Nightingale could imagine as her own fate: Cassandra dies at the age of thirty, 'withered, paralyzed, extinguished.' In her youth she had 'dreamed of Institutions to show women their work and to train them how to do it' and had 'sacrificed my individual future' of marriage for 'glimpses of a great general future'" (64). Although Showalter's study is extremely useful in reconstructing the complete history of Nightingale, I believe that this reading of Cassandra's death oversimplifies what Nightingale achieves in "Cassandra."
55. Showalter, "Nightingale's Feminist Complaint," 399.
56. Watson, "On Power and the Literary Text," 112.
57. Throughout her life, writing performed an important role in maintaining Nightingale's mental health. As with *Suggestions for Thought*, writing became a conduit to channel unsatiated energies that her forced passivity could not quench. After her first tenure in the Crimea, Nightingale, suffering from Crimean fever, was instructed simply to rest; but in "her delirium [Nightingale] was constantly writing. It was found impossible to keep her quiet unless she wrote, so she was given pen and paper" (Woodham-Smith, *Florence Nightingale*, 152). A few years earlier, at thirty, Nightingale had considered the possible directions for her life, writing "I had 3 paths among which to choose . . . I might have been a married woman, or a literary woman, or a hospital sister" (Woodham-Smith, *Florence Nightingale*, 55); but writing, while crucial to her stability and development, was always only a poor second for living. Nightingale explains this in her response to Mary Clarke's suggestion that she focus on

expressing herself through writing: "You ask me why I do not write some-thing. . . . I had so much rather live than write—writing is only a substitute for living. . . . I think one's feelings waste themselves in words, they ought all to be distilled into actions and actions which bring results" (Woodham-Smith, *Florence Nightingale*, 36).

58. Showalter, "Nightingale's Feminist Complaint," 397–98.

59. Jane P. Tompkins provides an important reevaluation of literary power in "Sentimental Power: *Uncle Tom's Cabin* and the Politics of Literary History," in *The New Feminist Criticism: Essays on Women, Literature, and Theory,* ed. Elaine Showalter (New York: Pantheon, 1985): 81–104.

60. Showalter, "Nightingale's Feminist Complaint," 400.

61. Strachey, *Eminent Victorians,* 158.

62. Woodham-Smith, *Florence Nightingale,* 199. In the end it is ironic that Nightingale, who so strongly rejected marriage, resisting the common practice of working "through" one's husband, would ultimately "work through" Sidney Herbert in the War Office. With Herbert, however, she retained a power and independence that would have been most likely lost legally, if not practically, in marriage at that time.

63. Cook, *Life of Nightingale* 2:366–67.

Chapter 3. Radical Protestantism versus Privileged Hermeneutics: The Religion and Romance of Brontë's Spirituality

Thomas James Wise and John Alexander Symington, eds., *The Brontës: Their Lives, Friendships and Correspondence* (1933; reprint, Oxford: Basil Blackwell, 1980), 2:216. Subsequent quotations from this work are cited in the text as *B*.

1. Charlotte Brontë, *Shirley* (Oxford: Oxford University Press, 1981), 174. Subsequent quotations from this work are cited in the text as *S*.

2. The cultural consensus about the inappropriateness of middle- and upper-class women writing professionally can be vividly illustrated by one of Brontë's contemporaries. Margaret Maison writes of Charlotte Yonge: "Before she published her first story there was a family council to decide whether or not to allow publication. 'In consenting,' her biographer tells us, 'there was an understanding that she would not take the money herself for it, but that it would be used for some good work—it being thought unladylike to benefit by one's own writings'" (*Victorian Vision,* 31–32).

3. Brontë's unequivocal faith in God has contributed to this critical oversight. For instance, Robin Reed Davis writes that "Charlotte Brontë never seriously questioned the foundations of Evangelical belief, and her adult life was singu-larly free from the religious conflict that tormented so many of her contempo-raries" ("Anglican Evangelicalism and the Feminine Literary Tradition, From Hannah Moore to Charlotte Brontë" [Ph.D. Diss., Duke University, 1982], 193). To read Brontë's life as free from "religious conflict," however, is to define that conflict in purely traditional (and I will argue androcentric) terms and miss what I identify as the characteristically female spiritual crisis—that between the individual and her culture, which appropriates sacred allusion for a secular agenda. Recently, in *The Brontë Sisters and George Eliot: A Unity of Difference* (Totowa, N.J.: Barnes & Noble, 1988), Barbara Prentis has provided a useful

starting point for discussions of Brontë's spiritual beliefs; see especially her chapter "Matters of Belief: Religious and Ethical Attitudes," 37–66.

4. The specific historical context in which the Brontës lived must have contributed significantly to their social instability, both potentially debilitating and empowering. Terry Eagleton notes that they were near some of the most intense English class-struggles; they experienced "an aspect of the events which Karl Marx describes in *Capital* as the most horrible tragedy of English history" (*Myths of Power: A Marxist Study of the Brontës* [London: Macmillan, 1975], 3).

5. Ellen Nussey writes that "Every morning was heard the firing of a pistol from Mr. Brontë's room window—it was the discharging of the loading which was made every night. Mr. Brontë's tastes led him to delight in the perusal of battle-scenes, and in following the artifice of war; had he entered on military service instead of ecclesiastical he would probably have had a very distinguished career" (*B*, 1:114).

6. The dialectical tensions of Brontë's life are reproduced in her two closest friends—Ellen Nussey (church member and ultra conservative) and Mary Taylor (independent and vocal feminist). These tensions also manifest in her fiction: Eagleton analyzes the "ambiguity about power" in Brontë's fiction, suggesting that "It parallels and embodies the conflicting desires of the oppressed outcast for independence, for passive conformity to a secure social order, and for avenging self-assertion over that order" that circumscribed her life (Eagleton, *Myths of Power*, 31).

7. Eagleton explains the Brontë sisters' social ambiguity, noting that "They were *isolated* educated women, socially and geographically remote from a world with which they nonetheless maintained close intellectual touch. . . . And as if all this were not enough, they were forced to endure in their childhood an especially brutal form of ideological oppression—Calvinism" (*Myths of Power*, 8).

8. She once wrote, in fact, that "You not unfrequently meet with Clergymen who should have been farmers, officers, shopkeepers—anything rather than Priests—and great scandal do they bring on their sacred calling by their natural unfitness to fulfill its duties" (*B*, 2:225). Later, she would explicitly portray this phenomenon through an unfavorable presentation of the curates in *Shirley*.

9. See Judith Farr's "Charlotte Brontë, Emily Brontë and the 'Undying Life' Within" for a discussion of how these two authors transform the "language of Christian teaching into a private dialectic which contained religious ideas rarely associated with conventional nineteenth-century Protestantism" (*Victorian Institute Journal* 17 [1989]: 87). This analysis proves useful in establishing the connection between the Brontës' writing and their spirituality but does not recognize the spiritual crisis that circumscribes the two.

10. Michael Wheeler notes that although rich biblical allusions permeate her adult fictions, Brontë's juvenilia are without religious allusion (*The Art of Allusion in Victorian Fiction* [London: Macmillan, 1979], 27). Winifred Gerin analyzed this significant absence and asserts that "The explanation lies, rather, in the too great hold that religion took upon their inflammable imaginations, in the terrors it awakened, in the sorrows it recalled" (*Charlotte Brontë: The Evolution of Genius* [Oxford: Clarendon Press, 1967], 33). I, however, would like to suggest an alternative explanation. Unlike in her childhood, the adult Brontë was forced not only to interact with her culture and what she perceived as its appropriation of God but also to come to terms with her place in that culture. By reappropriating sacred allusion as a narrative strategy, not simply as evidence of her religious beliefs, she authorizes her chosen nontraditional career of writing fiction.

11. Both Anglo-American and French feminists have analyzed women's relationship to writing as one of power and liberation. Barbara Bellow Watson in "On Power and the Literary Text" provides a useful study of the power women can achieve through their fictional productions. Examining this dynamic of women and writing, Hélène Cixous reaches a slightly different conclusion—that writing *is* liberation, not a vehicle for it ("The Laugh of the Medusa," trans. Keith Cohen and Paula Cohen, in *New French Feminisms*, ed. Elaine Marks and Isabelle de Courtivron [New York: Schocken Books, 1981], 250). Cixous also theorizes about the explosion of phallocentric binaries, which would make these two mutually exclusive, and allows both these principles to work toward Brontë's liberation ("Sorties," trans. Ann Liddle, in *New French Feminisms*, 96–97).

12. Gilbert and Gubar suggest that Brontë's writing can be seen as a "paradigm" for other nineteenth-century women who participated in a kind of "trance" writing, exploring their "feelings of enclosure" and their "desire to flee" feminine roles (*Madwoman in the Attic*, 313).

13. For critical overviews of the proliferation of religious novels in the nineteenth century, see Margaret Maison's *Search Your Soul, Eustace: Victorian Religious Novels* (New York: Sheed & Ward, 1961) and Robert Lee Wolff's *Gains and Losses: Novels of Faith and Doubt in Victorian England* (New York: Garland, 1977).

14. See Showalter's *A Literature of Their Own* for an analysis of the missing female literary tradition.

15. For an extensive analysis of Brontë's use of typology in her fiction, see George P. Landow's *Victorian Types, Victorian Shadows: Biblical Typology in Victorian Literature, Art, and Thought* (Boston: Routledge & Kegan Paul, 1980).

16. In "The Laugh of the Medusa," Cixous, locating her analysis of women's articulation in "the language of men and their grammar," suggests that a woman can "dislocate this 'within,' . . . explode it, turn it around, and seize it; to make it hers" (*New French Feminisms*, 257). Irigaray, in *Speculum*, argues that to be understood in the confines of symbolic order, women must mimic patriarchal scripts, that in Freud's consideration of the female position in the castration complex, the little girl must pretend to be the little man, must mime gender-specific behavior (21–27, 60). Translated into the female author reproducing traditional scripts that recreate such gender dynamics, mimicking the romance script for instance, the reality of her femaleness, by definition, changes rhetorically that script and produces different political effects (Moi, *Sexual/Textual Politics*, 140–41). Barry Qualls, considering Brontë in a tradition of Victorian writers who graft sacred images onto secular fiction, reaches a complementary conclusion; he writes that "Brontë's novels [are] English *Bildungsromane*, novels of the self's development—radically different from other spiritual biographies of the period only because three of them focus on the development of a woman's inner life" (*Secular Pilgrims*, 50).

17. Gilbert and Gubar focus long overdue attention on *Shirley* in their discussion in *Madwoman in the Attic*, where they identify the novel's central concern as impotence. I would like to suggest, however, that while the theme of impotence is important to understanding the novel, that theme is subsumed by her exposure of the inherent subjectivity of hermeneutics: with the radical protestantism for which Caroline Helstone argues, any individual could empower herself, as Brontë did, through claiming a divine authority to challenge patriarchal restrictions or inactivity, as the case may be.

18. Christine Froula's "When Eve Reads Milton: Undoing Canonical Authority" provides an important reexamination of images of authority. In this context,

however, I am not considering the images of authority but the exegetical function associated with authority, a privilege Froula quite rightly identifies as traditionally exclusive to an elite male coterie.

19. In *Writing Beyond the Ending*, Rachel Blau duPlessis argues that narrative patterns both parallel the social scripts available to women and in turn reinforce extant cultural models of behavior.

20. Helene Moglen identifies a similar theme, the "misuses of power" (*Charlotte Brontë: The Self Conceived* [New York: Norton, 1976], 158).

21. Eagleton also reads Brontë's novels as exploiting myths, although secular; he writes that her novels are "'myths' which work towards a balance or fusion of blunt bourgeois rationality and flamboyant Romanticism, brash initiative and genteel cultivation, passionate rebellion and cautious conformity; and those interchanges embody a complex structure of convergence and antagonism between the landed and industrial sectors of the contemporary ruling class" (*Myths of Power*, 4).

22. G. H. Lewes described *Shirley* as such in the January 1850 edition of the *Edinburgh Review*. Criticism has traditionally dismissed *Shirley* as a failed novel because of what is considered a flawed plot. For examples, see Asa Brigg's "Private and Social Themes in *Shirley*" (*Brontë Studies Transactions* 13, no. 3 [1958]: 203–19) and Mrs. Humphrey Ward's "Introduction" to The Haworth Edition of *Shirley*. Jacob Korg's "The Problem of Unity in *Shirley*" (*Nineteenth-Century Fiction* 2, no. 2 [1957]: 125–36) sees the novel somewhat unified by a theme of "romantic philosophy" (136); Moglen sees the novel as less than perfect but admires that Brontë would dare as much as she does and argues that although *Shirley* moves toward a radical criticism of Victorian England, it pauses and does not complete that criticism" (*Charlotte Bronte*, 156); Gilbert and Gubar suggest that the "inorganic development" of *Shirley* is really Brontë's efforts to articulate the "inextricable link between sexual discrimination and mercantile capitalism" (*Madwoman in the Attic*, 375). The Marxist-Feminist Literature Collective argues that "*Shirley* is a novel which conceals its feminist argument within an historical framework—the Napoleonic Wars and Luddism—with the result that Brontë's contemporaries and modern critics alike have failed to acknowledge the thematic complexity which Brontë ambitiously attempted in this work" ("Women's Writing: *Jane Eyre, Shirley, Villette, Aurora Leigh*," *Ideology and Consciousness* 2 [1977]: 27–48). I would argue that, in addition to this link between women's and workers' exploitation, the development of *Shirley* points to Brontë's conscious manipulation of patriarchal narrative scripts to expose the complicity between the patriarchy and the Church to keep hermeneutical privilege secure.

23. Considering the narrative structure of *Shirley*, Gilbert and Gubar write that it appears Brontë intended to subvert both literary sexual images and the roles of courtship, "But she could find no models for this kind of fiction; as she explains in her use of the Genesis myth, the stories of her culture actively endorse traditional sexual roles, even as they discourage female authority" (*Madwoman in the Attic*, 395). I argue, however, that Brontë does succeed in subverting those narrative and social scripts through her exaggerated mimicking of those patterns and, as I have already suggested, that because Brontë saw herself writing out of religious duty, she gains an authority independent of any cultural limitations.

24. Analyzing this passage, Gilbert and Gubar write that the narrator chastises Caroline for loving "without being asked to love," that the narrator is "pitiless" in her allusions to "the opposition of food and stone, as well as the

necessity of self-enclosure and self-containment for women" (*Madwoman in the Attic*, 377). I would suggest an alternative reading of the narrative voice; rather than castigating her, the narrator describes, with distinctly evocative Christian imagery, Caroline's situation, lamenting women's cuturally imposed powerlessness.

25. For an extensive analysis of this power attributed to women, see Nina Auerbach's article "The Rise of the Fallen Woman" (*Nineteenth-Century Fiction* 35 [1980]: 29–52) and her book *Woman and Demon: The Life of a Victorian Myth* (Cambridge: Harvard University Press, 1982).

26. Gilbert and Gubar also see parallels between the workers' aggressive revolt at the mill and the women (*Madwoman in the Attic*, 384).

27. Ironically, just as her characters did, Brontë dauntlessly tried to answer Carlyle's cry for salvation through work, but for women, "work" was defined within the domestic sphere, not the public. Brontë wrote to her publisher that even though she liked Carlyle more and more, she did not "quite fall in with his hero-worship" (*B*, 2:326). This distinction between Carlyle's call for the individual to find salvation through work and his vision that invests a handful of men as heroes proves useful in understanding Brontë's alternative vision—a spirituality that empowers each individual believer with a radical Protestantism, not one built on a hierarchical economy.

28. Quoting Q. D. Leavis, Qualls points to a parallel example in *Jane Eyre* where "Religion has thus become a means for imposing class distinctions *based on money*" (*Secular Pilgrims*, 46).

29. Cynthia A. Linder sees this chapter as explicitly alluding to *Pilgrim's Progress*, "to a passage in which Christian has to combat the spectres of his imagination" (*Romantic Imagery in the Novels of Charlotte Brontë* [London: Macmillan, 1978], 83).

30. In their article "Women's Writing: *Jane Eyre, Shirley, Villette, Aurora Leigh*," The Marxist-Feminist Literature Collective argues for the "revolutionary" potential of Brontë's narrative strategy that examines the "male proletarian struggle from the perspective of, and by analogy with, oppressed bourgeois women," that these analogies are so polemic "they cannot be spoken, but must lurk disguised within a text which is then read as structurally deficient" (36).

31. In the chapter on *Shirley* in her *Romantic Imagery in the Novels of Charlotte Brontë*, Cynthia A. Linder writes: "It should be clear that Charlotte Brontë is not decrying the Church, she is merely portraying the effect of practical Christianity on a community" (77). Linder's reading, however, oversimplifies the complex relationship Brontë saw between the Church and patriarchy, between organized religion and God; to understand fully Brontë's embrace of organized religion, one must not conflate it with the Church of England.

CHAPTER 4. TO "STAND WITH CHRIST AGAINST THE WORLD": GASKELL'S SENTIMENTAL SOCIAL AGENDA

1. Elizabeth Gaskell, *Ruth* (Oxford: Oxford University Press, 1985), 351. Subsequent quotations from this work are cited in the text as *R*.

2. This challenge to replace the prevailing Hebraic values with a radical Christian model occurs throughout Gaskell's oeuvre despite the traditional division of her fiction into three categories (the early social-problem novels, the later domestic novels, and the abundance of supernatural stories). With the clamor

from industrialists that surrounded *Mary Barton* (1848) and *North and South* (1854–55), the moral uproar that accompanied the publication of *Ruth* (1853), and the biographical challenges that dominated her first edition of *The Life of Charlotte Brontë* (1857), it is not surprising that Gaskell, like Hardy after her, would turn away from such a polemical vision and produce instead less overtly controversial fiction, although maintaining a consistent agenda.

3. Even while foregrounding the social-problem theme in *Mary Barton* and *North and South,* Gaskell still structures these narratives by an explicit appropriation of Christian allusion to criticize her culture. Early in *Mary Barton* John Barton sees the struggles between the masters and workers in distinctly religious terms. He criticizes the masters' "lack of Christian brotherhood" and claims that the "workers and masters are separate as Dives and Lazarus," a theme that gives shape to the unfolding story of Manchester life (*Mary Barton* [Harmondsworth: Penguin, 1985], 45; subsequent quotations from this work are cited as *MB*). The novel even concludes with a reminder of Christ's poverty and "man's responsibility to help those with less" (*MB*, 457).

With a more balanced presentation, Gaskell returns to these problems between masters and workers in *North and South.* Here, though, Gaskell extends her critical vision beyond just the tensions between industrialists and their workers to include the Established Church and the legal and conventional codes that govern England. By an act of conscience, Mr. Hale leaves the Church of England, transplanting his family from the rural South to the industrial North (*North and South* [Oxford: Oxford University Press, 1982], 33; subsequent quotations from this work are cited as *NS*). His son, Frederick, is falsely accused of mutiny (*NS,* 109), and Margaret lies to the police about her brother's visit to England (*NS,* 283). Outside the Church of England and English law, neither Mr. Hale nor his son will ever be able to be fully reintegrated into their culture; by definition neither can reconcile their moral vision with society's codes. Gaskell does not attempt to provide a solution for these ideological challenges of conscience. She does, however, portray a growing understanding between laborers and masters; through the learned compassion for one another, Higgins (the worker) and Thornton (the owner) begin to understand the plight of the other. Mr. Hale describes the workers' union as having the potential to be "Christianity itself" (*NS,* 233), and Thornton establishes a co-op commissary for his workers (*NS,* 361). The novel concludes, again voicing what Gaskell saw as a New Testament vision, that "we have all of us one human heart" (*NS,* 419).

4. Significantly, Bradshaw's dismissal of Benson's philosophy as sentimental anticipates the label most twentieth-century critics have given Gaskell's fiction. Even while acknowledging the historically explosive and controversial qualities inherent in her fiction, modern criticism continually points to structural flaws, a moralizing tone, and *sentimental* values in her early novels. For instances of her fiction being dismissed as sentimental, see A. B. Hopkins's *Elizabeth Gaskell, Her Life and Work* (New York: Octagon Books, 1971); as pious, see Arthur Pollard's "The Novels of Mrs. Gaskell," *Bulletin of John Rylands Library* 43 (1960–61): 403–25; or as moralizing, see Enid L. Duthie's *The Themes of Elizabeth Gaskell* (Totowa, N.J.: Rowman and Littlefield Press, 1980) and Edgar Wright's *Mrs. Gaskell: The Basis for Reassessment* (London: Oxford University Press, 1965). Consequently, the major project of reexamining Gaskell's fiction remains.

5. Tompkins, "Sentimental Power," 83–85.

6. Tompkins's redefinition of "sentimental" in her reading of *Uncle Tom's Cabin* is an important challenge to patriarchal aesthetics; although using her

redefinition as a starting point, my reconsideration of sentimentalism in Gaskell diverges from Tompkins's argument in the crucial nongendered component fundamental to Gaskell's Unitarianism.

7. As a young woman Gaskell attended Avonbank, situated in Stratford-upon-Avon, and when her father became ill, she returned to live with him, upon which he superintended her studies in Latin, French, and Italian (Hopkins, *Elizabeth Gaskell*, 31, 40).

8. Wright, *Mrs. Gaskell*, 25–26, 43. For further discussion of the nonhierarchical and nondogmatic foundation upon which Unitarianism based its beliefs, see Tessa Brodestsky (*Elizabeth Gaskell* [Oxford: Oxford University Press, 1986], 4). Significantly these qualities find important parallels in feminist readings of theological and literary canons; two important examples of this criticism include Elaine Pagels's *The Gnostic Gospels* and Christine Froula's "When Eve Reads Milton: Undoing Canonical Economy."

9. Carol Gilligan, *In a Different Voice: Psychological Theory and Women's Development* (Cambridge: Harvard University Press, 1982), 167.

10. M. D. Wheeler, "The Sinner as Heroine: A Study of Mrs. Gaskell's *Ruth* and the Bible," *Durham University Journal*, n.s., 5 (1976): 149.

11. Wright, *Mrs. Gaskell*, 25–26.

12. Although her liberal religious heritage enabled Gaskell to challenge her culture's reductive dismissal of female talent, she (as wife and mother) still possessed a mildly conservative perspective of balancing one's domestic responsibilities and one's career. In an 1850 letter to Eliza Fox, she wrote: "One thing is pretty clear, *Women* must give up living an artist's life, if home duties are to be paramount. It is different with men, whose home duties are so small a part of their life. . . . I am sure it is healthy for [women] to have the refuge of the hidden world of Art. . . . I have felt this in writing. . . . I have no doubt that the cultivation of [both "home duties and the development of the Individual"] tends to keep the other in a healthy state" (*LG*, 106). Her genuine commitment to challenge cultural rejections of nonconformist women, however, can best be illustrated through her efforts (enlisting Dickens's assistance) to help a young, orphaned woman who had been seduced by a surgeon when she had been ill emigrate to Australia. For details regarding this effort on Gaskell's part, see *LG*, 98–100. Even with exemplary behavior like Gaskell's own efforts to aid her society's victims, I am not trying to suggest that all Church of England members were pharisaical or that all Dissenters were socially progressive. Significantly the confrontation that illuminates Gaskell's agenda in *Ruth* takes place between two male Dissenters, Benson and Bradshaw. Similarly, some of her husband's congregation, like Bradshaw, could not revise their values to include Gaskell's controversial vision. In an early February 1853 letter to Eliza Fox, Gaskell writes: "I think I must be an improper woman without knowing it, I do so manage to shock people. Now *should* you have burnt the 1st vol. of Ruth as so *very* bad? even if you had been a very anxious father of a family? Yet *two* men have; and a third has forbidden his wife to read it; they sit next to us in Chapel and you can't imagine how 'improper' I feel under their eyes" (*LG*, 222–23).

13. Hopkins writes that Gaskell's "purpose belongs also with the Christian Socialists, among whom she counted many good friends: Francis William Newman (heterodox brother of the Cardinal), F. D. Maurice, Thomas Hughes, and Charles Kingsley" (*Elizabeth Gaskell*, 131–32). In a letter to William Robson, Gaskell asks him to distribute a pamphlet and two papers authored by Maurice and

Kingsley (*LG*, 105), and to Eliza Fox, she copies lines from Kingsley, whom she calls "my *hero*" (*LG*, 90).

14. For a detailed analysis of this phenomenon, see Taylor, *Eve and the New Jerusalem*, 126–27.

15. Nina Auerbach provides a more complete discussion of this hidden power in the myth of Victorian womanhood in both her article "The Rise of the Fallen Woman" and her book *Woman and the Demon*.

16. Gaskell strongly believed that her fiction was a means to "speak [her] mind" (*LG*, 220–21) even though much of the impetus behind the production of her first novel, *Mary Barton*, was to refocus her energies after the death of her young son, William—an activity her husband suggested.

17. The organic quality that Gaskell attributed to her fiction can be seen in a letter in which she tells a young author who solicited her advice about writing that "The plot must grow, and culminate in a crisis; not a character must be introduced who does not conduce to this growth and progress of events. The plot is like the anatomical drawing of an artist; he must have an idea of his skeleton, before he can clothe it with muscle & flesh, much more before he can drape it" (*LG*, 542).

18. In "Elizabeth Gaskell and the Novel of Social Pride," Angus Easson argues for the powerful recreation of the living conditions of Victorian workers in Gaskell's fiction, adding that Gaskell was alone among the period's major novelists in living in an industrial rather than urban area (*Bulletin of John Ryland Library* 67 [1984–85]: 693).

19. For a detailed study of this transfer of biblical allusions from religious to secular discourse, from allegorical to a more realistic presentation, during the Victorian period, see Barry Qualls's *The Secular Pilgrims of Victorian Fiction*.

20. Wheeler, "The Sinner as Heroine," 149.

21. The narrative divisions which I see in *Ruth* do not correspond with the three-volume divisions of the text: the first volume followed Ruth's story until her arrival, with the Bensons, at Eccleston; the second volume ended with Ruth rejecting Bellingham's marriage proposal (Easson, "Elizabeth Gaskell," 109).

22. Much of the Victorian public reaction to *Ruth*, however, was hostile if not outraged (see note 7). When told by his wife that *Ruth* had been burnt in some places, Archdeacon Hares replied: "Well, the Bible has been burnt" (Hopkins, *Elizabeth Gaskell*, 126). While the *Examiner* and the *North British Review* wrote favorably of *Ruth*, and individuals, including the leading Christian Socialists and Richard Monckton Milne, responded favorably to it, many more magazines and individuals condemned the novel as well as the author. In an early February 1853 letter to Eliza Fox, Gaskell writes: "one of your London librarians . . . has had to withdraw it from circulation on account of 'its being unfit for family reading' and Spectator, Lity Gazette, Sharp's Mag; Colborn have all abused it as roundly as may be. Litery [sic] Gazette in every form of abuse 'insufferably dull' 'style offensive from affectation' 'deep regret that we and all admirers of Mary Barton must feel at the author's loss of reputation'" (*LG*, 223).

23. I use the term phallic mother to identify a female complicit in the subjection of women by a patriarchal culture. This term, although originating with Freud (explaining the child's fantasy that the mother has a phallus), has been transformed by the French feminists to the more metaphoric quality I define above. The phallic mother's power results largely from its hidden quality; doubly veiled by both gender and social position, the phallic mother provides a crucial socializing factor in reproducing an androcentric culture. For a more detailed

definition and analysis of the phallic mother, see Julia Kristeva's "The Novel as Polylogue" in *Desire in Language* and Jane Gallop's chapter "The Phallic Mother: Fraudian Analysis" in *The Daughter's Seduction.*

24. Significantly, Thurston Benson's religious and ideological marginalization is mirrored by his physical carriage: he is an outsider by appearance as well as belief; when Ruth first meets him in Llan-dhu, she "saw a man [with] the stature of a dwarf . . . he was deformed" (*R*, 67).

25. For a useful theoretical discussion of these issues, see Margaret Homans's *Bearing the Word: Language and Female Experience in Nineteenth-Century Women's Writing* (Chicago: University of Chicago Press, 1986). Homans's first chapter, "Representation, Reproduction, and Women's Place in Language" (1–39), provides an important discussion in which she uses "Lacanian terms [to] transform Chodorow's psychological theory into a revisionary myth of women and language" (6). From this she proposes that "Articulations of myths of language, and specifically of their relation to the literal and to the literalization, appear generally in the form of four recurrent literary situations or practices," which she designates as "bearing the word" (29). Her theory, and her work on Gaskell, have important implications for this chapter. Writing about Gaskell, Homans asserts that "mother-present language . . . is always and inextricably bound up with and interdependent upon paternal power and its determination of women's subordinate linguistic role as transmitters of men's words" (234–35); I argue, however, that for Gaskell, especially in *Ruth*, this language representation becomes more complex. The figurative/symbolic that reveals the law of the Father replaces not just the absent mother, but also the absent God. The biblical language which Gaskell has her characters learn teaches a code of behavior in contrast to her androcentric culture, not one complicit with it. See also Sara Ruddick's "Maternal Thinking" for a useful delineation of the qualities that characterize this perspective; as part of this description, she identifies "inauthenticity," which she defines as a quality similar to submission and obedience found in "some versions of Christianity" (in *Mothering: Essays in Feminist Theory*, ed. Joyce Treblicot [Totowa, N.J.: Rowman & Allanheld, 1984], 221). In this way, Ruddick establishes the distinction that I argue defines Gaskell's contrast between "mother-love" and the patriarchally complicit women exemplified by Bellingham's mother. Similarly, the "attentive" love present in maternal thinking anticipates the emphasis of sympathetic projection, which, translated into Christian doctrine as the Golden rule, reflects qualities that I see in Gaskell's revisionist social vision (220). See also Virginia Sickbert's "The Significance of Mother and Child in Christina Rossetti's *Sing-Song*" (forthcoming in *Victorian Poetry*) for an important analysis of the role of the mother in Rossetti's poetry.

26. For an insightful analysis of Gaskell's use of metonymy and the significant role of women to connect public and private spheres in *North and South*, see Gallagher's *The Industrial Reformation of English Fiction*, esp. pp. 166–84.

27. Tompkins asserts that one of the important features of sentimental fiction is that salvation is achieved through the model of motherly love ("Sentimental Power," 83).

28. Faith Benson serves an important role as a mirror of public sentiment, reflected by her initial rejection and ultimate acceptance of Ruth. First she shrinks from this fallen woman, but once she develops a history with Ruth she becomes the character's champion. It is also Faith that persuades her brother to allow Ruth to be the Bradshaws' governess, an act which both instigates Ruth's

second dismissal and sets in motion the transfer of sentimental values from the domestic to the public arena.

29. Both Bellingham and Ruth have assumed new names when they reencounter each other here: he has taken the family name Donne, which provides him with greater position, property, and financial power (R, 440); she has taken the name Mrs. Denbigh (Benson's mother's name), which provides her with requisite respectability for a woman with a child (R, 130). The implications of these name changes underscore the significantly different values associated with the culture's gender-based morals. For men, value is abstract and connected to positions of power; for women, value is closely tied to their relation to men and the harnassing of their reproductive capacity within patriarchal constraints.

30. This image also metaphorically reveals the passion Ruth still feels for Bellingham.

31. Wheeler, "The Sinner as Heroine," 154.

32. Although the modern reader would interpret Ruth's choice to nurse the sick as an extension of "woman's work" from private to public mothering, nursing was considered nearly scandalous in the nineteenth century, attracting immodest and intemperate women before Florence Nightingale's transformation of it into what she believed to be, and what Gaskell's character supports, a "blessed" calling. Gaskell conflates the contemporary notion of nursing with that of the nineteenth century by having Ruth, as fallen woman, bring to that vocation a holy and pure quality.

33. Ruth's nursing the sick and dying in the fever ward is much more than what Coral Lansbury has argued it to be—a kind of unconscious modeling of Benson's care of the sick (Elizabeth Gaskell: The Novel of Social Crisis [New York: Barnes & Noble, 1975], 80). Instead, Ruth chooses to tend the sick partly because Mr. Wynne (the parish doctor) asks her to do so and partly because she needs the employment—she sees it as an opportunity to end her socially imposed idleness while comforting others (R, 388–89); the Bensons, in fact, try to talk her out of this endeavor.

34. While this scene outside the fever wards may be one of the most explicit cases, Gaskell, throughout the novel, has characterized Ruth with biblical allusions; all of the following (with distinct allusions to Christ) occur after her seduction. The narrator likens Ruth to Christ while she is at Benson's Sunday school: "Ruth sat on a low hassock, and coaxed the least of the little creatures to her" (R, 151). Later, the mutual salvation of Ruth and her son is described: "The child and the mother were each messengers of God—angels to each other" (R, 369). Benson, in an attempt to give Ruth strength to face her public detractors, reminds her of Christ's thorny life, paralleling her martyrdom (R, 358).

35. The verse that Gaskell revises is: "Her children rise up and call her blessed; / her husband also, and he praises her: / 'Many women have done excellently, / but you surpass them all'" (Proverbs 31:28–29).

36. See Rachel Blau duPlessis's Writing Beyond the Ending for a useful analysis of similar strategies by modern women writers. Although Gaskell is not included in her project, duPlessis's theory of women writers redefining narrative conventions provides useful insights into Gaskell's strategies. By delineating various narrative strategies that women writers used to write beyond the traditional endings of fiction, duPlessis provides a theory with which to illuminate women authors' conscious rewriting of narrative patterns to include female experience.

37. Because Unitarianism tended not to believe in Christ's divinity, Gaskell's conflation of biblical history (male and female) into Ruth's history becomes more

credible; the ability to be a prophet of God's word is opened to those who believe and accurately reveal God's word.

38. Examples of negative critical response to Gaskell's decision to conclude her novel with Ruth's death range from sympathetic incredulousness to simplistic condescension. Charlotte Brontë, for example, wrote "Why should she die? Why are we to shut up the book weeping?" (quoted in Gaskell, *Life of Brontë*, 475). Modern critics have echoed Brontë's question. Patricia Beer writes, "if Ruth is really an innocent victim of circumstances, why does she have to be so severely punished?"; she concludes it can only be because Gaskell believed "sexual intercourse outside marriage was a kind of disease with after effects" (*Reader, I Married Him: A Study of Women Characters of Jane Austen, Charlotte Brontë, Elizabeth Gaskell, and George Eliot* [New York: Macmillan, 1974], 146). In her biography of Gaskell, Hopkins writes, "Ruth was already saved; her death is purely gratuitous" (*Elizabeth Gaskell*, 130). Angus Easson, writing in his *Elizabeth Gaskell*, wonders if Gaskell "in presenting her character sympathetically, contrived to make her sinless in the event and yet to react afterwards as though she has sinned? That is, Gaskell seems to confound society's view of what has happened with God's despite quoting 'God judgeth not as man judgeth'" (118). And Margaret Ganz calls the description of Ruth's death as saintly, "mere mystical twaddle" (*Elizabeth Gaskell: The Artist in Conflict* [New York: Twayne, 1969], 112).

39. Tompkins argues, in her discussion of *Uncle Tom's Cabin*, that one of the defining features of sentimental fiction is the power obtained through a character's death; replicating Christ's example, those who die for someone else's salvation are more powerful than those they die for ("Sentimental Power," 85).

40. The passage alluded to from Shakespeare's *Cymbeline* is "Fear no more the heat o' the sun / Nor the furious winter's rages; / Thou thy worldly task hast done, / Home art gone, and ta'en thy wages. / Golden lads and girls all must, / As chimney-sweepers, come to dust." Wheeler, analyzing the effect of Gaskell's allusion on the Victorian reader, writes "The anticipatory effect of [this] quotation relies upon the reader's knowledge of the play. Imogen is not dead. Nor is Ruth, as a Christian, 'dead' in any final sense at the end of the novel, in the eyes of Thurston Benson, when he reads from Revelation" ("The Sinner as Heroine," 159).

41. Angus Easson sees Ruth's death as that of a conventional victim. Reading the novel's conclusion in this fashion, though, forces him to miss Gaskell's subversion of that literary motif. He writes: "Gaskell's purpose was partly to show that the fallen woman could lead a full and useful life, yet she couldn't escape the conventional idea that Ruth, the heroic dignified expansive creature, is also a victim, who must have her tragedy. She has not yet grasped fully, as she was to in *Sylvia's Lovers*, that to live can be more tragic than to die" (*Elizabeth Gaskell*, 125).

42. This range of Gaskell's narrative strategies can be best illustrated in her shorter works of fiction. With "Lois the Witch" (1861) and *Sylvia's Lovers* (1863) Gaskell continues to detail the conflict between God's and man's laws by using the Salem witch trials and the British press gangs as violent metaphors of oppression against those who deviate from the dominant ideology. These safer veiled challenges, distanced both historically and metaphorically, nonetheless call into question her culture's politics and reveal the tragic outcome of those who defy or reject the established values—Lois, hanged as a witch; and Daniel Robson, Sylvia's father, hanged as a rioter.

This tension between the defiant or victimized and their culture, which occurs throughout Gaskell's fiction, becomes transformed in her later fiction into a presentation of the power of a community of women, the dynamic of which essentially replicates Christian love. In "The Well of Pen-Morfa" (1850), *Cranford* (1851), "The Three Eras of Libbie Marsh" (1853), and "Half a Life-Time Ago" (1855), women help and aid other women, even, as in the case of Susan Dixon, when it is a former lover's widow and children. Through charity to one another, women find their salvation, taking in orphans, "idiots," and lame women— those rejected by patriarchal culture.

Written a few years before *Ruth*, Gaskell's short story "Lizzie Leigh" (1850) can be read as a preliminary engagement with the same issues to which she would later return in her most polemic novel. This narrative of two daughters' falls—one figurative and the other literal—rejects patriarchal codes for an ethical system built on love and forgiveness. Like *Ruth*, this story grafts biblical and religious imagery onto the narrative of a fallen woman and challenges traditional ideological assumptions about men and women. The narrator writes that "Milton's famous line might have been framed and hung up as the rule of [the Leighs'] married life, for he was truly the interpreter, who stood between God and [Mrs. Leigh]" (*Four Short Stories* [London: Pandora Press, 1983], 48). It is significantly Mrs. Leigh's rejection of her husband's harsh translation of God's words about fallen women and their daughter that eventually enables her reunion with Lizzie. Although, unlike Ruth, Lizzie does not die at the story's end, her daughter's death provides the catalyst for Lizzie's redemption. Although this story contains images of female prophets and Christ figures (it concludes with a picture of female compassion likened to Christ's), "Lizzie Leigh" does not present as revolutionary an agenda as does *Ruth*.

CHAPTER 5. THE "HIDDEN HEROISM" OF "SOCIAL SYMPATHY": GEORGE ELIOT'S ETHIC OF HUMANITY

George Eliot, *The George Eliot Letters*, ed. Gordon S. Haight (New Haven: Yale University Press, 1954), 1:125. Subsequent quotations from this work are cited in the text as *GEL*. See also note 12, chap. 1.

1. George Eliot, *Middlemarch* (Harmondsworth: Penguin, 1979), 25. Subsequent quotations from this work are cited in the text as *M*.

2. Those critics who insist on Eliot's irony here generally do so because they fail to see how this question is part of the overall challenge to patriarchal standards. Albert J. Palko, for instance, completely misses the crucial point of the opening question, asserting that "The tragedy of the new Theresas is that none ever achieves an ideally noble existence; all remain unheroic and unsung" ("Latter-day Saints: George Eliot's New Saint Theresa in Image and Symbol" [Ph.D. diss., Notre Dame, 1973], 203). While critics like Franklin E. Court and Harriett Farwell Adams recognize Eliot's intended contrast between the Victorian world and that of Saint Theresa, they persist in arguing that these changes devalue Dorothea's passions, as Court suggests that readers "look with suspicion and a certain degree of amusement on the motives of [Dorothea's] 'vocation'" ("The Image of St. Theresa in *Middlemarch* and Positive Ethics," *Victorian Newsletter* 68 [1985]: 22; "Prelude and Finale to *Middlemarch*," *Victorian Newsletter* 63 [1983]: 21–25).

3. In addition to providing an important contrast between the past effectiveness of religion and the present failure, the Theresa allusion also serves as a

significant model for Dorothea in a world which traditionally fails to consider women in historical analyses. One only needs to remember Carlyle's assertion that "Universal History . . . is at bottom the History of the Great Men" to understand Eliot's choice of Theresa as spiritual ancestor for Dorothea (*On Heroes, Hero-Worship and the Heroic in History* [Lincoln: University of Nebraska Press, 1966], 1). For an extended discussion of the importance and general absence of such female precursors, see Elaine Showalter's *A Literature of Their Own.*

The Saint Theresa allusion also invokes other important associations. Hilary Fraser correctly suggests that Theresa's "blend of sensuality and mysticism" contributes to Eliot's "treatment of the sexual attraction between Dorothea and Ladislaw" ("Saint Theresa, Saint Dorothea, and Miss Brooke in *Middlemarch,*" *Nineteenth-Century Fiction* 40, no. 4 [1986]: 401). Gilbert and Gubar see Theresa as Eliot's "attempt to discover a symbol of uniquely female divinity" as she struggled with her own place in a patriarchal world (*Madwoman in the Attic,* 468).

4. Knoepflmacher provides a useful analysis of this theme of intervening uncles ("*Middlemarch*: an Avuncular View," *Nineteenth-Century Fiction* 30, no. 1 [1975]: 53–81).

5. Knoepflmacher expands upon this idea of the life available to Theresa vis à vis Dorothea by positing that Eliot "can no longer believe in the sacramental universe that still existed for a sixteenth-century mystic—a universe in which an action, no matter how small, could be seen as part of a larger plan" ("Avuncular View," 54).

6. George Eliot, *Essays,* ed. Thomas Pinney (New York: Columbia University Press, 1963), 203. Subsequent quotations from this work are cited in the text as *GEE.*

7. Although many have interpreted this swan metaphor as an allusion to the Hans Christian Andersen fable, an alternative antecedent might be possible. Nightingale's mother, referring to Florence, confessed to friends, "We are ducks who have hatched a wild swan" (Gaskell, *LG,* 307). Because of Evans's acquaintance with the Nightingale family and the parallels between Florence's life and that which Eliot crafts for Dorothea, I believe this echo cannot be ignored.

8. Elaine Showalter writes that "George Eliot was virtually alone among feminine novelists in speculating about the psychological and moral impact of women's experience on the structure and content of the novel" (*A Literature of Their Own,* 96). For an extended analysis and theoretical explanation of women writers' manipulation of traditional narratives in the twentieth century, see Rachel Blau duPlessis's *Writing Beyond the Ending;* for a collection of essays which consider both the internalized landscape of the female *bildungsroman* and the characteristic shift in the genre beginning not with adolescence but marriage, see *The Voyage In,* ed. Elizabeth Abel, Marianne Hirsch, and Elizabeth Langland (Hanover: University Press of New England, 1983).

9. Two important aspects of *Middlemarch* as epic need to be further clarified: the "religious" component of epic and the subversion of traditional epic criteria. Kenny Marotta, as well as other critics, declares the "home epic" "oxymoronic"; he points to the novel's "uneasy relation . . . to the epic genre" that results from "combining domesticity with grandeur" ("*Middlemarch*: the 'Home Epic,'" *Genre* 15 [1982]: 403). Such critical perspectives misunderstand Eliot's reason for constructing the new genre and the point of the home epic for the same reason others misread the opening question—the failure to recognize Eliot's feminist agenda. The second element of epic which needs to be clarified is the "religious" component inherent in the epic. Whether to Greek gods or Milton's Christian

God, humanity's relationship to those gods forms the basis of the narratives. Knoepflmacher suggests that "Like *Paradise Lost, Middlemarch* is an epic effort at justification and persuasion" ("Avuncular View," 81). For the purposes of this study, the larger characteristic of humanity's relationship to a god (or the implied moral superstructure) is more to the point. Labeling *Middlemarch* epic, even as the revisionist "home epic," Eliot reinforces the absence of that grand plan in the nineteenth century; here the individual negotiates his or her life in relation to one another ("man's kinship to man," as Knoepflmacher identifies it), not his or her relationship to a god or gods.

10. Although Gilbert and Gubar also find the weaving imagery significant to Eliot's development of the novel, they point to it as a metaphor for the plot's intricacy; a contrast to Casaubon's goal to determine the single key to mythologies, this image reveals the impossibility of reducing history to a single interpretive act (*Madwoman in the Attic*, 526).

11. In his essay "George Eliot's Hypothesis of Reality," George Levine expands upon this concept of inescapable environmental interconnectedness; he writes that "For Lewes and George Eliot, following Darwin, the highest organism is both the most completely differentiated from its rudimentary origins and the most integrated in other organisms. The human organism exists in a 'medium' that is, quite literally, another organism—society" (*Nineteenth-Century Fiction* 35, no. 1 [1980]: 8).

12. From the beginnings of her literary career, Eliot saw *Antigone* as an essential model of human interaction. In her 1856 essay "Antigone and its Moral," she explains the play's significance, suggesting that the tragedy's turning point is not

"reverence for the dead and the importance of the sacred rites of burial," but the *conflict* between these and obedience to the State. Here lies the dramatic collision: the impulse of sisterly piety which allies itself with reverence for the Gods, clashes with the duties of citizenship; two principles, both having their validity, are at war with each. . . . Is it not rather that the struggle between Antigone and Creon represents that struggle between elemental tendencies and established laws . . . Wherever the strength of man's intellect, or moral sense, or affection beings him into opposition with the rules which society has sanctioned, *there* is renewed the conflict between Antigone and Creon. (*GEE*, 263–65)

Later, Eliot would describe "her sole purpose in writing" *The Mill on the Floss* as illustrating this same struggle, to show "the conflict which is going on everywhere when the younger generation with its higher culture comes into collision with the older. . . . [the] want of education made a theoretic or dogmatic religion impossible, and since the Reformation, an imaginative religion had not been possible" (*GEL*, 8:465).

13. Martin J. Svaglic addresses this apparent contradiction: "Of English novelists of the first rank, George Eliot is easily the most paradoxical. She appreciates the importance of religion in human life and writes novels to enforce it; but she does not believe in God" ("Religion in the Novels of George Eliot," in *A Century of George Eliot Criticism*, ed. Gordon S. Haight [Boston: Houghton Mifflin, 1965]: 285–86).

14. While the "ideal" may evolve from a Christian concept of God to a more Darwinian/scientific sense of development, as George Levine writes, "The 'ideal' had become for [Eliot] an essential component of reality" ("Eliot's Hypothesis of Reality," 3). This belief by Eliot becomes especially important in a work like

Middlemarch; it is not Dorothea's attempts at reaching an ideal which should be considered inappropriate, but the cultural opinion that checks and patronizes such efforts.

15. In a letter to the wife of Lewes's son, Eliot writes: "I was brought up in the Church of England, and never belonged to any other religious body. . . . As to its origin historically, and *as a system of thought,* it is my conviction that the Church of England is the least morally dignified of all forms of Christianity" (*GEL,* 4:213–14).

16. Writing to Sara Sophia Hennel, Evans asks: "Are we to go on cherishing superstitions out of a fear that seems inconsistent with any faith in a Supreme Being?" (*GEL,* 1:163).

17. The intensity with which Evans first embraced and then rejected Christianity can be evidenced through her letters. The early letters explode with an Evangelical passion marked by extensive biblical allusions as mottos for life. While these religious allusions saturate the early letters, when she quits the Church, they disappear completely. The biblical references return in her later letters, but instead of being morally charged, they function on a par with any other literary allusion.

18. Robert Evans's strong reaction to his daughter's agnosticism mirrors the social ostricization she would continue to face for her nonconformist views and lifestyle. Her father's disapproval forced her out of her home and exaggerated her marginalized and dependent position, forcing her to stay with her brother's family until peace could be made with her father.

19. While reaching similar conclusions to mine about Evans's human ethic, critics have traditionally considered her beliefs in more traditional dimensions— from that of an agnostic and unbeliever to a proponent of religious humanism. For examples of this scholarship, see C. B. Cox, "George Eliot: The Conservative Reformer," in *The Free Spirit: A Study of Liberal Humanism in the Novels of George Eliot, Henry James, E. M. Forster, Virginia Woolf, and Angus Wilson* (London: Oxford University Press, 1963); Bernard J. Paris, "George Eliot and the Higher Criticism," *Anglia* 74 (1966): 59–73 and "George Eliot's Religion of Humanity," *English Literary History* 29 (1962): 419–43; Sara Moore Putzell, "The Search for a Higher Rule: Spiritual Progress in the Novels of George Eliot," *Journal of the American Academy of Religion* 57 (1979): 389–407; Martin J. Svaglic, "Religion in the Novels of George Eliot"; George Levine, "George Eliot's Hypothesis of Reality"; and U. C. Knoepflmacher, *Religious Humanism and the Victorian Novel: George Eliot, Walter Pater, and Samuel Butler* (Princeton: Princeton University Press, 1965).

20. Eliot was referring to a chapter motto from *Felix Holt:*

> Yea, it becomes a man
> To Cherish memory, where he had delight
> For kindness is the natural birth of kindness
> Whose soul records not the great debt of joy
> Is stamped for ever an ignoble man. (510)

Subsequent quotations from this work are cited in the text as *FH.*

21. Haight also notes this in his edition of *GEL.*

22. Knoepflmacher, *Religious Humanism,* 16.

23. Ibid., 12.

24. Margaret Homans analyzes what she sees as the transitional phase of Evans's life, after she had left Church and family but before she wrote fiction, while she worked as a translator: "Translation requires, like other kinds of liter-

ary transmission, the suppression of self, for the translator writes not in her own words, but someone else's" (*Bearing the Word*, 177). Significantly, Evans did not begin writing fiction—discourse in which she, as author, totally controlled and directed its shape and content—until she completely rejected cultural codes and lived openly with Lewes. Even though she continually faced social ostricization, her relationship with Lewes appears crucial to her literary productivity. In her essay "George Eliot," Virginia Woolf writes: "The books which followed so soon after her union testify in the fullest manner to the great liberation which had come to her with personal happiness" (*Collected Essays*, ed. Leonard Woolf, vol. 1 [New York: Harcourt, Brace, and World, 1951], 199).

25. Barry Qualls argues in *The Secular Pilgrims* that the Victorian novel supplanted earlier religious literature as the medium to reveal to humanity the remnant of the god-like in the physical world. But unlike earlier religious literature, the Victorian novel superimposed these sacred values onto the secular genre. "Teaching is [George Eliot's] emphasis, as it was for Bunyan and the later religious writers," Qualls writes, but correctly qualifies her intent as not didactic, adding that "She wants no diagrams" (140). But while Qualls's study explains the predominance of biblical allusion at a time of growing doubt, it does not explain why Eliot also joins this pattern to a critique of patriarchy.

26. In her own experience, Evans found literature to provide this very alternative perspective. After reading Newman's *Apologia Pro Vita Sua*, she felt both sympathy for the author and indignation toward Kingsley. In a letter to Sara Sophia Hennel, Evans wrote that the *Apologia* was "as the revelation of a life—how different in form from one's own, yet with how close a fellowship in its needs and burthens—I mean spiritual needs and burthens" (*GEL*, 4:159).

27. The history of the composition of *Middlemarch* also helps to illuminate this controlling motif in that the novel is the joining of two separate works: the first, begun in early 1869 about Lydgate and entitled *Middlemarch*; and the second, begun late 1870, to be called *Miss Brooke*. In less than a year (spring 1871) Eliot recognized that the two separate works were really one and had combined them into one novel. It is Dorothea, I would contend (in addition to the obvious setting of Middlemarch), which ties the two stories together; it is her influence which effects the "resolution" of the Lydgate narrative.

28. In *Madwoman in the Attic* Gilbert and Gubar also point out Farebrother's nonaggressive behavior, characterising it as closer to "'feminine' renunciation" than that of a muscular Christianity (528).

29. Eliot had earlier in *Felix Holt* provided a similar meditation upon the generational changing state of religion, which reveals both the benefits and drawbacks of such changes. The narrator begins the novel considering religion 35 years earlier: "There was no sign of superstition near, no crucifix or image to indicate a misguided reverence: the inhabitants were probably so free from superstition that they were in much less awe of the parson than of the overseer" (77). She adds, with the coal pits came increasing Dissenting chapels: "Here was a population not convinced that old England was as good as possible; here were multitudinous men and women aware that their religion was not exactly the religion of their rulers . . ." (79).

30. Gilbert and Gubar address the ethnocentricity of Casaubon's project as well as its anachronism and representation of the Church's hierarchy, noting that through Casaubon Eliot confronts her own biblical criticism. In contrast to his goal, however, Eliot "sought to rescue the mythic value of the Bible from its historical origins, and to dissect traditional forms of faith only to resurrect rever-

ence for them" (*Madwoman in the Attic*, 502). Although they correctly point to the interrelation of Eliot's own nonfiction to this criticism of the church via Casaubon, I would suggest a slightly different emphasis—that Eliot's own deep immersion in biblical criticism intensified her belief in the outdated effects of organized religion and its doctrines.

31. F. R. Leavis dismisses Will vis-à-vis Lydgate, whom he considers "real and a man" (*The Great Tradition: George Eliot, Henry James, Joseph Conrad* [New York: New York University Press, 1969], 77). Influenced by more traditional romance plots, Knoepflmacher incredulously ponders Dorothea's choice of Will when she and Lydgate complement each other so well (*Religious Humanism*, 83). At the other end of the critical assessment of Will, Gilbert and Gubar write that "Will is Eliot's radically antipatriarchal attempt to create an image of masculinity attractive to women" (*Madwoman in the Attic*, 529).

32. In addition to Dorothea's craving for a vocation which will give meaning to her life and the allusions to Theresa, Eliot defines and describes her character with other religious allusions. She is described by Will's German artist friend as having "the consciousness of Christian centuries in [her] bosom. But she should be dressed as a nun; I think she looks almost what you call a Quaker; I would dress her as a nun in my picture" (*M*, 220). In protest to Will's reluctance to introduce Dorothea to him, he tells Will: "If you were an artist, you would think of Mistress Second-Cousin as antique form animated by Christian sentiment— a sort of Christian Antigone—sensuous force controlled by spiritual passion" (*M*, 221). After Dorothea volunteers to work clearing Lydgate's name, he reflects: "This young creature has a heart large enough for the Virgin Mary. She evidently thinks nothing of her own future, and would pledge away half her income at once, as if she wanted nothing for herself but a chair to sit in from which she can look down with those clear eyes at the poor mortals who pray to her" (*M*, 826).

33. The other side of such a cultural restriction on marriage as the only voca- tion for women can be seen with the character Mary Garth. Eldest daughter of a large family, Mary has been raised with the reality that she most likely will have to support herself, so she has been trained to be able to teach. Rosamond addresses this very issue of the alternatives of marrige or being self-supporting, contemplating: "'one wonders what such people do, without any prospect [of marriage]. To be sure, there is religion as a support. But,' she added, dimpling, 'it is very different with you, Mary. You may have an offer'" (*M*, 141). Rosa- mond's remark also reveals the cultural view of religion—religion pacifies earthly tribulations like a balm rather than addressing the real problems faced by individuals.

34. George Eliot, *Adam Bede*, ed. John Paterson (New York: Houghton Mifflin, 1968), 102–3.

35. George Eliot, *The Mill on the Floss* (New York: New American Library, 1965), 365. Subsequent quotations from this work are cited in the text as *MF*.

36. George Eliot, *Daniel Deronda* (Harmondsworth: Penguin, 1982), 694. Sub- sequent quotations from this work are cited in the text as *DD*.

37. Much interest has been sparked by the simple fact that Eliot allows none of her characters, here Dorothea, either to defy cultural restrictions on male- female relationships or to be as productive as she was herself. While some see this as a latent conservativism in Eliot, I suggest that this pattern reflects her realistic rather than utopian portrait of the individual suffering caused by the culture. Eliot suffered a great deal for her "freedoms," and she recognized that

few women would have either her opportunities or strength to confront and reject patriarchal restrictions of women.

38. Like Florence Nightingale, the character Dorothea Brooke finds herself in conflict with cultural prescriptions that ordain work as the medium through which to achieve an earthly spirituality, but prohibits women from working—except through a husband.

39. Qualls also analyzes Dorothea as a Victorian Christian, citing her continual questioning "Tell me what I can do" as having a "Bunyanesque resonance" (*Secular Pilgrims*, 165). See also Vincent Newey's "Dorothea's Awakening: The Recall of Bunyan in *Middlemarch*," *Notes and Queries* 31 (1984): 497–99, for a brief delineation of the parallels between Dorothea and Christian. Neither Qualls nor Newey, however, places Dorothea's pilgrimage within a feminist context.

40. Although many critics recognize movement in Dorothea's personal and spiritual perspective, they generally misread both the starting and ending points. Albert J. Palko sees the movement as a kind of "battle of myths" between paganism and Christianity ("Latter-Day Saints"); Gilbert and Gubar as that between a female Fate and God the Father (*Madwoman in the Attic*). Palko also sees Dorothea's personal growth as that from selfishly naive illusions to a final maturity of expanded consciousness ("Latter-Day Saints," 3). While I would agree with Palko as to the enlarged scope of Dorothea's perspective, I disagree that she begins from a selfish naivety, as I will argue. Susan J. Rosowski situates Dorothea's growth in terms of a two-stage awakening about love seen in her movement from Casaubon to Will and the subsequent renunciation of material considerations ("The Novel of Awakening," in *The Voyage In: Fictions of Female Development*, ed. Elizabeth Abel, Marianne Hirsch, and Elizabeth Langland [Hanover: University Press of New England, 1983], 49–68). Robert F. Damm and Knoepflmacher see Dorothea's movement, correctly, as that toward a human, not abstract spirituality, but both qualify the human focus as a "middle-ground" (Damm, "Sainthood and Dorothea Brooke," *The Victorian Newsletter* 35 [1969]: 22) or, translated into her marriage to Will, a "Victorian 'second best' . . . the 'middle march' between her soaring aspirations and the ground force of a prosaic reality" (Knoepflmacher, *Religious Humanism*, 76). To see Dorothea's growth as a settling, however, is to miss Eliot's point: human sympathy is *the* method of moral advancement for nineteenth-century England, not a *qualified* choice among various paths.

41. George Eliot, *Romola* (Harmondsworth: Penguin, 1981), 309. Significantly for Romola, this ability to identify sympathetically with other women's suffering in marriage prevents any egoism from motivating her actions toward Tessa—the common-law wife of Romola's husband, Tito. Once she processes the full meaning of Tessa's situation—believing herself married to Tito, having borne him children, essentially alone after his death, facing the political/religious upheaval brought on by Savonarola's death—Romola takes in Tessa and her children and creates a nurturing, loving environment for them—a striking contrast to the patriarchal alternative both women had experienced previously.

With this idea of one woman rejecting her socially prescribed role (to "compete" with other women for men—specifically for husbands), Eliot portrays radically rejected patriarchal standards for the relationship between women and by extension society as a whole. This model Eliot presents echoes distinctly one which Gaskell had illustrated earlier in a number of her shorter works, most notably in "Half a Life-Time Ago," where Susan Dixon takes in the widow of her former lover, Michael Durst, who had abandoned Susan because she would not institutionalize her retarded brother.

42. To fully understand Eliot's use of marriage as a metaphor, the role of the individual—the solitary pilgrim—must be understood. One need not marry to experience the sympathetic projection that recognizes another's "equivalent centre of self"; marriage simply provides two people with the most fruitful opportunities to do so. Eliot creates similar opportunities for this interpersonal growth for characters not married to one another: Chettam and Dorothea and Rosamond and Will in *Middlemarch* as well as Gwendolyn and Daniel Deronda in *Daniel Deronda*.

43. In her essay "Margaret Fuller and Mary Wollstonecraft," Eliot meditates on men like Casaubon and Lydgate:

> Men pay a heavy price for their reluctance to encourage self-help and independent resources in women. The precious meridian years of many a man of genius have to be spent in the toil of routine, that an "establishment" may be kept up for a woman who can understand none of his secret yearnings, who is fit for nothing but to sit in her drawing-room like a doll-Madonna in her shrine. No matter. Anything is more endurable than to change our established formulae about women, or to run the risk of looking up to our wives instead of looking down on them. (*GEE*, 204–5)

44. One of the most consistently misread themes in Eliot's fiction is that of renunciation, by feminist and canonical critics alike. Gilbert and Gubar see the preponderance for renunciation by Eliot's characters as a kind of punishment for her own success (*Madwoman in the Attic*, 466). I believe that Eliot's recurring motif of renunciation is not this kind of self-denial, when appropriately embraced, but instead the result of a sympathetic understanding which counteracts egoism.

45. Eliot herself attests to this common thread which runs throughout her fiction: in a letter to Sara Sophia Hennel (15 February 1869) she writes, "The various elements of [*Middlemarch*] have been soliciting my mind for years— asking for a complete embodiment" (*GEL*, 5:16); and, in a letter to Elizabeth Stuart Phelps (16 December 1876), "The principles which are at the root of my effort to paint Dinah Morris are equally at the root of my effort to paint Mordecai" (*GEL*, 6:318).

CHAPTER 6. AFTERWORD: WOMEN WRITERS AND THE VICTORIAN SPIRITUAL CRISIS

1. Ellis makes several references to this distinction between God and humanity: see esp. *D*, 19, 262, and 275–76.

2. William S. Peterson, *Victorian Heretic: Mrs. Humphry Ward's 'Robert Elsmere'* (Leicester: Leicester University Press, 1976), 14.

3. Ibid., 6.

4. Peterson notes Ward's "ambivalent feelings" toward her character Catherine, that "she responds to her heroine's intense spiritual fervour yet insists that such a childish faith in the modern age is, intellectually speaking, an anachronism" (*Victorian Heretic*, 142). It is significant, however, that Ward portrays her female character as maintaining this "anachronistic" faith and that her male character has the traditional spiritual crisis.

5. Interestingly, as Peterson points out, Ward strongly resisted any compari-

son of her work with that written by Eliot; instead, she preferred to see her work influenced by the Brontës, especially Charlotte (*Victorian Heretic*, 103).

6. Mrs. Humphry Ward, *Robert Elsmere* (Oxford: Oxford University Press, 1987), 576. Subsequent quotations from this work are cited in the text as *RM*. See also Peterson, *Victorian Heretic*, 157.

7. Davis, "Anglican Evangelicalism," 193.

8. Cook, *Life of Nightingale* 1:440.

9. See Knoepflmacher's *Religious Humanism and the Victorian Novel* for a detailed analysis of Eliot's humanism. Although this important work provides a careful consideration of her evolution from an agnostic and unbeliever to a proponent of a human-based spirituality, he fails to take into consideration the inescapable influence of gender on her beliefs and their manifestations.

10. Kingsley, *Letters and Memories* 3:188.

11. See Margaret M. Maison, "'Thine, Only Thine!': Women Hymn Writers in Britain, 1760–1835," in *Religion in the Lives of English Women, 1760–1930*, ed. Gail Malmgreen (Bloomington: Indiana University Press, 1986), 11–40.

12. Helsinger, Sheets, and Veeders, eds., *The Woman Question* 1:183.

13. R. F. Kinloch, *An Historical Account of the Church Hymnary*, rev. ed. (Cambridge: W. Heffer & Sons, 1928), 79; Adam Fox, *English Hymns and Hymn Writers* (London: Collins, 1947), 39; Horton Davies, *Worship and Theology in England: From Watts and Wesley to Maurice, 1690–1850* (Princeton: Princeton University Press, 1961), 208–9.

14. My discussion is based on the hymns found in *The Hymnal Companion to the Book of Common Prayer, with Accompanying Tunes*, ed. Joseph Thomas Cooper, rev. ed. (London: Sampson Low, Marston, Searle, & Rivington, 1880). Quotations from this work are cited in the text by line numbers.

15. Kinloch, *Historical Account*, 79–80. For an important analysis of this quality in Christina Rossetti's hymns, see Virginia Sickbert, "Dissident Voices in Christina Rossetti's Poetry" (Ph.D. diss., SUNY Stony Brook, 1990), esp. chap. 4, "The Maternal Jesus."

16. William Jensen Reynolds, *A Joyful Sound: Christian Hymnody*, ed. Milburn Price (New York: Holt, Rinehart & Winston, 1978), 60.

17. An interesting example is provided by Kinloch, who wonders whether women's hymns are really any good (*Historical Account*, 82).

Bibliography

Adams, Harriett Farwell. "Prelude and Finale to *Middlemarch*." *Victorian Newsletter* 63 (1983): 21–25.

Allen, Donald R. "Florence Nightingale: Toward a Psychohistorical Interpretation." *Journal of Interdisciplinary History* 6, no. 1 (1975): 23–45.

Anderson, Olive. "Women Preachers in Mid-Victorian Britain: Some Reflexions on Feminism, Popular Religion and Social Change." *The Historical Journal* 12, no. 3 (1969): 467–84.

Arnold, Matthew. *Poetry and Criticism of Matthew Arnold.* Edited by A. Dwight Culler. Boston: Houghton Mifflin, 1961.

Atkinson, Clarissa W., Constance H. Buchanan, and Margaret R. Miles, eds. *Immaculate and Powerful: The Female in Sacred Image and Social Reality.* Boston: Beacon Press, 1985.

Auerbach, Nina. "The Rise of the Fallen Woman." *Nineteenth-Century Fiction* 35 (1980): 29–52.

———. *Woman and the Demon: The Life of a Victorian Myth.* Cambridge: Harvard University Press, 1982.

Beer, Patricia. *Reader, I Married Him: A Study of the Women Characters of Jane Austen, Charlotte Brontë, Elizabeth Gaskell, and George Eliot.* New York: Macmillan, 1974.

Behnke, Donna A. *Religious Issues in Nineteenth-Century Feminism.* Troy, N.Y.: Whitston Publishing, 1982.

Briggs, Asa. "Private and Social Themes in *Shirley*." *Brontë Studies Transactions* 13, no. 3 (1958): 203–19.

Brodestsky, Tessa. *Elizabeth Gaskell.* Oxford: Oxford University Press, 1986.

Brontë, Charlotte. *Shirley.* Oxford: Oxford University Press, 1981.

Carlyle, Thomas. *On Heroes, Hero-Worship and the Heroic in History.* Lincoln: University of Nebraska Press, 1966.

———. *Sartor Resartus.* Edited by Charles Frederick Harrold. New York: Odyssey Press, 1937.

Carpenter, Mary Wilson. *George Eliot and the Landscape of Time: Narrative Form and Protestant Apocalyptic History.* Chapel Hill: University of North Carolina Press, 1986.

Casteras, Susan P. "Virgin Vows: The Early Victorian Artists' Portrayal of Nuns and Novices." In *Religion in the Lives of English Women, 1760–1930,* edited by Gail Malmgreen, 129–60. Bloomington: Indiana University Press, 1986.

Christ, Carol. *Diving Deep and Surfacing: Women Writers on a Spiritual Quest.* Boston: Beacon Press, 1980.

Cixous, Hélène. "The Laugh of the Medusa." Translated by Keith Cohen and

Paula Cohen. In *New French Feminisms*, edited by Elaine Marks and Isabelle de Courtivron, 245–64. New York: Schocken Books, 1981.

———. "Sorties." Translated by Ann Liddle. In *New French Feminisms*, edited by Elaine Marks and Isabelle de Courtivron, 90–98. New York: Schocken Books, 1981.

Cook, Sir Edward. *The Life of Florence Nightingale*. 2 vols. New York: Macmillan, 1942.

Cooper, Joseph Thomas, ed. *The Hymnal Companion to the Book of Common Prayer, with Accompanying Tunes*. Rev. ed. London: Sampson Low, Marston, Searle, & Rivington, 1880.

Cormie, Lee. "The Hermeneutical Privilege of the Oppressed: Liberation Theologies, Biblical Faith, and Marxist Sociology of Knowledge." *Proceedings of the Annual Convention of Catholic Theological Society of America* 32 (1978): 155–81.

Court, Franklin E. "The Image of Saint Theresa in *Middlemarch* and Positive Ethics." *Victorian Newsletter* 68 (1985): 9–11.

Cox, C. B. "George Eliot: The Conservative Reformer." In *The Free Spirit: A Study of Liberal Humanism in the Novels of George Eliot, Henry James, E. M. Forster, Virginia Woolf, and Augus Wilson*. London: Oxford University Press, 1963.

Craik, W. A. *Elizabeth Gaskell and the English Provincial Novel*. London: Methuen Press, 1975.

Daly, Mary. *Beyond God the Father: Toward a Philosophy of Women's Liberation*. Boston: Beacon Press, 1973.

Damm, Robert F. "Sainthood and Dorothea Brooke." *The Victorian Newsletter* 35 (1969): 18–22.

Davies, Horton. *Worship and Theology in England: From Watts and Wesley to Maurice, 1690–1850*. Princeton: Princeton University Press, 1961.

———. *Worship and Theology in England: From Newman to Martineau, 1850–1900*. Princeton: Princeton University Press, 1962.

Davis, Robin Reed. "Anglican Evangelicalism and the Feminine Literary Tradition, From Hannah More to Charlotte Brontë." Ph.D. diss., Duke University, 1982.

duPlessis, Rachel Blau. *Writing Beyond the Ending: Narrative Strategies of Twentieth-Century Women Writers*. Bloomington: Indiana University Press, 1985.

Duthie, Enid L. *The Themes of Elizabeth Gaskell*. Totowa, N.J.: Rowman & Littlefield Press, 1980.

Eagleton, Terry. *Myths of Power: A Marxist Study of the Brontës*. London: Macmillan, 1975.

Easson, Angus. *Elizabeth Gaskell*. London: Routledge & Kegan Paul, 1979.

———. "Elizabeth Gaskell and the Novel of Local Pride." *Bulletin of John Ryland Library* 67 (1984–85): 688–709.

Eliot, George. *Adam Bede*. Edited by John Paterson. New York: Houghton Mifflin, 1968.

———. *Daniel Deronda*. Harmondsworth: Penguin, 1982.

———. *Essays*. Edited by Thomas Pinney. New York: Columbia University Press, 1963.

———. *Felix Holt, The Radical*. Harmondsworth: Penguin, 1982.

————. *The George Eliot Letters*. Edited by Gordon S. Haight. 9 vols. New Haven: Yale University Press, 1954–78.

————. *Middlemarch*. Harmondsworth: Penguin, 1979.

————. *The Mill on the Floss*. New York: New American Library, 1965.

————. *Romola*. Harmondsworth: Penguin, 1981.

Elliott-Binns, L. E. *Religion in the Victorian Era*. 1936. Reprint. London: Lutterworth Press, 1964.

Ellis, Sarah Stickney. *Education of the Heart: Woman's Best Work*. London: Hodder & Stoughton, 1869.

————. *The Daughters of England: Their Position in Society, Characters, and Responsibilities*. New York: D. Appleton, 1842.

Farr, Judith. "Charlotte Brontë, Emily Brontë and the 'Undying Life' Within." *Victorian Institute Journal* 17 (1989): 87–103.

Fiorenza, Elisabeth Schussler. *Bread Not Stone: The Challenge of Feminist Biblical Interpretation*. Boston: Beacon Press, 1984.

————. "Interpreting Patriarchal Traditions." In *The Liberating Word: A Guide to Nonsexist Interpretation of the Bible*, edited by Letty M. Russell, 39–61. Philadelphia: Westminster Press,1976.

"Florence Nightingale as Leader in the Religious and Civic Thought of Her Time." *Hospitals* 10 (1936): 78–84.

Fox, Adam. *English Hymns and Hymn Writers*. London: Collins, 1947.

Fraser, Hilary. "Saint Theresa, Saint Dorothea, and Miss Brooke in *Middlemarch*." *Nineteenth-Century Fiction* 40, no. 4 (1986): 400–11.

Froula, Christine. "When Eve Reads Milton: Undoing Canonical Authority." *PMLA* 10 (1983): 321–47.

Frye, Northrop. *The Secular Scripture: A Study of the Structure of Romance*. Cambridge: Harvard University Press, 1976.

Gallagher, Catherine. *The Industrial Reformation of English Fiction: Social Discourse and Narrative Form, 1832–1867*. Chicago: University of Chicago Press, 1985.

Gallop, Jane. *The Daughter's Seduction: Feminism and Psychoanalysis*. Ithaca: Cornell University Press, 1982.

Ganz, Margaret. *Elizabeth Gaskell: The Artist in Conflict*. New York: Twayne, 1969.

Gaskell, Elizabeth. *Four Short Stories*. London: Pandora Press, 1983.

————. *The Letters of Mrs. Gaskell*. Edited by J. A. V. Chapple and Arthur Pollard. Cambridge: Harvard University Press, 1967.

————. *The Life of Charlotte Brontë*. Harmondsworth: Penguin, 1983.

————. *Mary Barton*. London: Penguin, 1985.

————. *North and South*. Oxford: Oxford University Press, 1982.

————. *Ruth*. Oxford: Oxford University Press, 1985.

Gerin, Winifred. *Charlotte Brontë: The Evolution of Genius*. Oxford: Clarendon Press, 1967.

Gilbert, Sandra M., and Susan Gubar. *The Madwoman in the Attic: The Woman Writer and the Nineteenth-Century Literary Imagination*. New Haven: Yale University Press, 1979.

Gilligan, Carol. *In a Different Voice: Psychological Theory and Women's Development*. Cambridge: Harvard University Press, 1982.

Gross, Rita M., ed. *Beyond Androcentrism: New Essays on Women and Religion.* Missoula, Mont.: Scholars Press, 1977.

Haddad, Yvonne Yazbeck, and Ellison Banks Findly, eds. *Women, Religion, and Social Change.* Albany: State University of New York Press, 1985.

Haight, Gordon S. *George Eliot: A Biography.* New York: Oxford University Press, 1968.

Helsinger, Elizabeth K., Robin Lauterbach Sheets, and William Veeders, eds. *The Woman Question: Society and Literature in Britain and America, 1837–1883.* 2 vols. New York: Garland Press, 1983.

Holloway, John. *The Victorian Sage: Studies in Argument.* 1953. Reprint. Hamdem: Archon Books, 1962.

Homans, Margaret. *Bearing the Word: Language and Female Experience in Nineteenth-Century Women's Writing.* Chicago: University of Chicago Press, 1986.

Hopkins, A. B. *Elizabeth Gaskell, Her Life and Work.* New York: Octagon Books, 1971.

Houghton, Walter E. *The Victorian Frame of Mind, 1830–1870.* New Haven: Yale University Press, 1957.

Irigaray, Luce. *Speculum of the Other Woman.* Translated by Gillian C. Gill. Ithaca: Cornell University Press, 1985.

Jacoff, Rachel. "God as Mother: Julian of Norwich's Theology of Love." *Denver Quarterly* 18, no. 4 (1984): 134–39.

Jay, Elizabeth. *The Religion of the Heart: Anglican Evangelicalism and the Nineteenth-Century Novel.* Oxford: Clarendon Press, 1979.

Jenkins, Ruth Y. "Rewriting Female Subjection: Florence Nightingale's Revisionist Myth of 'Cassandra.'" *Weber Studies* 11, no. 1 (1994): 16–26.

Joint Commission on the Revision of the Hymnal of the Protestant Episcopal Church in the United States of America. *The Hymnal 1940 Companion.* New York: The Church Pension Fund, 1949.

Kingsley, Charles. *His Letters and Memories of His Life.* Edited by Mrs. Kingsley. 4 vols. London: Macmillan, 1901.

Kinloch, T. F. *An Historical Account of the Church Hymnary.* Rev. ed. Cambridge: W. Heffer & Sons, 1928.

Knoepflmacher, U. C. "*Middlemarch*: An Avuncular View." *Nineteenth-Century Fiction* 30, no. 1 (1975): 53–81.

———. *Religious Humanism and the Victorian Novel: George Eliot, Walter Pater, and Samuel Butler.* Princeton: Princeton University Press, 1965.

Korg, Jacob. "The Problem of Unity in *Shirley.*" *Nineteenth-Century Fiction* 2, no. 2 (1957): 125–36.

Kristeva, Julia. *Desire in Language: A Semiotic Approach to Literature and Art.* Translated by Thomas Gora, Alice Jardine, and Leon Roudiez. Edited by Leon S. Roudiez. New York: Columbia University Press, 1980.

Landow, George P. *Elegant Jeremiahs: The Sage from Carlyle to Mailer.* Ithaca: Cornell University Press, 1986.

———. *Victorian Types, Victorian Shadows: Biblical Typology in Victorian Literature, Art, and Thought.* Boston: Routledge & Kegan Paul, 1980.

Lansbury, Coral. *Elizabeth Gaskell: The Novel of Social Crisis.* New York: Barnes & Noble, 1975.

Leavis, F. R. *The Great Tradition: George Eliot, Henry James, Joseph Conrad.* New York: New York University Press, 1969.

Levine, George. "George Eliot's Hypothesis of Reality." *Nineteenth-Century Fiction* 35, no. 1 (1980): 1–28.

Linder, Cynthia A. *Romantic Imagery in the Novels of Charlotte Brontë.* London: Macmillan, 1978.

Lockhead, David. "Hermeneutics and Ideology." *the ecumenist* 15, no. 6 (1977): 81–84.

Maison, Margaret M. *Search Your Soul, Eustace: Victorian Religious Novels.* New York: Sheed & Ward, 1961.

———. "'Thine, Only Thine!': Women Hymn Writers in Britain, 1760–1835." In *Religion in the Lives of English Women, 1760–1930,* edited by Gail Malmgreen, 11–40. Bloomington: Indiana University Press, 1986.

———. *The Victorian Vision: Studies in the Religious Novel.* New York: Sheed & Ward, 1961.

Mantripp, J. C. "Florence Nightingale and Religion." *The London Quarterly and Holborn Review,* July 1932, 318–25.

Marotta, Kenny. "*Middlemarch:* the 'Home Epic.'" *Genre* 15 (1982): 403–20.

Martin, Hazel T. *Petticoat Rebels: A Study of the Novels of Social Protest of George Eliot, Elizabeth Gaskell, and Charlotte Brontë.* New York: Helio Books, 1968.

Marxist-Feminist Literature Collective. "Women's Writing: *Jane Eyre, Shirley, Villette, Aurora Leigh.*" *Ideology and Consciousness* 2 (1977): 27–48.

Mill, John Stuart. *The Autobiography of John Stuart Mill.* New York: Columbia University Press, 1924.

Miller, Nancy K. "Emphasis Added: Plots and Plausibilities in Women's Fiction." *PMLA* 96 (1981): 36–48.

Mintz, Alan. *George Eliot and the Novel of Vocation.* Cambridge: Harvard University Press, 1978.

Moglen, Helene. *Charlotte Brontë: The Self Conceived.* New York: Norton, 1976.

Moi, Toril. *Sexual/Textual Politics: Feminist Literary Theory.* London: Methuen, 1985.

Munich, Adrienne Auslander. "Notorious signs, feminist criticism and literary tradition." In *Making a Difference: Feminist Literary Criticism,* edited by Coppélia Kahn and Gayle Greene, 238–59. London: Methuen, 1985.

Newey, Vincent. "Dorothea's Awakening: The Recall of Bunyan in *Middlemarch.*" *Notes and Queries* 31 (1984): 497–99.

Newton, Judith Lowder. *Women, Power, and Subversion: Social Strategies in British Fiction, 1778–1860.* Athens: University of Georgia Press, 1981.

Nightingale, Florence. *Cassandra and Other Selections from Suggestions for Thought.* Edited by Mary Poovey. New York: New York University Press, 1992.

———. *Ever Yours, Florence Nightingale: Selected Letters.* Edited by Martha Vicinus and Bea Nergaard. Cambridge: Harvard University Press, 1990.

———. "A Note of Interrogation." *Fraser's Magazine,* n.s., 7 (1873): 567–77.

———. "A Sub-Note of Interrogation: What Will Be Our Religion in 1999?" *Fraser's Magazine,* n.s., 8 (1873): 25–36.

———. *Suggestions for Thought to Searchers After Religious Truth.* 3 vols. London: Eyre & Spottiswoode, 1860.

Ochshorn, Judith. *The Female Experience and the Nature of The Divine.* Bloomington: Indiana University Press, 1981.

Pagels, Elaine. *The Gnostic Gospels.* New York: Random House, 1979.

Palko, Albert J. "Latter-Day Saints: George Eliot's New Saint Theresa in Image and Symbol." Ph.D. diss., Notre Dame, 1973.

Paris, Bernard J. "George Eliot and the Higher Criticism." *Anglia* 74 (1966): 59–73.

———. "George Eliot's Religion of Humanity." *English Literary History* 29 (1962): 419–43.

Peterson, William S. *Victorian Heretic: Mrs. Humphry Ward's "Robert Elsmere."* Leicester: Leicester University Press, 1976.

Plaskow, Judith, and Joan Arnold, eds. *Women and Religion.* Missoula: Scholars Press, 1974.

Pollard, Arthur. *Mrs. Gaskell: Novelist and Biographer.* Cambridge: Harvard University Press, 1966.

———. "The Novels of Mrs. Gaskell." *Bulletin of John Rylands Library* 43 (1960–61): 403–25.

Poovey, Mary. *Uneven Developments: The Ideological Work of Gender in Mid-Victorian England.* Chicago: University of Chicago Press, 1988.

Prelinger, Catherine M. "The Female Diaconate in the Anglican Church: What Kind of Ministry for Women?" In *Religion in the Lives of English Women, 1760–1930,* edited by Gail Malmgreen, 161–92. Bloomington: Indiana University Press, 1986.

Prentis, Barbara. *The Brontë Sisters and George Eliot: A Unity of Difference.* Totowa, N.J.: Barnes & Noble, 1988.

Putzell, Sarah Moore. "The Search for a Higher Rule: Spiritual Progress in the Novels of George Eliot." *Journal of the American Academy of Religion* 57 (1979): 389–407.

Qualls, Barry. *The Secular Pilgrims of Victorian Fiction: The Novel as Book of Life.* Cambridge: Cambridge University Press, 1982.

Reynolds, William Jensen. *A Joyful Sound: Christian Hymnody.* Edited by Milburn Price. 1963. Reprint. New York: Holt, Rinehart & Winston, 1978.

Ringe, Sharon H. "Biblical Authority and Interpretation." In *The Liberating Word: A Guide to Nonsexist Interpretation of the Bible,* edited by Letty M. Russell, 23–38. Philadelphia: Westminster Press, 1976.

Rosowski, Susan J. "The Novel of Awakening." In *The Voyage In: Fictions of Female Development,* edited by Elizabeth Abel, Marianne Hirsch, and Elizabeth Langland, 49–68. Hanover, N.H. University Press of New England, 1983.

Rowbotham, Sheila. *Women, Resistance, and Revolution.* New York: Random House, 1972.

Ruddick, Sara. "Maternal Thinking." In *Mothering: Essays in Feminist Theory,* edited by Joyce Treblicot, 213–30. Totowa, N.J.: Rowman & Allanheld, 1984.

Ruether, Rosemary Radford. *Womanguides: Readings Toward a Feminist Theology.* Boston: Beacon Press, 1985.

Ruskin, John. "Of Queens' Gardens." In *The Works of John Ruskin,* vol. 18. London: George Allen, 1905.

Sheehan, Thomas. *The First Coming: How the Kingdom of God Became Christianity.* New York: Random House, 1986.

Showalter, Elaine. *A Literature of Their Own: British Women Novelists from Brontë to Lessing.* Princeton: Princeton University Press, 1977.

———. *The Female Malady: Women, Madness, and English Culture, 1830–1980.* New York: Pantheon, 1985.

———. "Florence Nightingale's Feminist Complaint: Women, Religion, and *Suggestions for Thought.*" *Signs* 6 (1981): 395–412.

Sickbert, Virginia. "Dissident Voices in Christina Rossetti's Poetry." Ph.D. diss., State University of New York at Stony Brook, 1990.

———. "The Significance of Mother and Child in Christina Rossetti's *Sing-Song.*" *Victorian Poetry.* Forthcoming.

Sprague, Rosemary. *George Eliot: A Biography.* Philadelphia: Chilton Book, 1968.

Stone, Merlin. *When God Was a Woman.* New York: Dial, 1976.

Strachey, Lytton. *Eminent Victorians: Cardinal Manning, Florence Nightingale, Dr. Arnold, and General Gordon.* New York: Capricorn, 1963.

Svaglic, Martin J. "Religion in the Novels of George Eliot." In *A Century of George Eliot Criticism,* edited by Gordon S. Haight, 285–94. Boston: Houghton Mifflin, 1965.

Tarrant, William George. *Florence Nightingale as a Religious Thinker.* London: British and Foreign Unitarian Association, 1917.

Taylor, Barbara. *Eve and the New Jerusalem: Socialism and Feminism in the Nineteenth Century.* New York: Pantheon, 1983.

Tennyson, Alfred. *Tennyson's Poetry.* Edited by Robert W. Hill, Jr. New York: Norton, 1971.

Tompkins, Jane P. "Sentimental Power: *Uncle Tom's Cabin* and the Politics of Literary History." In *The New Feminist Criticism: Essays on Women, Literature and Theory,* edited by Elaine Showalter, 81–104. New York: Pantheon, 1985.

Vicinus, Martha. *Independent Women: Work and Community for Single Women, 1850–1920.* Chicago: University of Chicago Press, 1985.

Ward, Mrs. Humphry. *Robert Elsmere.* Oxford: Oxford University Press, 1987.

Watson, Barbara Bellow. "On Power and the Literary Text." *Signs* 1 (1975): 111–18.

Webb, R. K. "The Victorian Reading Public." In *From Dickens to Hardy,* vol. 6 of *The New Pelican Guide to English Literature,* edited by Boris Ford, 198–219. Harmondsworth: Penguin, 1982.

Wheeler, Michael. *The Art of Allusion in Victorian Fiction.* London: Macmillan, 1979.

Wheeler, M. D. "The Sinner as Heroine: A Study of Mrs. Gaskell's *Ruth* and the Bible." *Durham University Journal,* n.s., 5 (1976): 148–61.

Winnifrith, Tom. *The Brontës.* New York: Macmillan, 1977.

Wise, Thomas James, and John Alexander Symington, eds. *The Brontës: Their Lives, Friendships and Correspondence.* The Shakespeare Head Brontë. 4 vols. 1933. Reprint (4 vols. in 2). Oxford: Basil Blackwell, 1980.

Wolff, Robert Lee. *Gains and Losses: Novels of Faith and Doubt in Victorian England.* New York: Garland, 1977.

Woodham-Smith, Cecil. *Florence Nightingale, 1820–1910*. New York: McGraw-Hill, 1951.

Woolf, Virginia. "George Eliot." In *Collected Essays*, edited by Leonard Woolf, vol. 1, 196–204. New York: Harcourt, Brace & World, 1967.

Wright, Edgar. *Mrs. Gaskell: The Basis for Reassessment*. London: Oxford University Press, 1965.

Index